Smarter
Trading

Smarter Trading

Improving Performance in Changing Markets

Perry J. Kaufman

McGraw-Hill, Inc.

New York   San Francisco   Washington, D.C.   Auckland   Bogotá
Caracas   Lisbon   London   Madrid   Mexico City   Milan
Montreal   New Delhi   San Juan   Singapore
Sydney   Tokyo   Toronto

Library of Congress Cataloging-in-Publication Data

Kaufman, Perry J.
    Smarter trading : improving performance in changing markets /
Perry J. Kaufman.
        p.   cm.
    Includes index.
    ISBN 0-07-034002-1 (alk. paper)
    1. Program trading (Securities)   I. Title.
HG4515.5.K38   1995
332.64'5—dc20

94-23636
CIP

    3 4 5 6 7 8 9 0   DOC/DOC   9 0 9 8

ISBN 0-07-034002-1

*The sponsoring editor for this book was David Conti, the editing supervisor
was Nancy Land, and the production supervisor was Donald Schmidt. This
book was set in Palatino by McGraw-Hill's Professional Book Group composi-
tion unit.*

Printed and bound by R. R. Donnelley & Sons Company.

This book is printed on recycled, acid-free paper containing a
minimum of 50% recycled de-inked fiber.

Contents

Part 3. Making a Trading Strategy Robust

Preface

You can't dig a new hole by making the old one deeper *But ISN'T IT A NEW HOLE*

Trading is a difficult business. Finding a way to build steady profits takes long, hard work or very good luck. Sometimes the effort fails; no matter how much energy is applied, there is no answer to be found. Other times, a successful program has only a short lifespan before the market changes. *Smarter Trading* tries to be realistic about how to find broad-based trading strategies that can survive change. It uses a *lateral* solution rather than a *vertical* one. *what does that mean? See below*

Vertical and Lateral Solutions

A *vertical solution* is where each new part reinforces the previous work. A *lateral solution* is where the parts fit side by side, resting on their own foundation. Think of searching for buried treasure. You know it's in the back yard. You can dig one hole deeper and deeper or dig a series of holes in different places.

An 50-floor skyscraper is a vertical solution to living space. Building on the same foundation makes the final result dependent on all the previous work. But markets change causing some assumptions to fail. The top of the building becomes very fragile when you start removing bricks from the middle.

The vertical solution is dependent
The lateral solution is INdependent

Consider NLP as tools for AWARENESS

hence,
independent

The *lateral solution* builds a wide base by taking the pieces, each one of which can stand on its own and combining them side-by-side into a single structure. None of the parts are complicated and none of them duplicate another piece. If one part fails, the others continue to work.

P+L is such a lateral solution

A Lesson from Supercomputers

At one time, the biggest "supercomputers," used only for high-powered research, were the creation of a few brilliant engineers. They became so sophisticated that each wire and connection between parts needed to be as short as possible to enable the electric current to travel at maximum speed. The main processing units were designed as a sphere so that each wire was an equal distance from the center.

Faster computers are now built with a lot of slower, off-the-shelf parts. In this design, called "parallel processing," the slower components operate on different parts of the problem at the same time. The computer companies that had invested tremendous resources in building complex systems were put out of business by someone who simply divided the problem into many little pieces and solved them using inexpensive, ready-made parts.

Not all problems can be divided into many small parts, but most can be divided. This book will teach the most important lessons about different aspects of trading, including profit-taking, trends, stops, risk and return, and testing methods. Using any one will improve results; using all of them will improve performance even more.

Thus, he is using an object oriented approach
So how does one identify the objects in P+L?

Looking for What Is Not There

INSERTION
FILTERING
DELETION

Omissions cause the biggest problems, and they are the hardest to find because they are not there. The mind's eye often fills the empty spaces with what it *expects* to be there. In the same way that we fill these omissions, we often overlook repeated, small events. We do not hear the ticking of a clock that once seemed too loud.

We will try to understand what to expect, then question the results that are either much better or worse than expected. We are always fast to look for ways to fix losses, but slow to question profits.

Learning is the result of experience. You do the best you can to analyze the problem, find a solution, and see if it works. Most often it

This is a mistake. We should examine profits as closely as losses.

does not work the first time because you failed to see the complete picture, underrated the importance of some factors, or missed an important part altogether. That is the normal way things work. Do not assume that anyone comes up with the perfect answer without trial and error. The process is not glamorous, but it is necessary. Being successful means being tenacious. *PERSISTANT*

→ TESTING HYPOTHESES

Wandering from the Path

Branches do not necessarily change sets

→ not necessarily the same as his lateral solution

Lateral thinking benefits from not following one path. It may take the best from each area, applying those parts in which we have great confidence, rather than developing the "ultimate" indicator. As we get more complicated, the benefits derived from the effort become questionable, and the solution may not be as lasting. Making very small improvements takes much more time and effort once you have extracted the essence of an idea. It is often a good time to switch to another approach when you feel that your efforts are becoming unproductive. *marginal utility strikes again.*

One approach to lateral thinking is to reverse an idea. For example, baby Jane—by playing with the ball of wool—is annoying Grandma, who is trying to knit. A likely solution would be to put baby Jane into her playpen where she cannot reach the wool. Another solution would be to put Grandma and the wool into the playpen to protect them from baby Jane. Either solution could work although most people would not consider asking Grandma to get in the playpen. Later in the book, *?where* we look at using the worst test results rather than the best.

Lateral thinking is results oriented. The goal is to get the best answer. A lateral solution often develops from a stumbling block, a point where you can no longer go forward. You shift to another area where there is a possible solution. In doing this, you may discover that parts of each direction can work together to create a better result.

→ a system that is wrong all the time is the perfect system. just do the reverse of the signals.

Generalists

We will try to keep our perspective about the value of the techniques used to build a robust trading strategy. We will be generalists, rather than specialists. We want to know, "Should we take profits or should *OR BOTH* we wait for a trend reversal?" We could always find one case where taking profits is better than staying with the trend. Our objective is to find out if it is a good rule in most cases.

It is unproductive to try to prove that an exponentially weighted trend is better than a simple moving average. Does the accuracy of one approach really make a difference to the direction of prices? If a system worked using an exponential calculation but did not work with a simple moving average, one would be forced to question the validity of the "trend." As a realistic analyst, I can say that all techniques are imperfect but many have value. When you are estimating answers, you should not calculate them to the 10th decimal place,

Significant digits

Realists

OF COURSE NOT!

In dealing with a market problem, we must ask if we are looking at the real cause of the price move. Patterns may be coincidental. Even if we know the cause, can we predict the result? Throughout this book, we will return to the need for a logical solution, rather than one that is computer-generated. *PRICE IS EFFECT*

Trading programs cannot be perfect, but we need to know what to expect. Is a stop-loss a good way to control risk, or does it only give us unfounded confidence? It is not important whether a stop-loss is good or bad, only that we know the right answer.

This book will also present some new ideas, such as an adaptive, or self-adjusting, moving average and a detailed plan for creating a robust trading program. In the spirit of a lateral solution, it will take a new look at simple ways to improve most trading models, extracting the essential aspects from each idea. Examples will use forex, futures, stock, and stock index markets to show how readily these techniques apply to all markets, and trading in general.

PERRY J. KAUFMAN
Wells River, Vermont

Acknowledgments

Writing a book is a long process that takes time from those closest to you. Without the encouragement and support of Barbara, this volume would have been long delayed. Credit must be given to our dog Terra, who always knew when it was time to take a break.

P.J.K.

PART 1

How Changing Markets and Technology Affect Results

Following moving averages is like playing a game of crack the whip with the trader being at the trailing end of the whip. He gets flipped off well after the trend changes. Can the trader find ways to move to the front of the line?

1

The Impact of Change on Markets and Trading

This book is about how to improve your trading in the stock, foreign exchange and futures markets. Although many technical solutions and spreadsheet applications appear in these pages, *Smarter Trading* is really about making decisions and solving problems. It will identify why many trading strategies and forecasts fail and will show how to improve results and create more lasting solutions.

The approach taken here tries to be realistic; trading systems have limitations, as do the tools and the traders. The techniques for improving profits and assessing risk focus on those areas that offer the greatest improvement, rather than the subtleties of fine tuning. Most of the more difficult topics are concerned with risk. Experienced traders usually know what to do with profits; even for novice traders, profits often take care of themselves. It is an unreasonably optimistic attitude toward risk that gets many traders into trouble; therefore, sections of this book keep returning to risk evaluation and control. We're in this for the long term.

→ How robust is this idea? Do people generally understand benefits, but are unreasonably optimistic toward risk.

Changing Factors Affecting Markets and Prices

Recent years have seen political and economic changes of large proportion. The emergence of China, the instability of the European Monetary System, and the faltering of Russia are all poised to produce massive changes in trade. At the same time, technology has made immense

QUICK TOOL: Set modest goals, take profits.
Set tight stops based on price action and S/R.

3

advances. More powerful computers come in smaller packages. Prices can be displayed for any time period in an array of multicolored windows.

Methods that once worked do not work anymore. IBM stumbles, patterns change, markets are more volatile than ever, and even seasonals are not the same. Program trading has been declared "disruptive" all over the world. Traders sit behind screens in massive bank trading rooms, surrounded by high-powered displays, looking for arbitrage opportunities between any two markets in any two countries. All this continues 24 hours each day.

This evolution of markets is a structural change that moves in only one direction. The introduction of the automated exchanges in the United States and United Kingdom aren't anomalies, but a trend. Eventually, the floor traders will disappear—not all at one time, but edged out by automated exchanges that will surround them and slowly infringe on the sanctity of even the largest trading floors. Adapting may take more effort than simply retesting a program, adjusting for inflation, or changing the value of a stop-loss, but it cannot be ignored.

Along with increasing complexity is additional competition. Floor traders once had the advantage of being aware of every price tick. Now we can recall prices and volume instantly, and catch up on market action even when we have been away from the picture for hours or days. It requires more to compete successfully. This book will help identify the problems. It will provide solutions and an understanding of new tools and how to use them.

Changing Technology for Market Analysis

Advances in technology have caused great changes in the trading industry. New tools and techniques are absorbed quickly. The goal of improving returns by a fraction of a point has tremendous rewards,

Figure 1-1. Technology evolves, markets evolve,.....

enough to motivate and finance major research projects. And as machines increase in their ability to process more of everything, pushing those limits becomes a compulsion.

There is also a fascination with the new tools and the ability to display graphics and analyze prices. Real-time data from all over the world is being processed at speeds measured in nanoseconds. We can do more faster and cheaper, even when we're not always sure what we are doing.

Fundamentals at the Root

"Fundamentals" will always be the reason for price change. Fundamental analysis is the study of information that can influence corporate earnings, dividends, and interest rates, resulting in a price change. In both stock and commodity markets, forecasts are the result of comparing current and past economic data, and determining the effects of government policy on interest rates and growth. Unexpected events introduce volatility and uncertainty.

In general, the direction of stock prices is related to the health of business, which might include data on the Gross National Product (GNP), Consumer Price Index (CPI), retail sales, employment, and interest rates. If the economy is expanding, you can expect equity markets to rise. It is still a challenge to look further for the industries and sectors that will perform independently, or without correlation, to the market as a whole.

Supply and demand determine the price of goods and materials: how much there is versus how much is wanted. The more material, the lower the price; the more that is wanted, the higher the price. The fundamentals of price change are clear. It is the changes in those factors or the anticipation of change that causes prices to move.

One of the first computer applications for price forecasting used a technique called *multiple regression* (Box 1-1). Data on imports, exports, *p6* production, consumption, interest rates, inflation, technology, and other essentials could be analyzed in conjunction with the price. Fundamental analysis *explains* what has happened in the past by assigning "weighting factors" to the information put into the computer. If you don't put in the right data, you don't get a good answer. Putting in too much data isn't as bad, but it takes a longer time to process. Sometimes, too much data allows the computer to find answers that are only coincidental, which we call "overfit."

The answer to a regression analysis is assigned a *confidence* level, which indicates its accuracy. It is stated as "plus or minus" an error factor (e.g., interest rates will drop to $5\frac{1}{2}$ percent $\pm$ 1 percent by May).

Fundamentals also fail because of their static (linear) assumptions - "all things being equal". Markets are NON LINEAR.

Box 1-1. DETERMINING A COMMODITY PRICE WITH FUNDAMENTALS

A simple regression model calculates a commodity price from the history of fundamental factors. In this example, the price of soybeans is simply the weighting of supply and demand:

Est_Price = constant + (weightS $\times$ supply) + (weightD $\times$ demand)
$\pm$ error

where Est_Price is the current estimated value
supply is the total production
demand is the total distribution
error is the error reflecting the accuracy of the results
and constant, weightS, and weightD are calculated using a
regression program.

Data from 1964 to 1975 gives constant = -1.64, weightS = 3.97 and weightD = 0.81, indicating that changes in the supply of soybeans, represented by the much larger value of weightS, are much more important than demand. The error factor would be large because only a few years were used in the calculation.

A regression analysis of fundamental data tells where prices *should* be, in the same sense as an option fair value calculation. It is very structured and provides only a single price range, which is considered "normal." It may not include data that cause the market to anticipate changes.

In general, this classic approach is not helpful to a trader because it says nothing about risk. If the current price level is below the calculated one, but prices start to fall instead of rise, when do you say that something is wrong? The forecast only shows where the price should be; it does not tell anything about how it will get there. *or whether it will.*

Fundamental analysis still makes sense, but it remains the domain of institutions and long-term traders. It requires a well-capitalized investor to absorb fairly large equity swings during periods when less important factors cause market volatility. For others, the risk is too high, the analysis takes too much time and effort, and the profits are too far off.

This method of econometric analysis can be applied to the stock index, but not to individual shares; however, results are still very general.

Newer methods, such as neural networks and expert systems, which are discussed in later chapters, have replaced econometric analysis, offering some additional accuracy when used in the traditional way, and much more flexibility.

Technical Analysis

Technical analysis is a broad area that uses price and related data to decide when to buy and sell. It tries to bridge the problems that fundamental analysis has about the specifics of timing and risk. The methods used can be as interpretive as chart patterns and astrology, or as specific as mathematical formulas and spectral analysis.

From the time chart interpretation first appeared to the early use of the home computer, technicians have been separated from fundamentalists. More recently, the line between them has become gray. Fundamentals provide the reason and direction of price movement, and technicals give the timing and risk control.

The two methods can be kept separate by making a decision and commitment based on fundamentals, then creating and implementing the plan using technicals. Or, the process can be integrated with an expert system approach, a sophisticated neural network, or simply a combination of individual programs. It is only necessary that each make sense and satisfy the preset objectives.

Automating the Trend

Computerized technical analysis is associated most with the *moving average* (Box 1-2). It came into greatest popularity in the early 1980s and has remained the basis for many technical programs. All factors that influence the market are assumed to be netted out as the current price. A simple moving average applied to those prices gives a trend. The longer term 200-day average is a benchmark indicator of price direction for most stock issues. Short-term 5-, 10-, and 20-day trends, related to weekly and monthly periods, are often used for timing entries and exits and for leveraged futures and options markets.

A moving average, or similar technical indicator, is frequently used to confirm a decision to enter the market. Although there may be reason to believe prices will move higher, fundamental analysis can be complex, and occasionally unexpected external factors overwhelm the normal situation. By waiting for a moving average to turn up, the program may sacrifice some initial profit for a greater chance of being correct and of using capital effectively.

Box 1-2. EASIER NEW WAYS OF CALCULATING MOVING AVERAGES

A moving average is now a "function" in a strategy testing program or a spreadsheet. A 3-day moving average may appear as:

@Average(close,3) = (close + close[1] + close[2])/3

or the spreadsheet form:

@AVG(B3..B5)/3

An exponential trend is simply another function, @Exp_MA(close,10), all of which makes price analysis very easy to perform. The trendline formed by the daily averages produces a buy signal when it turns up and a sell when it turns down.

Trend trading was very successful during the 1970s and into the 1980s. Even now, it is just as important to know the direction of prices, but it has become more difficult to trade a simple trend system. What was once a strong commitment to "the trend is your friend," we now hear that there are too many systematic trend-followers who are "pushing the market" and "triggering stops."

Trend following proved to many investors that technical analysis is viable. Some analysts, equipped with real-time intraday data, were able to continue trading the trend by applying the same logic to hourly or 15-minute prices. Others looked for additional indicators or more sophisticated tools, often adapted from another industry.

Indicators

Timing indicators, such as *relative strength* and *stochastics* have become very popular. Most quote equipment provides a broad selection of techniques that users can modify. The Relative Strength Index (RSI), developed by Welles Wilder, is a ratio of the total daily upmoves to total daily downmoves over the past 14 days, expressed from 0 to 100:

@RSI(close,14) = 100 × (RS/(1 + RS)

where

RS = @SUM(Total_Up_Moves,14)/@SUM(Total_Down_Moves,14)

Because of the flexibility of computers, any trader can substitute another time period for the standard 14-day interval.

The *stochastic,* developed by George Lane, is equally popular. It gives the relative position of the closing price within the previous high-low range, determined by the length of the period used for the calculation. The raw stochastic, called FastK, which ranges from a value of 0 to 100, is not normally used for trading because it is too sensitive to price change. Instead, the SlowK (also called %D) and SlowD, a 3-day smoothing of SlowK, have become the popular values for trading. The 5-period stochastic is given as

$$@FastK(series,5) = 100 \times (close - @Lowest(5)/(@Highest(5)$$
$$- @Lowest(5))$$

$$@SlowK(series,5) = @Moving\_Average(@FastK(series,5),3)$$

$$@SlowD(series,5) = @Moving\_Average(@SlowK(series,5),3)$$

As with the RSI, traders vary the period of the stochastic to make it more or less sensitive to price movement.

Stock Market Advance/Decline Indicators

In addition to indicators that use price, a wide selection of calculations are based on volume, or the number of advancing and declining stocks. It is interesting to see how the same numbers are used with slightly different emphasis:

Bolton-Tremblay: $\quad$ BT = (Advancing − Declining)/Unchanged

Schultz A/T: $\quad$ SAT = Advancing/(Advancing + Declining + Unchanged)

McClellan Oscillator: $\quad$ McC = Advancing − Declining

For each of the indicators, an index is created by adding the current value to the accumulated index value for the previous day, as in the Bolton-Tremblay Index:

$$BTX = BTX[1] + BT$$

While there is virtue in simplicity, it is not clear that an index such as the one based on advancing and declining issues improves a moving average signal. The indexes themselves require interpretation and selection because they do nothing to filter noise, nor is it apparent how to use those days with significantly greater advancing or declining issues. Instead of just one difficult price series to work with, you now have the original price data plus an equally difficult index.

Status of Technical Analysis

Simple moving averages and indicators do not give the complete picture of technical analysis. There are sophisticated graphics programs that allow the user to draw trendlines and channels. They can perform spectral analysis to find cycles; give Gann lines and angles, Fibonacci spirals, and Elliott waves; and create ARIMA (Autoregressive Integrated Moving Average) models, which constantly recalculate the best moving average for every new piece of data.

Testing software has also pushed the industry forward. Anyone with an untried trading strategy or theory can enter simple instructions and test the rules on a wide selection of data. The most popular examples of this software are Dow Jones' *TeleTrac*, Omega's *System Writer*, and Equis' *MetaStock*. These programs eliminate the need for a computer specialist, by providing standard "functions" (as described earlier in this chapter) for calculating a moving average, true range, highest and lowest price, and many other convenient values, in an easy-to-use form. For example,

@Average(Price,Length)

@Bollinger_Band(Price,Length,StdDev)

@Bullish_Divergence(Price,Osc,Strength,Length)

@Linear_Regression(Price,Length)

are the functions for a simple moving average, a Bollinger band, bullish divergence, and the angle from the horizontal of a linear regression line. They are all easy to understand even without a manual. Length is the number of periods used in the calculation, and price is any data series, whether daily, hourly, or user defined.

Strategy-testing software takes two forms: (1) a spreadsheet style system, such as *TeleTrac*, in which each calculation becomes a new row, and each day appears as a column; (2) the *System Writer* design, which allows all the power of computer programming, similar to the BASIC language (Box 1-3). In Omega's software, the individual calculation can be displayed by day on request.

a blooper →  AN IMPORTANT BOX ?

Box 1-3. PROGRAMMING SYSTEMS USING NEW COMPUTER SOFTWARE

An "efficiency ratio" is calculated as 10-day price changes divided by the sum of 10 daily closing price differences. The *EfRatio* gives the efficiency, or relative noise, of price movement over the 10-day period, and is used for the Adaptive Moving Average in Chapter 8.

TeleTrac allows the calculations to be entered in their own spreadsheet format. The first column is the name of the value being created and the second gives the formula. Results are shown for each time interval selected, from ticks to monthly. This example has daily data:

		18 Feb 93	23 Feb 93	24 Feb 93	25 Feb 93
diff	Abs_val(close-close[1])	0.64	0.97	0.45	0.57
noise	Sum(diff,10)	3.969	4.521	4.839	5.124
signal	close-close[10]	1.29	2.68	2.09	1.81
EfRatio	Abs_val(signal)/noise	0.325	0.593	0.433	0.353

System Writer uses Omega's fully programmable *Easy Language* to find the same ratio:

```
noise = @Summation(@AbsValue(close[0] − close[1], length)
signal = close[0] − close[10]

if noise <> 0, then Efficiency_Ratio = signal/noise
```

The last line of the *System Writer* code tests that the noise is not equal to ("<>") zero before dividing. In the first line, it "nests" the first two lines of the *TeleTrac* code.

any questions?

Buy and sell signals, as well as moving average lines, oscillators, and user-defined values can be displayed on split-screen graphics. Every calculation and detailed statistics of the test results can be easily retrieved and printed.

New Technology

As computers have become more powerful and scientists try to synthesize the human brain, some new techniques have become more practical for market analysis. The area called *artificial intelligence* includes the most promising *neural networks*, as well as simple *pattern recognition*, *expert systems*, and *fuzzy logic*. These will be covered later in this book.

Neural networks are already replacing regression analysis as the best method for finding how fundamental factors change price. But the power of neural nets is still untouched. It is primarily used to find the same continuous relationships between dividends, economic conditions, and price—or supply, demand, and price—that was the technique of the older tools. It has the ability to identify how today's set of factors compares with specific cases in history, an equally sophisticated and practical approach.

Evolution and Obsolescence   *A FASCINATING SECTION*

It is easy to argue that communications and computers have changed world and local economies, trading tools, and market participants. The extent of these changes requires us to look at the process as an evolution. It should not be a surprise that simple systems that worked well during the 1970s and 1980s are no longer profitable.

Economic changes have altered price relationships. Countries have floated their currencies and interest rates, as gold was allowed to be traded in the United States in 1975. Other countries have tried to control the fluctuation by forming pacts, such as the European Monetary System or OPEC (Organization of Petroleum Exporting Countries). For each of these events, there is a change in price patterns, sometimes more volatile; other times less volatile; and still other cases go unnoticed. A simple way of looking at this evolution is by comparing the performance of a trend-following system in different types of markets.

Maturing Markets and Price Trends

As markets become familiar and accepted, participation increases, and with more participation comes a higher level of "noise." The U.S. stock market has been a main investment for pension funds, individuals, and other countries for many years. Broad interest takes on the characteristic of a constant level of activity resulting from unrelated objectives of its participants, much like the undercurrent of constant talking at larger and smaller meetings. A pension fund adds to its positions because of new investment capital; a corporation liquidates a stock portfolio to invest in a shopping center, or a family withdraws from a mutual fund to pay medical bills. Much of the price movement has little to do with economic trends or clever timing of entry and exit points.

a definition of noise - i.e. noise represents entry and exit for reasons unrelated to economic trends.

New or emerging markets do not have this broad participation; therefore, the level of noise is not nearly as high. That makes it easier to trade a simple trend-following system profitably. Table 1-1 and Box 1-4 compare more and less mature markets. They show that it is easier to trade a newer market with a simple system, and just as impossible to use that same approach for a broadly traded, mature market.

p14

Comparing New and Mature Markets

Results show that the newest, active world markets, the Hong Kong *Hang Seng Index* and MATIF's *CAC-40* are still very profitable for all trend speeds tested. The Hang Seng has a higher annualized return for faster trends, indicating that short-term price swings are sustained with a relatively low level of noise, even though the longer term trend did not develop as well. Had the noise been greater, the trend would have reversed frequently, causing whipsaw losses.

The *CAC-40* shows a drop of about 50 percent in trend returns for the most recent five years compared with the earlier period. It also posted larger profits in faster trading for the earlier period but has evolved to a more uniform distribution as the market matured. There is now only a slightly declining pattern in the rate of return as you move from the shortest 5-day trend speed to the longest 75-day period.

The Deutsche mark, along with other major currencies, has always been actively traded. In the past five years, however, Deutsche mark activity has increased as the mark assumed a dominant role in the European economic structure, combined with greater world trading activity. The first five years, 1983–1987, show greater profits and a tendency toward longer term trends than the more recent years. Both periods show that the fastest trends are the most difficult, the likely result of short-term volatility, frequent price shocks, and intense competition in active Forex trading. The "optimum" trend may vary based on long-term economic shifts, confidence in the European Community, and the ability of the United States to compete in trade. As the foreign exchange markets continue to mature, the ability to produce trending profits with faster trading should decline.

IBM is shown for only the first five-year period, to allow you to study its change. With the exception of the 5-day trend, it shows a clear increase in profits as a longer-term position is taken. With transaction costs included, the smaller profits posted in the 15- to 45-day trends are likely to disappear. The profit of 18 percent for the 5-day trend may seem unusual but would have presented a window of opportunity for some small investors.

Box 1-4. THE ABILITY TO PROFIT FROM A TREND-FOLLOWING SYSTEM

Changes in price patterns as markets mature can be illustrated with a simple trend-following system. It shows that newer or emerging markets have clear trends. As they mature, the increased participation increases noise and makes the price patterns more complex. Orders entering continually, for different reasons, obscure the trend.

Table 1-1 shows the results of a simple trend-following system tested for a selection of markets. The system uses the following rules:

1. An exponential moving average determined the trend.
2. *Buy* when today's exponential trend value turns up.
3. *Sell* when today's exponential trend value turns down.
4. The system is always in the market.
5. No transaction costs were charged.

Table 1-1. Comparison of Trend Performance

Exp MA Days	Hang Seng 1988– 1993	CAC-40 1983– 1987	CAC-40 1988– 1992	D-Mark 1983– 1987	D-Mark 1988– 1992	IBM 1982– 1987	Dow 1983– 1987	Dow 1988– 1992	Crude Oil Dec 1992
5	22.3	40.5	16.6	5.7	1.3	18.0	(47.5)	(36.2)	(0.17)
15	17.5	33.1	20.7	9.7	4.9	4.0	(22.3)	(26.8)	0.27
25	12.1	32.8	19.9	6.7	7.4	4.3	(22.7)	(16.1)	(0.41)
35	9.8	30.0	19.7	9.3	6.2	6.9	(18.9)	(14.9)	(0.43)
45	8.7	29.1	10.8	8.5	9.3	8.6	(12.9)	(14.4)	(0.91)
55	11.7	28.5	13.5	9.3	6.3	11.7	(0.7)	(8.7)	(1.19)
65	11.1	27.7	18.3	11.7	5.8	11.1	0.8	(6.6)	(0.85)
75	18.0	27.8	13.5	11.2	5.8	18.0	(0.7)	(11.6)	(0.17)
Avg	10.4	31.2	16.6	9.0	6.2	10.3	(15.6)	(16.9)	(0.48)

Results show

1. The most mature market, the Dow, cannot be traded using any trend within the tested range.
2. Developing markets, such as the Hang Seng and CAC-40 (from 1983 to 1987) show characteristic short-term trends. As they mature, they begin to show greater profits in long-term trends, rather than short-term.
3. The D-mark is a deep market, as are all the other major currencies, and shows a tendency toward declining, smaller profits.
4. IBM shows long-term trends with the exception of a small opportunity window for the 5-day trend, which is difficult to trade.
5. Crude oil volatility, the result of large commercial dominance and attempted OPEC manipulation, overwhelms the price trend.

We might assume that institutions cannot trade a short-term trend because they cannot trade a large enough position and tend to move the market too far for the expected profit. Small, independent traders can take advantage of this slot only if their commissions and other transaction costs are low. A 5-day trend may have traded as much as once each week. With commissions at $\frac{1}{2}$ percent, an 18 percent profit becomes an 8 percent loss for the year.

The Dow represents the most mature market. The large losses at nearly every trend speed indicates that the daily market volatility is very high compared with the net movement of stock prices. Mature markets have broad participation, representing traders with diverse interests. Constant institutional buying and selling to fill portfolios, or speculative liquidation to invest in real estate or other assets, adds a high level of noise to the daily activity. As other world markets mature, they should follow the pattern of the Dow.

The last example looks at a single futures contract of NYMEX crude oil. It also shows losses in nearly every trend period. But crude oil is not as much a mature market as it is a manipulated one. Attempts by OPEC to limit production cause sharp moves and discourage small, individual traders from participating. The cash and futures markets, dominated by very large commercials, are used to buy and sell cargoes for delivery and hedging. This combination—attempted price controls and traders with large orders and deep pockets—adds volatility that overwhelms the trend.

Conclusion: more noise = less effectiveness of trend following, less noise = more effectiveness of trend following

Structural Change: Seasonality

Can you make the same type of trading decisions today as you could in 1960? No. Many of the markets with the greatest volume form a relatively new "derivatives" group. Foreign exchange futures, options on futures, stock index futures of all types in many countries, and short- and long-term interest rates, including the European Currency Unit or ECU (which is more a concept than a hard currency that you could use to pay a lunch bill) are all very different from the markets only 10 years ago.

Even agricultural markets, the oldest of the exchange-traded commodities, have changed. Crops are still planted and harvested according to their season, but the seasonal price patterns that survived for centuries are no longer dependable. In the 1980s, U.S. grain prices rose with surplus production, confusing traders and delighting farmers. Afterward, the phenomenon was recognized as "parity," the ability of a freely traded product to hold a constant world value. As the U.S. dollar declined, U.S. grain became more attractive to non-U.S. buyers, causing export demand and price to rise.

It seems odd to think that the normal seasonal patterns have also changed. Beginning in the mid-1970s, farmers built more storage facilities. Before there was adequate storage, farmers needed to forward price their production with a local grain elevator or be subject to selling everything that couldn't be stored at harvest. They could rent storage space, but only if they booked in advance and paid a minimum 3-month fee. On-farm storage relieved the pressure on harvest prices and farmers could recoup their cost by adding carrying charges to the crop price each month after harvest. With 100 percent storage, it is possible to eliminate the price drop at harvest.

With their own storage facilities, carrying charges become "soft dollars" to the farmers. When crops were stored in a rented space, farmers paid out-of-pocket costs to elevator operators. On-farm storage is similar to price "bundling"; it is harder to distinguish the cost of the parts, and the total price becomes more flexible.

Orange juice presents two more seasonal wrinkles. Crop freezes are no longer devastating to consumers. Prices may jump sharply when temperatures hold under freezing in central Florida, but not for long. For the past few years, Brazil has been anxious to fill the gap in U.S. supply, and consumers are equally agreeable to paying lower prices at the expense of domestic U.S. growers. Because the government bowed to the pressure and permitted juice to be imported from tremendous Brazilian reserves, what will happen the next time there is a freeze? Do prices jump on a sharp reduction in supply, or will traders anticipate a fast substitution of Brazilian product? In either case, the seasonal pattern is disrupted.

The second twist is the result of the opposite North American–South American crop years. Orange juice, soybeans, and eventually other crops can be produced in quantity in the opposite season. When the U.S. farmers are harvesting in the fall, Brazilian farmers are planting in the spring. Just when carryover stores are dwindling, crops from the other hemisphere are being harvested. When U.S. crop production is not good, Southern Hemisphere stocks and plantings can be abundant. The world import market is fungible. If the Russians need grain, they will go to the best price, not just to the U.S. market. What does this do to the seasonal patterns? It makes supply and demand a global concept, and far less predictable.

The Evolution of Markets

This is not just an agricultural phenomenon. It is no secret that financial markets have been globalized. These effects are permanent. Even if governments change and exchanges disappear, the United States will never again be the only center of activity. Undoubtedly, the People's Republic of China (PRC) and Russia will play an increasing role in world trade. Despite the PRC's apparent resistance to political change, it has shown an aversion to cutting off its Hong Kong arm. Regardless of inconsistency, China—with a quarter of the world population—wants to enter into world trade more actively. Russia has already made it clear that it wants a market economy. The effects on supply-and-demand equilibrium will be enormous. If the transition is fast, the imbalance will provide short-term opportunities in business and speculation that are unprecedented. Either way, the future will not look the same as the past.

2

Assessing Market Reality

Trading looks easier than it is. Think of how clear the trends and patterns seem on an old chart of the DOW, or gold, or bonds. The recession that started in 1990–1991 was severe and prolonged, and it caused bond prices to move steadily higher for three years. It is perfectly clear that interest rates could do nothing other than decline. But how many "traders" just held bonds rather than bought and sold throughout the whole period? Not many. Whether people are trading stocks or selling crops, they usually buy and sell when they are forced to, or when they can no longer stand the stress of holding the position.

Change is difficult. We tend to be resistant, slow to recognize change, and often slower to react. Awareness of change often comes when it becomes obvious that the old way doesn't work anymore. Only then do we look for new solutions. This chapter looks at changes in the market structure, its participants, and in the way we use the new tools. Recognizing the problems can be a convincing argument for changing some of your trading methods.

The Screen Is History   *The screen is NOT the market*

Prices that appear on the quote screen are already part of history. In a fast futures market, the price you see may have traded 5 minutes ago. At any time, the market is more likely to be trading at a price that is different from the one you see on the screen. The screen shows where the price traded *last*, not where it's going to trade *next*. When execution timing is critical, you cannot wait for a screen price. The screen is not the market. ✓ It lags the market in the same way a trend lags actual price movement.

That's not to say that you always get a poor execution price. There are those times when, because you were too slow, you got in at a better price later. But they are exceptions. Even when you can make the entry gracefully, exiting a trade can be a rushed event. Use of spontaneous judgment only gives you the opportunity to delay the exit, hold onto that losing trade, and wait for a worse price to come along.

The screen is a poor substitute for a resting order, which gets executed immediately. Unfortunately, Stops and Limit orders only work for small lots. However, anticipating a trade, whether a computerized or intuitive system, will improve the ability to get a target price for smaller, individual traders as well as institutions. The importance of anticipation will be discussed later in this chapter.

Nonexistent Spread Profits

During the trading day, screens often show prices within a single market, such as crude oil, that appear out of line. Or, a part of the yield curve, such as the 10-year note, may be too high with regard to the 5- and 20-year instruments. Box 2-1 shows the prices as they might appear at midday, with the November quote clearly out of line with respect to other delivery months.

If you try to spread those markets, to profit by selling the apparent distortion, you find that the bid-asked is perfectly in line with the other months, although the screen price only reflects the last trade. The price was higher or lower on the screen simply because one forward month had not traded while activity in the neighboring delivery months had moved those prices lower.

In general, spreads that are constructed by matching two separate price series will suffer the same problem. The traded spread price is not often saved as historic data because it seems easy enough to create a spread once you have the prices for each of the components. It simply involves getting the prices at the same time.

Frequently, two markets do not trade at exactly the same time. The spread will appear to move in and out based entirely on one market trading while the other remains quiet. This is especially the case for a nearby versus deferred delivery of the same futures market. In reality, the spread price (the difference between the two months) may have remained unchanged during the entire time.

Closing Prices

It is more common to use the closing prices to generate a spread. For financial markets that close at the same time, these prices can be reason-

Box 2-1. MIDDAY CRUDE OIL PRICES IN AUGUST 1993

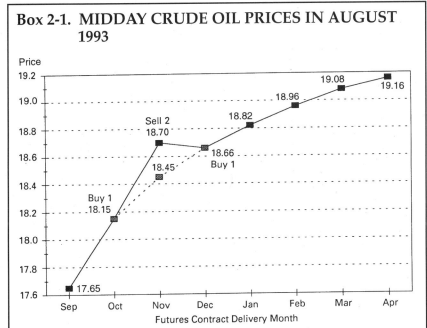

Figure 2-1. Distortion in crude oil forward prices. A relative price distortion is shown for the November contract.

The November quote of 18.70 should be closer to 18.45 if the carrying charge pattern is to remain uniform. A butterfly spread that buys one Oct and one Dec and sells two Nov would capture certain profits. When the spread prices are quoted, however, you find that Nov is bid at the equivalent of 18.45. The distortion only exists on the screen because Nov has not traded in 5 minutes while the other delivery months were more active.

able, if you consider the slightly higher transaction costs of executing a spread. However, creating a spread from the closing prices of two markets that did not close at the same time (and at the same exchange) creates an unrealistic spread price. If you trade only the IMM (International Monetary Market) currencies and the Swiss franc closes 5 minutes after the Deutsche mark, then the spread may appear to widen or narrow during those 5 minutes. The Deutsche mark will remain aligned with the Swiss franc in the cash market, and open the next day at the spread price that existed 5 minutes before the Swiss closed, when both markets were open. A trading signal based on prices quoted at different times could easily have been an error.

Execution Problems and Performance

Brokerage fees are often only a small part of transaction costs. *Slippage,* the difference between the price you wanted and the price you got, is a costly component in trading. This ignores the fact that some trades don't get filled at all. *Unables,* the trades that don't get executed, are the biggest problem and the greatest cost for large traders.

You can get filled on any trade if you *must* be in or out of the market. By placing an order "at the market," it will be filled; or, you can take the bid or asked price in the cash market, regardless of the amount. But most traders won't take *any* price; systematic trading generally requires a price relatively close to the signal or target price to produce profits.

"Unables"

Unables are usually orders that were canceled because the market moved too fast and too far. This applies to entering new positions much more than getting out of existing ones. Entering a position allows more selectivity; exiting a trade always seems to be an urgent matter.

Experience shows that a fast trend-following or breakout system can miss nearly all profitable trades under poor market conditions, and up to 30 percent of all profitable trades during a volatile 1-month period.

Intraday breakout systems show the typical problems. Buying a breakout that occurs during the trading day may not be possible. When government reports are released just after the opening of the U.S. financial markets, prices can leap to new levels. Only a few contracts in total may be executed during the price move that lasts only a few seconds. You can't expect to be filled by being fast or using a Stop order. You can only buy the top or not buy at all.

An individual with a small order may be pleasantly surprised once in a while, by getting an execution somewhere before the market reaches its extreme. If you trade larger lots, say 100 or more futures contracts, and limit the slippage that you will accept (by using Limit orders or waiting for a specific price level), expect that 5 percent to 30 percent of your trading volume won't be filled over the long term. Many times all of an order will be filled, other times very little.

Who Is Likely to Have Execution Problems?

Not all traders have difficulty getting fills. The worst performance comes from a combination of five features:

1. *High-volume traders, such as fund managers and institutions.* Large orders mean pushing the price, especially if you are exiting a position. It means that it may take from 10 minutes to 3 days to execute an order. It's difficult to get a specific price under those conditions.

2. *Short-term traders, holding positions for less than two days.* Fast trading keeps both profits and losses small. Slippage can take a large percentage from profits, in addition to increasing the size of each loss.

3. *Trend-followers, buying and selling in the direction of the price move.* Buying when the market is rising always results in sizable slippage, and occasionally an unpleasant surprise when prices jump. Good news is rare.

4. *Intraday traders, executing orders between the open and close.* Volume drops sharply between the open and close of an exchange trading session, and between traditional business hours in interbank markets. It is not always easy to find someone to take the trade, or the bid-asked moves to an unacceptable spread.

5. *Traders who use limit orders, such as "Or Better."* Rather than using "At the Market orders," professionals try to execute at a price. They can find themselves chasing the market more often than they expect. At some point, the price becomes unacceptable.

An institutional trader, such as a fund, using a short-term breakout system (considered to be trend-following) in which signals occur at any time during the day, would have the largest slippage and the most unables. Few traders and methods are immune from unables.

Only the Profits Don't Get Filled

It is easy to see that the unfilled positions would have all been profits. If prices had reversed after a breakout or trend signal, there would have been an opportunity to enter the whole trade. Therefore, it is the profitable move—where prices keep going (or pull back only a small amount)—that does not get executed. The losing trades are always filled and you miss only the winners.

Can you make money trading a system where 5 percent to 30 percent of the profitable positions aren't filled or when you must execute in a fast market? Box 2-2 shows that a single unexpected price jump p 24

Box 2-2. THE IMPACT OF SLIPPAGE

Example 1: Impact of normal slippage

A trend-following program has an average profit of $500, an average loss of $150, and is profitable 40 percent of the time, netting an average combined profit of $110 per trade after commissions, without slippage. Trades in the Deutsche mark, entered as *Stop* orders, are typically filled 4 pips from the signal price, but no less than 2 pips. For a Chicago International Monetary Market contract, traded in 8ths of a million, that means a cost of no less than $25, but normally at least $50 of added cost for each entry and exit. That leaves only $10 per trade as an expected profit!

Example 2: Impact of slippage in a fast market

The importance of slippage can be reduced by increasing the expected profits per trade. Using a slower trend-following approach, with larger profits and fewer trades, the program produces the same $500 average profits, $150 losses, and a 40 percent reliability, but this time *net of both* fees and normal slippage.

When the IMM Deutsche mark opens at 7:20 A.M. in Chicago, the price is at 58.10. The trend-following system has a *buy Stop* entered for 20 lots at 58.25. At 7:30, the U.S. Balance of Trade is released, showing a deficit of $12 billion, unchanged from the previous month, but $4 billion worse than expected. The fills come back from the floor: 2 at 58.30, 5 at 58.60, and 13 at 58.75, averaging 58.667. The total slippage is US$521 per contract. If this program has one trade per week, the expected returns would be:

21 Profits @ $500 =	$10,500
31 Losses @ $150 =	(4,650)
52 Trades total	$5,850

A single added loss of $521 is 9 percent of the annual returns.

---

could cost nearly 10 percent of the expected yearly profits. If you do not plan for execution problems during development, most programs will not survive.

Improving Results

The three ways of reducing the unpleasant effects of unables and slippage are to seek larger profits per trade, use realistic transaction costs in testing, and anticipate the trading signal (anticipation is discussed in Chapter 11). Larger profits can be accomplished in the following ways:

- *Holding long-term positions*. Trading only one to three times per year, with large expected profits, reduces the importance of slippage and allows a longer time to enter and exit a trade. An average price or a specific entry strategy can work well.

- *Targeting larger profits per trade*. When using a faster trading method, which is a necessity for many foreign exchange operations, profits per trade can be increased by selecting more volatile markets or by including a profit-taking strategy. Profit taking will improve the overall profile of a system and will contribute significantly to reducing slippage.

Test Criteria

The use of a realistic execution price when simulating a trading strategy can resolve all slippage and profitability problems. You cannot know if a strategy will be profitable unless you assign correct entry and exit prices. The following procedures are advisable:

- *Approximate "normal" slippage*. Box 2-3 shows that fill prices are p 26 based on a number of factors. The net transaction cost is difficult to determine in advance. A "worst-case scenario" may be too extreme, but something less than an optimistic approach is best.

- *Estimate fills for intraday trading*. It is safe to assume that you get the worst price during the 5–15 minutes following your order. That means taking the worst high or low during the interval, not just the price at the end of the period.

- *Test for "locked-limit" moves in futures markets*. In most cases, you can't buy if the closing price equals the high of the day; you can't sell if the close equals the low of the day. The exchange system of settlement, based on an average of the last one minute of trading, makes it unlikely that the close will settle at the high or low. Of course, when the high and low are the same, no trading occurred.

The best estimate comes from monitoring a system that is actually traded, as discussed in Chapter 11. Unfortunately, that does not help at the early stages of development. Previous experience will allow you to estimate the transaction costs for trend-following and other programs, even though those strategies are not identical to the current system.

Box 2-3. GUIDELINES FOR CALCULATING SLIPPAGE

The following guidelines are for *buy* orders: *reverse for sells*

	Small Orders	Large Orders
Variable slippage. Add a percentage of the high-low range to the fill price, e.g., Price $\pm$ .15 $\times$ (High $-$ Low)	15% above the system signal price	15% above the average of the execution interval price
Minimum slippage. Each market is assigned a minimum slippage that is larger than the normal bid-asked spread. For IMM Japanese yen or Deutsche marks, the spread is 8 pips, or US$50. For the S&P, it is often 20 ticks, or US$100. Use the minimum slippage if it is greater than the *variable slippage.*	For trend following: (Ask-Bid) $\times$ 1.5 Countertrend orders: (Ask-Bid) $\times$ 1.0	(Ask-Bid) $\times$ 3.0 (Ask-Bid) $\times$ 2.0
Orders on the Open or Close. Orders executed in the opening or closing range receive the worst price of the range.	Worst of the opening or closing range	Worst of the range $\times$ 1.5

Maximum volume. Assume that an order will not be entirely filled, at any price, if it exceeds 5 percent of the daily volume.

Screen trading execution lag. If Stop orders are not used, traders must assume that prices have moved past their price by the time that price appears on the screen. At best, the screen shows the *bid* price. The calculations above assume that the time to call the broker, quote the price, and place one or more orders results in larger slippage.

Small lot Stop orders. Small orders placed as Stops are usually filled at prices showing slippage greater than you would expect from the bid-asked spread. You often pay a premium for trading small.

Globalization: Simultaneous Absorption

The Nikkei drops 700 points, and the S&P opens 200 lower. The Bundesbank raises the rate on the bund by a half-point, and U.S. bonds drop. The old theories of isolationism no longer exist. Economic events in one financial center affect financial markets everywhere with nearly instant reactions. As Great Britain struggles with its economy, its equity market fails to react to rate changes by the Bank of England. Instead, it is pulled by the more influential trading partners in the European Monetary System.

Portfolio diversification is more difficult when markets are tied together, pulling at each other. Some of the new links between investments are not yet obvious because they have not been tested. Diversifying a portfolio into 30 percent selected stocks, 30 percent bonds, and 10 percent currencies seems safe until a political crisis surfaces. Then money runs to the safety of the U.S. dollar. Bonds move sharply higher, stocks move slightly higher, and the dollar gains, posting a loss in the Forex holdings. The currency allocation is reduced to compensate for the sudden increase in risk just when the international problems ease. Money flows away from the dollar, bond prices drop, the dollar drops, and stocks drop. Your holdings in currencies are too small to help the portfolio. So much for diversification.

Even though each investment group, individual stock, and commodity is directly affected by its own fundamental factors, the global picture can overwhelm all of them. The purpose of diversification is, foremost, to protect a portfolio from extreme risk. Normally, there is ample time to shift positions and take advantage of changing opportunities. With a crisis or price shock, it is too late. Investors pull funds from entirely unrelated investments to cover losses elsewhere. This causes all markets to reverse at the same time.

Factors That Always Exist

Noise

An unusual market move may cause you to forget that many underlying factors still exist. A fast move always includes some noise, which should be no less than in a normal market, perhaps larger. An anticipated price or target level may be over- or understated by the amount of market noise. Profit taking when high volatility has clearly favored your position is a way to take advantage of noise. Waiting to liquidate a position that has taken a bad loss on a price shock shows an understanding of noise.

Inflation

Inflation moves along at a relatively steady rate. If prices do not have an upward bias, then they are going down relative to other products. This relative decline can be confirmed by a long-term drop in volatility and a better return to risk ratio for purchases rather than sales.

Seasonality

A market that does not exhibit known seasonal tendencies is still seasonal. During the prolonged devaluation of the U.S. dollar in the 1980s, grain prices tended to move higher, sometimes during periods when seasonal patterns would have favored lower levels. Attractive exports, combined with price parity (a buyer in any country seeks the cheapest price) causes the price of freely traded commodities to maintain a constant world value. Seasonal patterns are overwhelmed by outside interest but still exert their influence on prices. During periods of lower supply, the commodity price will be that much higher to include a supply premium. Because seasonal factors cannot be removed, a period that overwhelms them, causing them to appear ineffective, is even more volatile and more unstable than it might seem.

Change and Evolution

An interesting phenomenon of change is that, when events stabilize, they are never quite the same as they were. Globalization and communications, broader markets, new technology, and better quote machines and analytic tools mean that markets are evolving. They will never respond to one another in the same way they have in the past.

The European Monetary System tries to regulate the variation (although not the volatility) between member currencies. The entry of Russia and China into the free market system can change both the supply and demand of nearly everything. It increases the chances of shortage and surplus. U.S. stock prices could double quickly if money could move freely between countries. Or, money could flow to the rapidly expanding Asian economies, shifting the center of finance.

Change means that the past does not help us to forecast the future as much as we would want. Unless you view the past as an evolving process, trading methods that worked in the past may no longer work. If market relationships change, you cannot use old data to forecast the future. You only know that the future is going to be different.

The assumption made by rigid systems, such as trend-following, fixed cycles, or patterns, that the current state of affairs will continue, contradicts reality. We are only passing through the current state. A trend-follower can only hope that unexpected changes do not cause extreme volatility that results in unreasonable losses. It is not the forecasting attributes of a trending system that allow profits, it is the risk controls.

To forecast successfully is to accept the inevitability of change and the risks associated with it. You cannot assume that the future will be the same as the past, that the risks and profits and patterns will repeat themselves. We can only try to develop systems that recognize the possibility of change and are flexible enough to profit from it.

3

Reasonable Expectations Give Achievable Results

The combination of technology, optimism, and the success of some highly visible traders can easily lead to unrealistic expectations. We see the profits before the risks, then we attack and eliminate the risks without questioning the validity of the profits. When developing a trading strategy, the failure to understand what is most likely to happen can waste time and effort, as well as cost a great deal of money.

Trade-Offs

Every profit opportunity has risk. Larger profits have larger risk. Each systematic approach to trading has its own risk and reward trade-offs. And a trade-off is always an unpleasant compromise. It is a mistake to think that you can find a trading strategy that has no losses, or an arbitrage that will absorb unlimited funds.

A pure *trend-following method* has smaller losses and larger profits. It is classified as a "conservation of capital" approach. To keep losses small, it is necessary to close out trades quickly. The system continually tries to find a trend but exits as soon as prices move in the wrong direction. Therefore, there are more losing trades than winning ones. If you increase your tolerance for risk, by using a slower trend or larger stop-loss, the system will have a larger percentage of winning trades but larger losses and equity swings. Make the trend very slow and the stop-loss far away and you have a passive portfolio of one open trade.

Countertrend strategies typically allow more risk to achieve frequent, small profits. When the strategy errs, there are large losses. Its trade-offs have the same, continuous relationship as a trend-following method, but in reverse. As the targeted profits get smaller, they are more frequent. In exchange, the fewer losses get larger.

Trend and countertrend traders have similar choices: smaller losses or smaller profits more often, offset by larger profits or smaller losses less often.

Commodity arbitrageurs compete for "riskless" opportunities, such as a *location arbitrage*. Profits can be made when the differential between the same product selling in separate locations is greater than the cost of transportation, insurance, and other carrying charges. Competition can be so keen that the arbitrageur accepts both small profits and small volume, a situation that, at some minimum, is not worth the effort.

There is no secret way to produce constant trading profits. Some methods are better than others, but none of them are immune from these trade-offs. It is important to identify and understand the alternatives before making a final choice (see Table 3-1).

Risk and Reward

We all know that there is higher risk with higher profits and that the only system that doesn't have losses is the one that doesn't trade. When you sit in front of a powerful computer with sophisticated tools, however, you tend to forget that these limitations still apply.

Profits seems to stand out when you look at the trading results of hundreds of strategies. The high leverage of options and futures pushes many of the test returns well above 100 percent per year. These are exceptionally high compared with most investment returns and can be intoxicating at first. But presented in a more traditional risk-adjusted form, with adequate capitalization to insure safety, results are scaled

Table 3-1. Trade-Offs

	For Every Positive	There Is a Negative
Trend-following	Large profits	Many small losses
	Small losses	More losses than profits
Countertrend	Many profits	Each one small
	Only a few losses	Each one large
Arbitrage	Very low risk	Few opportunities Very competitive Small profits
All systems	High profits	High risk

down to a more sensible range of 5 percent to 25 percent annually. This is discussed in Chapters 4 and 11. You may discover that the risk-adjusted returns of a very profitable trading method are no better than a conservative bond fund.

Be Wary of Unreasonably Good Results

Developing a trading method is hard work. The main idea can be the result of years of watching market patterns, or the formation of precise mathematical relationships. The process of testing and verifying is also difficult. Each calculation needs to be checked and entry and exit prices must be reviewed. It can be so tedious that, at some point, you would willingly accept good test results and stop looking for errors. You begin to look at larger individual losses without also reviewing the larger profits. But errors cause both good and bad results, and a program is not valid until it is error free.

A trading strategy that returns more than 20 percent annually, with a reward/risk ratio greater than 3.0, is an enviable achievement. If you add a stop-loss to a system to reduce its risk, you find that the returns also drop; or, by selecting specific trades with better opportunities, you reduce the frequency of trading so that each trade must generate larger profits to reach the original rate of return. Each day that you are out of the market, waiting for an entry signal, reduces the rate of return.

In the end, all systems must conform to the expected trade-offs. If they don't, you have reason to be suspicious. A system with no losses, a reward/risk ratio over 5.0, or annualized returns over 50 percent for 10 years must have compensating limitations for these benefits. You cannot accept their results at face value; you must find and understand their problems. There is no room for careless optimism.

Giving the Computer Free Rein

Computers excel in the manipulation of data. Great advances in technology are the result of the ability to consolidate massive amounts of information and produce solutions. What better application than solving a price-forecasting problem?

It is a simple task to input fundamental and economic data necessary for the interpretation of stock prices. Or information about supply and demand, which are the primary factors affecting the price of food, energy, and other commodities. It is also possible to add to the database less obvious influences (e.g. financial data, such as money supply, unemployment, and per capita income) that when combined with other events, will cause prices to shift.

The computer can be given sophisticated tools for finding relationships in the data that *explain* price movement. The most popular has been a form of multiple regression—finding constant relationships over time between numerous factors. More recently, neural networks are replacing regression analysis as the favorite method. For example, when crude oil stocks decline more than 10 percent below the average, prices rise. And, when OPEC calls an emergency meeting, prices rise. When the two happen at the same time, the prices rise higher. Fundamentals provide a reasonable, classic approach to predicting price movement.

In the past, the speed limitations of computers curtailed the amount of data that could be matched against each other. Calculations were lengthy and the results showed a clear relationship, but large variability. Because not all the price movement could be "explained," the predictive quality also had uncertainty. Newer, faster computers can analyze much more data. They should be able to reduce the variance and improve forecasting. Entering as much data as possible and letting the computer find the relationships is a simple extension of the same problem.

But the solution usually is not improved. Many choices of statistics, in combination, can "explain" the price movement. Which combination is the right one? Or are any of them correct? With enough data, countless patterns are produced. The power of the computer can find them all, without having any way to identify the *right* ones. GIGO

Recognizing Reliable Patterns

A common use of computer analysis is *pattern recognition*. In an attempt to find relationships not yet clear to others, the computer can scan, for example, unemployment data and find that a drop greater than 3 percent in November was followed by a rally of at least 4 percent in housing starts during the following May, for all of the 18 years available.

Is that a perfect solution or a coincidence? It depends on how much data the computer scanned. If you started with the premise that unemployment affects housing, and that more people working means more home sales, then you needed to scan only those two data series to confirm the relationship that you already believed to be true.

If you began with the entire database of U.S. statistics spanning the past 50 years, looking for a perfect relationship, this would have been one of many that you found. Another one may have been the infestation of gypsy moths relating perfectly to the import of Chilean grapes. Employment and housing sound right, but how do you know it is any more significant than moths and grapes? You can only know if you applied a logical argument, determined before testing, then validated the theory using the computer. Because we never would have thought of a trading program using gypsy moths, even the most astounding result must be ignored. Box 3-1 shows how to calculate when a relationship is "significant." *pp 36-37*

Throwing Microchips at It

Big companies have more choices than individuals. When they need to solve a more complicated problem, they can buy a bigger computer and get more crunching power. They also get a very impressive computer center and a higher electric bill.

Some solutions require long calculations. Finding meaningful relationships among thousands of data series can require hours of computing time even on large machines. Yet, figuring out the navigational sequences and landing instructions for putting a space team on the moon takes a small computer only a few minutes. Why is the difference so great? The computer that guides explorers to the moon has both objectives and well-defined physical relationships. The effects of planetary motion and gravity are precise, although intricate. Specify the time and everything else can be solved.

Although forecasting a price can be stated as a clear objective, the solution is not clear. The answer may not even be hidden in all the data stored in the computer. The method used to scrutinize the information may not be the way the market works.

You do not necessarily get a better solution by using more computer power, you just get a faster one. Power can overwhelm reason. No matter how big or fast, the computer only solves problems the way it is told. It does not claim to solve a problem that has no answer.

Oversimplifying a Solution

Indicators have been given credit for correctly signaling major price moves in stocks and financial markets. On-balance volume, short-interest, customer margin debt, "insider" trading, percentage of cash holdings of mutual funds, oscillators, contrary opinion, and countless others claim accurate forecasting ability. It is true that they have produced buy and sell signals at key points. But at other times, they signal the wrong moves or no move at all.

A indicator is an optimistic, oversimplification of a solution. It is an attempt to find a single, orderly solution to a complex problem.

Box 3-1. WHEN DOES 18 OUT OF 18 BECOME *SIGNIFICANT?*

You would think that finding a perfect pattern over 18 years is an impressive discovery. But not if the computer finds it by scanning a large database. For example, with 5 years of data, there are 2^5 = 32 possible up-down patterns:

1	Patterns	.	32

Year		
	1	U U U U U U U U U U U U U U U U U D D D D D D D D D D D D D D D
	2	U U U U U U U U D D D D D D D D D U U U U U U U U D D D D D D D D
	3	U U U U D D D D U U U U D D D D U U U U D D D D U U U U D D D D
	4	U U D D U U D D U U D D U U D D U U D D U U D D U U D D U U D D
	5	U D U D U D U D U D U D U D U D U D U D U D U D U D U D U D U D

If you scan 33 series of 5-year up-down patterns, *at least* two of those series *must* be identical although that doesn't prove they have anything in common. There is only a 1 in 32 chance that any two series will be identical. Therefore, if you were to take only two series that you thought depended on one another, and they proved to be identical, you would succeed with a 3.1 percent probability. If you were able to match 6 years, there would be a 1 in 64 chance, or 1.5 percent.

Rating the Results

Statistics say that there has to be *less* than a 5 percent chance of occurrence before an event is called *probably significant.* But that's of minimum

---

Combining multiple indicators does not seem to eliminate the bad signals, as you would want. Instead, the new composite indicator has the same erratic properties as its components.

This disappointing inconsistency is not the fault of the indicator, but of the user. Indicators are constructed to emphasize a particular market feature. On-balance volume will confirm a trend if there is one; stochastics and contrary opinion will show when a market is overbought or oversold, but not whether it's a good time to buy or sell.

A reliable strategy is one that uses relevant information or specific indicators *only when they are important.* At other times, these indicators have no value; forcing them to say something all the time is a misdirected approach to analysis. The market does not always have something to say.

Standard econometric analysis, often based on multiple regression analysis, tries to form continuous relations between the data. That requires all data to interact in the same way throughout history, even

interesting, but what's the evidence

Box 3-1. (*Continued*)

interest. It needs to have less than a 1 percent chance (1/100) of occurring to be called *significant*, and less than .1 percent (1/1000) to be *highly significant*.

When Is 18 Out of 18 Significant?

Finding the importance of a pattern of results requires only a few simple steps:

Step 1: *How many different combinations are there in a series of 18 ups and downs?*
There are 2 possibilities (up or down) for every one of the 18 items in the series. Then there are $2 \times 2 \times 2 \times \ldots \times 2$ (18 times), or 262,144 total combinations.

Step 2: *What are the chances of having two identical series?*
If you entered one more than the total combinations, or 262,145, series of 18 years into the computer, one of those series *must* be a duplicate. When half the data (131,072 series) have been tested, there is a 50 percent chance that one of them is a duplicate.

Step 3: *When is there a "significant" 1 percent chance?*
When you compare only two data series of 18 items, there is only a 1 in 262,144 chance of them being the same (which is *very* small). There is a 1 percent chance of finding two identical patterns in 2,622 series. Selected at random, statistics states that it is not likely to be coincidence.

when markets are being driven by different forces, or by nothing at all. That technique is similar to forcing a relationship. This problem can now be avoided by using a neural network for *threshold analysis* to isolate different market scenarios. A single event, or combination of events, will trigger the use of a selected set of information applying only to that situation. For example, an unusually large jump in inflation will turn the focus to interest rates, and begin monitoring the Producer Price Index, the Goldman Sachs Commodity Index, the yield curve, and the U.S. dollar, looking for confirmation. More about this can be found in Chapter 9.

Data Grows

An interesting feature common to price charts and system testing is that many of the patterns depend on the length of the chart. You cannot find a head-and-shoulders formation with only one week of daily data, or a major bull market with one year. Performance expectations are also distorted by using too little data, or selected data. It is not necessarily the profile of the profitable trades that change as you look at more price examples, but the risk. A sustained sideways market and an exceptionally volatile period will create prolonged large losses not seen in a smaller test.

The more data you use, the more patterns you see. A test of 500 days of data will have longer sustained moves than a test of 250 days; 1000 days is that much better than 500 days. More data means more of every price pattern and their combinations. There will be more new highs and new lows, whipsaw periods, and price shocks. In total, the risk gets greater as you use more data, and the profits rarely keep pace with them.

When you begin trading, you are adding the current data to your data history. After a year, you have increased a 1000-day test to 1250 days. The combined periods will contain new or more extreme patterns, just as though you had tested 1250 days, and as the data grows, so does the trading risk. As a result, when you begin trading, the risk may be larger than is seen in testing.

The Use of Systems

Computers and systems have added valuable structure to both individual and institutional trading. Arbitrage, strips, multiple decision-making programs, and expert systems would not be possible without current technology. It has also contributed to risk control and dynamic asset allocation. It allows theories to be tested without real losses.

The use of computerized strategies is not the "easy" answer. It is really a more disciplined and limited form than traditional trading. It requires users to carefully review their procedures and decision making, and put them in an orderly form. In doing this, many traders question what they have been doing. Discretionary trading—the ability to apply instinct and select outside factors—is what makes a great trader. A computer is not going to make an exception. For those traders who consistently benefit from their market judgment, a computerized program often serves as a guideline. It can tell them the trend direction, show key price levels, and give them an idea of how others are positioned.

Some successful traders already use systems as a basis for trading. They are able to select which trades have more potential, enter at a better price, or exit before profits disappear. You might find that they attribute much of their success to the system, while a careful, systematic test of the method will show that it does not produce net profits at all. The traders' skill is what actually makes it work. Yet these traders swear to the system's success.

Many traders are unsure whether computerized strategies improve their performance or only contribute to their peace of mind. It is said that, because life is a struggle against disorder, some traders would rather use a bad system than no system at all. Systems are good because they are definitive and can be validated by testing. Not all systems work simply because they are clear. This book is intended to help you understand systems and improve your trading performance.

Right Position, Wrong Reason

When a market technician holds a position supported by fundamentals, expectations of success increase. But the rules of most systematic trading are not compatible with the equity fluctuations needed to maintain a trade based on government policy, supply and demand, or corporate expectations.

The reason for technical analysis is to cope with the unpredictable way that prices react to fundamentals, the difficulty in assessing objectives, and the need to control risk. In exchange for improving control over an investment, it is necessary to sacrifice what seems to be an "obvious" bull move because prices retrace from their recent highs and exceed preset risk levels.

A technical system grinds out profits, alternating with losing trades. It may take a big loss on a short position during a bull move. Although traders can claim that they "know the system was wrong," it is the discipline of the program that ultimately succeeds.

Technical trading is not glamorous. It will never let you say that you bought at the lows and took profits at the top. But trading should be a business, and a systematic program is a plan to profit over time, rather from a single trade.

Why Does Everyone Know Except You?

*If you can keep your head, when all about you
are losing theirs, then maybe you haven't
heard the news.*
                                        —H. L. MENCKEN

Conversations with other traders can lead you to believe that they knew more than you did about a surprising market move. You lost and they profited. However, if the move was a price shock, then no one could have known it was going to happen. They were probably caught on the right side of the market while you were on the wrong side.

Newspapers highlight the big winners or those newsletters that gave the right advice. Considering the number of reports published, some must have been short before the October 1987 stock market crash. Their advice could have been mediocre before that and worse, but you always find out who was right after a price shock. You can always assume that half the traders you know were right about a move, and those are the ones most likely to talk about it.

Expectations

High expectations are essential to success, but unrealistic ones just waste time. Computers do not tell you how to profit in the market, they can only verify your own ideas. Using a computer to develop trading programs is a sensible, conservative approach. As with other tools, it requires skill, which comes from study and practice. As you become more proficient, you will learn more.

Because it is only a tool, results of system testing must be compared fairly with all other investments. Returns should be risk adjusted, and investments must be properly capitalized.

Be suspicious of unrealistic results, even when they are profitable. Strategies are trade-offs between many features. With more complex tools, there are many more chances for error. Check the details carefully before accepting the results. There is no substitution for careful work.

Use new technology cautiously. Increased computer power takes the pressure off the individual's need to conceive a profitable strategy before testing. Many of the new methods discussed later can be a great asset or a crutch; their benefits are entirely in the hands of the user.

Researching and developing trading programs are unique activities among businesses. There is no assurance that some problems have a solution. Other times, successful plans and opportunities are short-lived; even market patterns that have been reliable for many years can disappear. Part of developing a program is identifying when it no longer works.

4
Risk and Return

Amateur traders first look at profits while professionals first look at ✓
risk. It is far more interesting to search for a profitable system than to
concentrate on losses, but an understanding of risk is essential to every
aspect of trading. Otherwise, it is only a matter of time before a price
shock forces you out of the market, or a series of losses become enough
of a worry to stop your trading. In this book, you will find that some
trading methods are considered better than others. This chapter will
explain how those choices were made. The preferred methods are based
on sound rules that incorporate both risk and return. These techniques
can be applied to any trading method.

Figure 4-1 shows two equity plots for the same time period. The left one p 42
(a) shows much higher profits, but more risk. The price fluctuations above
and below the straight line (the rate of return) are clearly larger than in the
right plot (b). Which is better, the one with higher profits, or the returns
with lower risk? Is it investor "risk preference" that decides the answer?

The "best" performance is not based on whether the investor is conservative or risk-seeking. It is entirely a function of which performance
gives the highest returns for the lowest risk, which in turn will translate
back into higher profits. In Figure 4-1, it is difficult to decide which is
better without being given the exact risk and return for each chart.

Risk Preference

Risk preference is the investor's willingness to accept more or less risk in
exchange for profits. When two systems have the same returns, rational
investors will choose the system with the lowest risk. Similarly, when

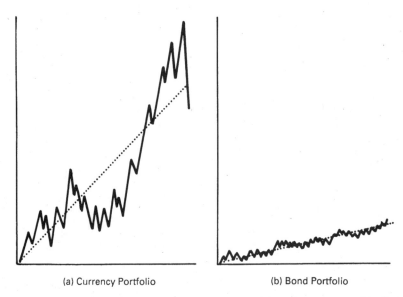

(a) Currency Portfolio   (b) Bond Portfolio

Figure 4-1. Which equity pattern is better? (a) *High returns and high risk.* A currency futures portfolio shows a 50% return and a 20% risk. (b) *Low returns and low risk.* A bond portfolio with an 8% return and a 2% risk.

two systems have the same risk, investors would choose the one with the highest returns. Among programs with the best combination of risk and reward, it is necessary to accept proportionately higher risk to increase returns by a small amount.

Standardizing Risk and Return

Before comparing the currency and bond portfolios in Figure 4-1, the returns and risk must be represented in a standard, convenient form. This allows different test periods to be compared equally with one another. The most popular approach is used extensively by equities and financial analysts:

- Return is the annualized, compounded rate of return.
- Risk is the annualized standard deviation of the equity changes.

Compounded Rate of Return

A *compounded* rate of return means that the accumulated funds are reinvested. In the case of a simple interest-bearing savings account, "daily compounding" means that the interest earned each day is added to the total savings and earns interest starting the next day.

Using *annualized* compounding, you may earn, for example, 5 percent on an investment, leaving the interest to accumulate. Because the interest is posted only once each year, a $1,000 investment is worth $1,050 at the end of the first year. At the end of the second year, the $1,050 has grown by another 5 percent to $1,102.50, and after the third year to $1,157.625. The same result can be found by multiplying the initial investment of $1,000 by the rate of interest *raised* to the number of years that the funds were invested.

This technique is useful for system evaluation when you have the starting and ending value of an investment and you want to find the compounded rate of return that would give those values. The calculation can simply be reversed, as shown in Box 4-1. p 44

Annualized Standard Deviation

The annualized standard deviation measures risk. It is simply *the standard deviation of the annual increase or decrease in equity* (*compounded returns*). Therefore, if the annualized return is only one value each of 20 years, the annualized standard deviation uses only those 20 values. You may use monthly changes in equity to get more accuracy. The next few sections will compare risk and return evaluated over different time periods, and show that they are not easily interchanged.

Using a Standard Deviation to Determine the Chance of Loss

The *standard deviation* is the classic measurement of distribution. It shows how data is clustered around the average value. It assumes that the pattern of results is symmetrical. For example, a chart of trading performance is shown in Figure 4-2(a). The rate of return is the solid angled line drawn upward through the center of the equity. The standard deviation of the monthly profits and losses (subtracting last month's equity, or accumulated profits and losses, from this month's value) will show how the returns are clustered above and below the rate-of-return line. p 45

It is easier to see the distribution of equity changes in Figure 4-2(b). By subtracting the equity value of each month from the previous month, the equity has been *detrended*. Fluctuations are centered above and below a zero line, rather than an upward regression line, as in Figure 4-2(a). The standard deviation is useful because it puts a value on the chance of loss. In Figure 4-2(b) bands are drawn parallel to the straight-

Box 4-1. CALCULATING THE RISK AND RETURN

Most market analysts have standardized their way of representing both risk and return. This book will adopt the same notation.

Returns are the annualized, compounded rate of return. This is given as

CROR = (Ending_Equity/Investment)^(1/Period) − 1

where CROR is the compounded rate of return
Ending_Equity is the last account value
Investment is the starting account value
Period is the number of years (for annualized returns)

The Period, or number of years, is expressed as a decimal fraction (e.g., $8\frac{1}{2}$ years is 8.5). Therefore, if your $1,000 investment is worth $1,300 after $4\frac{1}{2}$ years, you have earned a compounded rate of return equal to 6.00 percent:

CROR = (1300/1000)^(1/4.5) − 1

= 1.0600 − 1.00

= 6.00% per annum

For a monthly compounded rate of return, the period would be 54.0 months, or .487 percent per month.

Risk is the annualized standard deviation of the equity, which we will take as the standard deviation of the annual returns. Then

ASD = @SUM(Yearly_Returns^2)/Period

where ASD is the annualized standard deviation
@SUM is the program function that adds a list of values
Yearly_Returns is a list of yearly changes in returns
Period is the number of years (for annualized returns)

- *Spreadsheet.* This calculation is readily available on spreadsheet programs as a built-in function. In Quattro, it is simply specified as @STD(B4..B20) in order to find one standard deviation of the values in column B, rows 4 through 20.

- *TeleTrac* and *System Writer.* Both testing software programs have similar built-in standard deviation functions, Std_Dv(series,period) in *TeleTrac* and @StdDev(series,period) for *System Writer.* Each calculates and returns the value of one standard deviation.

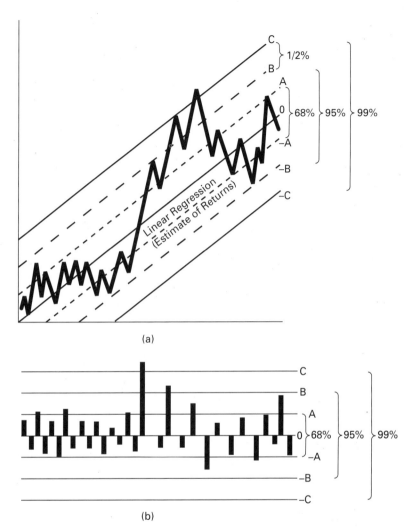

(a)

(b)

Figure 4-2. Standard deviation of equity and equity changes. (a) The
standard deviation of the equity shows the chance of a total profit or loss
swing with respect to the straight line approximation of the rate of return. (b)
The standard deviation of monthly equity changes shows the likelihood of
profit or loss during any one month.

line, detrended rate of return (0). These lines show the grouping of 1, 2,
and 3 standard deviations, as follows:

68% of all data falls between ± standard deviation
(the band from A to −A)
95% of all data falls between ± 2 standard deviation
(the band from B to −B)

99% of all data falls between $\pm$ 3 standard deviations
(the band from C to $-$C)

WHY

Because we are only interested in the risk of loss, we need to know the chance of equity falling below $-$A, $-$B, and $-$C. If 68 percent of the data falls between $+$A and $-$A then 32 percent falls outside. One half of the 32 percent will be above $+$A and the other half below $-$A. Therefore, there is only a 16 percent chance that losses will exceed 1 standard deviation, a 2.5 percent chance they will exceed 2 standard deviations, and a .5 percent chance they will exceed 3 standard deviations.

Choosing Between the Currency and Bond Portfolios

Once the returns and risk are in uniform notation, the comparison between the currency and bond portfolios becomes simple. The portfolios are risk-adjusted by dividing the larger risk (20 percent in the currency portfolio) by the smaller risk of the bond portfolio, giving 20/2 = 10. If the currency risk is reduced by a factor of 10, then the currency profit of 50 percent must also be divided by 10. The result is that the currency portfolio returns only 5 percent, compared with 8 percent for bonds, when they are both at the 2 percent risk level. The bond portfolio (Figure 4-1b) is 60 percent better.

p42

Leverage

The risk-adjusted return is a better measurement of performance because it is the simplest way of getting the most portfolio diversification, especially when futures or options programs allow leverage. The bond portfolio, with 8 percent returns, could have been leveraged as high as 20 times using the futures markets, returning 160 percent with a 40 percent risk.

Options and other derivatives allow the investor considerable flexibility in varying leverage. Portfolios that deleverage by holding cash reserves also have latitude for varying the investments based on risk and reward. Only the fully invested account (which can assume more risk than either the currency or bond portfolios) may choose the highest profits.

Actual System Test for Finding the Best Choice

A trend-following system was tested on two years of the Bombay stock p47 index, the SENSEX. Table 4-1 shows nine tests progressing from short-term, faster trends at the top to slower ones at the bottom. The best profits were 3681 points for test 8 and the lowest risk was 814 points for test 4. However, the best performance choice was test 2, with an adjusted, compounded rate of return of 34.5 percent. Profits and risk in columns 2 and 3 were both converted to percentages based on the current SENSEX price of 2700.

A fast way of arriving at the best choice is simply to divide the total profits (column 2) by the total risk (column 3). The greatest return/risk ratio will be the best choice, as long as standard measurements were used and both returns and risk were calculated over the same time period within the same test. Even if test 4 was evaluated over a slightly different length interval than test 9, the ratio would give a valid comparison.

Table 4-1. Risk-Adjusting Results of a Trending System

Test (1)	Profit (in SENSEX pts) (2)	Risk (3)	Return (%) (4)	CROR (%) (5)	Risk (%) (6)	Adjust Factor (7)	Riskadj CROR (8)	Prof/Risk Ratio (9)
Fast 1	3133	1208	216	47.0	45	1.50	31.3	2.59
2	3046	1093	213	45.9	40	1.33	34.5	2.79
3	2808	1113	204	28.3	41	1.37	20.6	2.52
4	2032	814	175	32.3	30	1.00	32.3	2.50
5	2069	827	177	33.0	31	1.03	32.0	2.50
6	2136	905	179	33.8	33	1.10	30.7	2.36
7	3220	1391	219	48.0	51	1.70	28.2	2.31
8	3681	1568	236	53.6	58	1.93	27.8	2.35
Slow 9	3311	1451	223	49.3	54	1.80	27.4	2.28

Finding the best risk-adjusted returns for the Bombay SENSEX trend-following program can be done by combining a spreadsheet and system tests. In this case, *profits* and *risk* (columns 2 and 3) were found using CompuTrac *SNAP* for 2 years of data. *Risk* was calculated as 1 standard deviation of the equity. *Percentage returns* (column 4) were calculated using 100, the initial investment, plus the gross returns divided by 2700, the current SENSEX price. The *compounded rate of return* for the 2-year period is the return (column 4) less the initial investment of 100, raised to the 1/2 power (see calculation for compounded rate of return). The *percentage risk* (column 6) is the risk in points (column 3) divided by the current SENSEX price of 2700. The *risk-adjustment factor* is the percentage risk (column 6) divided by the lowest percentage risk in column 6 (30 in test 4). The *risk-adjusted compound rate of return* (column 8) is the compound rate of return (column 5) divided by the adjustment factor (column 7). The *profit/risk ratio* (column 9) is the profit (column 2) divided by the risk (column 3).

Columns 8 and 9 both show that the best choice for trend speed was test 2, which had neither the highest profits nor the lowest risk. Although the ratio does not tell the relative rate of return, using the highest value is a fast way of identifying the best test.

Risk to Time

The standard deviation using the quarterly change in equity must be bigger than the standard deviation of monthly changes because longer time intervals allow larger fluctuations. Even though a quarter is 3.0 times longer than a month, the standard deviation is 4.74 times larger. As the time interval becomes even larger, however, the variation does not increase at the same rate. Most price or equity data will tend toward a maximum variance, regardless of the time interval. A typical *risk-to-time* curve is shown in <u>Figure 4-3.</u>

p49

Time Periods Tell Different Stories

Although equity changes get larger when annual data is used instead of monthly or daily returns, longer periods can also hide risk. During October 1987, the S&P 500 plunged 44 percent but recovered to show a smaller loss of 21 percent by the end of the month, and actually closed out the year up 2 percent.

Dec 87 S&P Futures	Sep 30, 1987	321.69 (closing price)	
	Oct 20, 1987	181.00 (low)	down 44%
	Oct 31, 1987	255.74 (closing price)	down 21%
Mar 87 S&P Futures	Dec 31, 1986	242.17 (closing price)	
Mar 88 S&P Futures	Dec 31, 1987	247.09 (closing price)	up 2%

Using monthly data, the chances are only 1 in 21 that the returns for the month will be the low of that month, therefore the performance is *smoothed*. The risk of loss is there, but you cannot see it from the numbers.

Maximum Drawdown

To assess risk it is always necessary to know the *maximum drawdown,* the largest peak-to-valley equity drop. The maximum drawdown is likely to be much larger than any monthly equity change, as seen in the S&P example. Even though you may not see a loss of that magnitude soon, it is inevitable that a swing as big or greater will occur sometime in the future. It is both naive and unrealistic to assume that a faster, larger rally or bigger plunge will never occur.

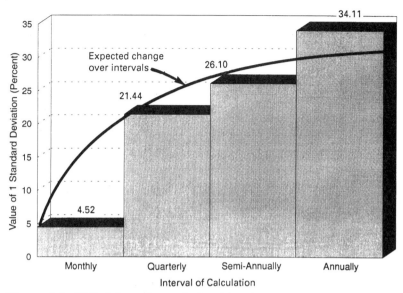

Figure 4-3. S&P risk to time relationship. The standard deviation of the S&P price changes from 1983–1992 shows that price change approaches a limit as the measurement time period gets larger.

The 50-Year Rule

Environmental planning uses a 10-year rule for water relief. Ditches are built along country roads to control the maximum runoff measured over the past 10 years. If the runoff overflows the ditch, there is unfortunate erosion (although no obvious harm to people). To protect farmers settling on the banks of the Mississippi River, levies were built to a height that satisfies the "50-year rule." What does that mean to a family living in a home along the river? It says that water *will* rise above the levy, but not very often. It may have overflowed the levy 75 years ago, but not during the past 50 years; therefore, flooding *could* happen once in the lifetime of each family member.

The same situation exists in trading. Professional traders will be faced with extreme moves and extraordinary price shocks during their careers. Those who plan to use the markets for only a short time may never see these moves and could take the chance that these extremes will not occur during their short trading stay. It is a classic risk-and-reward decision.

Trading safety relates directly to capitalization. Larger, more diversified investments, with proportionately greater reserves, are safer. If you are fortunate enough to profit from a small amount of capital, then decrease the relative risk by increasing the percentage of reserves. Traders who continue to leverage all their profits increase their chance of a complete loss.

Specifying Acceptable Risk

Standardizing the risk measurement is important because it allows you to specify the amount of risk you are willing to accept for any trading method. For example, as a foreign exchange trader, you are given US$10 million to trade. You are told that you should not risk more than 10 percent. Having traded for some time, you have a good idea about the fluctuations of your performance, and have a track record that can be measured. Or, as an experienced analyst, you expect to devise a method based on previously successful ideas.

Using annual figures, your performance shows an admirable 40 percent return with a 10 percent standard deviation. You know that 1 standard deviation means that there is an 84 percent chance that the equity *won't drop* more than 10 percent, and 3 standard deviations gives a 99.5 percent chance that equity *won't drop* more than 30 percent. Looking at the results in reverse, a risk of 10 percent means that there is a 16 percent chance that you *will lose* more than 10 percent during a year.

You cannot have such a large risk of losing 10 percent; therefore, you bring this down to a safe level by dividing by 4. This really means that you will use only one-fourth of the capital in the account to trade. The account is "deleveraged." The original 10 percent standard deviation becomes 2.5 percent and there is a

16.0% chance of losing more than 2.5% (1 standard deviation)

2.5% chance of losing more than 5.0% (2 standard deviations)

.5% chance of losing more than 7.5% (3 standard deviations)

which is about right for your risk limits. Because you divided the risk by 4, the returns must also be divided by 4, giving an adjusted annualized return of 10 percent—still pretty good. To implement this plan, you need to trade only one-fourth of the funds allocated to you, or $2.5 million instead of $10 million, holding the rest as reserve in the event of an undesirable (but possible) run of bad trades. You are experienced enough to know that a 0.5 percent chance means that you *will lose* more than 7.5 percent, but not often. Since this risk measurement used monthly values, a daily maximum drawdown is still needed to decide a safe level of capitalization.

Foreign Exchange
Trader's Dilemma

Even if everything works as planned, producing a 10 percent return with a 5 percent risk during the next year, there is still a problem. The trading manager calls you aside and asks, "Why aren't you using all the money? You returned 10 percent using only $2.5 million. If you had used all the money, you could have returned 40 percent. If you're not going to use it all, I'll have to give it to someone else."

That's the dilemma. You needed $7.5 million in reserve for bad times, but you didn't use it. You look brilliant, but too conservative. How do you explain that *you were using the money?* There was a 16 percent chance that you would need more than $2.5 million and a 2.5 percent chance of using more than $5 million. It is difficult to explain, but it needs to be done. If you trade a larger percentage, you will eventually be shut down by losing more than 10 percent. This same problem will be seen in Chapter 7, when we look at the effects of price shocks.

Graphing Risk and Reward

Graphing the risk and reward leads to important observations. This approach is often used by asset allocators, to show the trade-offs between systematic combinations of profits and losses. The returns and risk (in points) given in Table 4-1 have been plotted in Figure 4-4 and marked 1 through 9.   p47   p52

Results that are plotted higher and to the left have more profit and less risk. Those that are lower and to the right are worse choices because they have less profit and more risk. A rational investor would always choose a point directly above another one because it has a higher return for the same level of risk (given a choice of points 2 or 3, point 2 is the better one).

Efficient Frontier

A curve can be drawn through the points that return the highest profit at each level of risk. Note that the curve, seen as a broken line in Figure 4-4, flattens out as it goes to the right. This means that the investor or trader must assume a proportionately higher risk to gain a small increase in profits.

This curve is similar in concept to an *efficient frontier*, used in asset allocation. However, if you use the performance of a single trading system, one combination may show exceptionally good returns by chance. A curve drawn through the best cluster of points, rather than the absolute highest combinations, will give a more realistic appraisal of expectations.

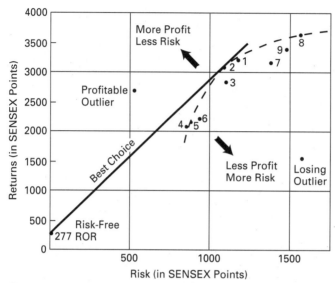

Figure 4-4. Plot of risk and returns. Plotting the risk and return of each test provides a clear picture of investment choices. Those points higher and to the left are better; those lower and to the right are worse. The standard selection is found at the point where a straight line, anchored at the risk-free rate-of-return on the left scale, touches the curve. The curve is called an *efficient frontier*.

The Best Choice

Investors are always free to choose the combination of risk and reward that satisfies their objectives. A rational choice must be on the efficient frontier. A more conservative investor will be more comfortable with a selection further to the left, while a risk seeker will prefer the higher profits even at the cost of increased risk.

What is normally considered the "best" choice is found by drawing a straight line from the risk-free rate of return (on the left scale), tangent to the efficient frontier curve, as seen in Figure 4-4. The risk-free rate of return assumes 5 percent over 2 years applied to the amount of money needed to buy the stock index at 2700 points. Keeping the calculation in SENSEX points,

$$2700 \times .05 \times .05 = 277$$

2700	×	.05	×	.05	=	277
(investment in points)		(year 1)		(year 2)		(interest in points)

The straight line drawn from 277 touches the efficient frontier at exactly test 2, the best choice.

Diversification and Risk Reduction

Diversification is the best form of risk reduction. Investing in more than one asset, each with a good return, will reduce risk by benefiting from equity variation that occurs at different times. Investment managers are constantly searching for ways to place funds that yield better-than-average returns and modest risk. Combining a number of medium-risk, diverse investments often nets a low-risk portfolio. Diversification can also be gained by using different trading strategies in the same market.

Applying Asset Allocation Techniques

Asset allocation is the process of distributing investment funds into one or more markets or vehicles to create an investment profile with the most desirable return/risk ratio. In its simplest form, asset allocation would use only one active investment, such as a stock portfolio, placing the remaining funds into risk-free, short-term government bonds. In its most complicated form, many investment vehicles are combined on a dynamic basis. Assets may vary from a passive gold portfolio to active international stocks and discretionary trading of foreign exchange markets.

Simple Risk Reduction

The stock market produces healthy long-term returns of about 10 percent per year (16.4 percent compounded rate of return from 1983 to 1992), with a return/risk ratio of approximately 1:1. If you were 100 percent invested in stocks, there would be a 16 percent chance of a loss greater than the annualized return *sometime during that year.* To reduce the risk, you simply trade a smaller amount of stocks and put the balance in a money market account or Treasury bills. Figure 4-5 shows that the risk and returns are reduced linearly by holding varying amounts in reserve.

Classic Stock and Bond Portfolio

A more popular alternative is to allocate a portion of the portfolio to bonds. Although risk-free when held to maturity, a passive bond portfolio will fluctuate in value in the same way as equity holdings. Therefore, the bond investor is subject to fluctuation in the underlying interest rates, profiting when interest rates drop and losing when they rise.

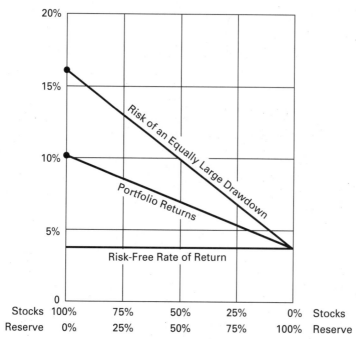

Figure 4-5. Combining stocks and cash reserves. As cash reserves increase, both risk and return decrease at the same rate.

Figure 4-6 compares the return/risk ratios of a stock and bond portfolio for varying percentage combinations of those two items. The monthly returns were combined using a spreadsheet, and the compounded rate of return and monthly standard deviations were recalculated on the new portfolio. The result is a classic relationship, where a small addition of a higher risk asset (in this case the stock market) adds more return than risk. When more than 20 percent equities are added to the portfolio, the incremental risk becomes larger than the return. In both cases, the final portfolio has lower risk than stocks alone, achieving the goal of the asset manager.

Adding Other Assets

To see whether a new trading method or alternate investment would improve the returns of a stock and bond portfolio, we can use the same spreadsheet technique that was applied in Figure 4-6. Because most fund managers use a portfolio of 60 percent stocks and 40 percent bonds as a benchmark, the following calculations assume that the new trading

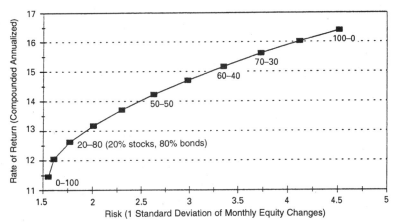

Figure 4-6. Combining stocks and bonds. Because stocks and bonds have different risk and return profiles, and provide portfolio diversification, plotting combinations of these assets results in a curve, rather than a straight line. The best choice favors a smaller allocation of stocks.

program or asset replaces a percentage of that standard portfolio. Each spreadsheet row, representing one month, becomes

$$\text{New Portfolio Return} = (1 - \% \text{ New Asset})$$
$$\times (.60 \times \text{Stock Return} + .40 \times \text{Bond Return})$$
$$+ \% \text{ New Asset} \times \text{New Asset Return}$$

where % New Asset is the percentage of the new asset used
Return is the compounded (annual or period) rate of return
Risk is the (annualize or period) standard deviation

Diversifying with Derivatives

If the new asset has better returns at lower risk than the old portfolio, then it will raise the efficient frontier everywhere. In fact, the new asset will be a better investment than the stock and bond portfolio. But that is rarely the case. The new asset will usually have a higher profit and a higher risk or a lower profit at a lower risk. By diversifying the original portfolio with a small allocation of the new asset, the portfolio returns will be improved at some investment levels.

Derivatives have become a closely watched asset for portfolio diversification. The most popular index for measuring performance of Commodity Trading Advisors is the *MAR Dollar-Weighted CTA Index* (compiled by *Managed Account Reports*). For the period 1983 through 1992, the Index showed a compounded rate of return of 12.84 percent with a monthly standard deviation of 5.62 percent. For the same period, the performance profile of stocks, bonds, and the CTA Index was:

	Monthly Returns, 1983–1992		
	S&P	LB Bonds	$W CTA
Monthly standard deviation	4.52	1.56	5.62
Compounded rate of return	16.40	11.45	12.84

MAR changed the Dollar-Weighted Index retroactively as of January 1, 1993.

We would not expect the CTA performance to improve the returns of a stock and bond portfolio because the risk was higher and the returns lower than stocks. The unique monthly patterns, however, prove that diversification can improve performance even though the cumulative statistics make it seem unlikely. Figure 4-7 shows the risk and return of a portfolio where different percentages of the CTA Index are combined with a 60 percent to 40 percent stock and bond portfolio. As allocations increase to a 20 percent use of the CTA Index, risk decreases while returns improve marginally. At the 20 percent level, risk has dropped more than 9 percent while returns are unchanged. As allocations become larger, the unfavorable profile begins to show and the total performance deteriorates. In this case, diversification alone improves results.

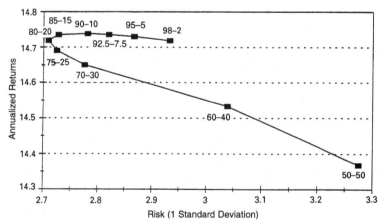

Figure 4-7. CTA Index with stocks and bonds. Adding derivatives to a stock and bond portfolio improves results when less than up to 20% is allocated. Risk declines due to diversification, although returns remain nearly unchanged.

Using Correlations to Select Assets

Risk is reduced when the assets in the portfolio are diversified using different strategies or unrelated markets. But diversification is not always obvious. Most investors would consider a portfolio of stocks and bonds to be diversified, offering some risk reduction because stocks might post a profit on the same day that bonds lose. That is true sometimes.

When an unfavorable economic report is released by the federal government, stock prices may react with a sharp drop. Traders expect the Fed to lower interest rates to offset this decline, therefore they buy bonds, moving prices higher (and rates lower). If you have a portfolio of stocks and bonds, this represents risk protection. The loss in stocks is partially offset by a profit in bonds.

But under most economic conditions, profits from stocks and bonds have similar movements. That does not mean that the stock market rises on one out of every two days that bond prices rise. When interest rates move slowly lower, as seen in the prolonged recession of the early 1990s, the stock market moves slowly higher. This may be a combination of higher earnings (more productivity, lower cost of money) and anticipation of economic stimulation. The result is that the price movements of stocks and bonds are fundamentally related and do not offer as much diversification as an entirely unrelated investment (see Figure 4-8).

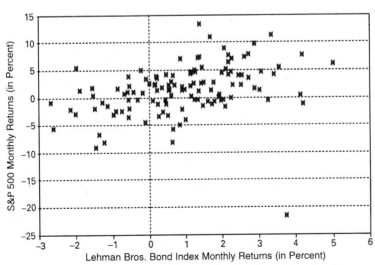

Figure 4-8. Scatter diagram of monthly stock and bond returns.
The elongated pattern shows returns of passive portfolios of stocks and bonds. This similarity limits the potential diversification.

Correlations and Risk Protection

The similarity of two price series can be measured by calculating the *correlation coefficient, r,* which compares how two corresponding sets of numbers in a times series vary with respect to one another. The results of the relationship are expressed on a scale from +1 (perfect positive correlation, where the two series move exactly together) to 0 (no relationship between the data movements) to −1 (perfect negative correlation, where the two items move exactly in opposite directions).

Correlation coefficients are a good indication of how much diversification you will get by combining markets or strategies in a portfolio. As

---

Box 4-2. CALCULATION AND INTERPRETATION OF CORRELATIONS

The *correlation coefficient* measures the variation in the corresponding values of two data series. Formally, it is the ratio of the *unexplained deviation* to the *total deviation* of each value from the average or trend. It can be expressed for two equity series in the following general notation:

R = @SUM(Equity1_deviations*Equity2_deviations,N)/
(@SQRT (@SUM(Equity1_deviations^2,N)
*@SQRT(@SUM(Equity2_
deviations^2,N)))

For a spreadsheet, it is necessary to create a new column with the difference between each equity value and the average equity:

Spreadsheet solution. Assume there are 100 rows of equity values entered. Each row below is copied down from 2 through 100.

Cells	Formulas	Description
A1-A100	Date of the Entry	Daily, Monthly, or Yearly
B1-B100	Equity1	1st Equity values
C1-C100	Equity2	2nd Equity values
D1	B1 2 @AVG(B1..B100)	Deviations of Equity 1
E1	C1 2 @AVG(C1..C100)	Deviations of Equity 2
F1	D1*E1	Products of Deviations
G1	D1^2	Square of Equity 1 Deviations
H1	D2^2	Square of Equity 2 Deviations

The following is calculated once after rows 1–100 are complete:

R = @SUM(F1..F100)/(@SQRT(@SUM(G1..G100)))
*(@SQRT(@SUM(H1..H100)))

the positive correlations become stronger, the potential diversification declines. When a correlation is +1.00, there is no diversification. But when the correlation is zero (where there is no predictable relationship between the two items), it is still not clear how much risk reduction is to be gained (see Box 4-2).

A comparison of the average of the standard deviation and rate of return with the same values found using a spreadsheet portfolio, shows the real effect of diversification for three passive portfolios (see Table 4-2). Using stocks, bonds, and a simple foreign exchange basket, more risk reduction is gained when the correlation is .00 for the FX index with stocks or bonds, compared with a higher .34 correlation for stocks and

---

Box 4-2. (*Continued*)

The results r are interpreted as follows:

$r = +1$	A perfect positive correlation exists. For every move in one data series, there is an equivalent move in the other series.
$+1 > r > 0$	The similarity of price movement increases as the value of r moves from 0 to 1.
$r = 0$	There is no relationship between the two sets of points.
$-1 < r < 0$	The *negative* similarity increases as the value of r moves from 0 to -1.
$r = -1$	A perfect negative (opposite) correlation exists. For every move in one data series, there is an opposite, equivalent move in the other series.

Note that results are more meaningful when the series is detrended by taking the first differences of the prices.

Example

The scatter diagram (Figure 4-8) shows an elongated pattern, indicating a modest relationship between monthly stock and bond price movements. When bond prices rise during one month, there is a reasonable chance that stock prices will rise. The result of the calculation is $r = .34$; there is a 34 percent positive correlation between annual stock and bond price movement.

Built-In Spreadsheet Functions

The correlation coefficient can be found for most spreadsheet programs, under the "Tools" menu. The result is instantaneous. Just select *TOOLS/ADVANCED MATH/REGRESSION* in Quattro, or the equivalent in other programs. Most spreadsheets give R Squared, (r^2) rather than r; therefore the correlation value ranges from 0 to +1, rather than -1 to $+1$. If you have r^2, you must compare the slopes of the individual series. If they are the same, then r is positive; if they are moving in opposite directions, r is negative.

Table 4-2. Risk Reduction Associated with Correlations

a. S&P vs. Bonds with a .34 Correlation (Modest Pattern)

	S&P500	Bonds	Average	Equal Allocation
Avg Return	16.78	11.05	13.92	13.92
St Dev	10.65	4.89	7.77	7.04 (−9.4%)

b. S&P vs. FX with a .00 Correlation (No Pattern)

	S&P500	FX	Average	Equal Allocation
Avg Return	16.78	2.90	9.84	9.84
St Dev	10.65	14.52	12.58	8.92 (−29.1%)

c. Bonds vs. FX with a .00 Correlation (No Pattern)

	Bonds	FX	Average	Equal Allocation
Avg Return	11.05	2.90	6.98	6.98
St Dev	4.89	14.52	9.70	7.80 (−19.6%)

bonds. It is still necessary to create a portfolio using a spreadsheet to find the expected level of risk reduction.

The 9.4 percent risk reduction for the S&P bond portfolio is less than either of the two FX portfolios. That is expected because the correlation of .34 is higher than the other portfolios. However, the Stocks-FX and Bonds-FX portfolios had very different amounts of risk reduction, even though they both had zero correlations. Correlations are helpful, but not complete.

Fast-Netting Method for Asset Allocation

Computers allow us to shortcut the mathematics and go directly to the answer. The purpose of standard deviations and correlation coefficients is to find out which combination produced the greatest return for the lowest risk. Although the traditional method is correct, it still leaves a large degree of uncertainty.

Spreadsheets can find more complete, understandable answers quickly. How did we know that the two FX portfolios in Table 4-2 reduced risk by 29 percent and 19 percent? By putting the annual returns in spreadsheet columns, it is a simple matter to create another column by adding half of the Stocks return plus half the FX returns. Then calculate the standard deviation of the new column. That is as definitive as you can get. The same procedure can be followed for monthly and daily returns. The computer may only take another 3 seconds to calculate a portfolio of daily, rather than monthly returns.

Computers now allow us to perform operations directly, rather than estimate the results. Some of us need time to adjust to this way of operating, of using the power available in the computer. The spreadsheet solution is much simpler, but requires such a large number of calculations that we would never have considered doing this manually. The correlation coefficient is a smart, uniform way of estimating relationships, but not as good as the spreadsheet solution.

There are still error factors and probabilities to be considered in the "fast netting" approach. Past performance is likely to show less risk than the future; one standard deviation represents the *probability* of 68 percent occurrence; and using 10 years of annual data gives a sample *error* of 1/SQRT(N-1), or 32 percent.

Adding Common Sense to Statistics

Probability and statistics are not a substitute for common sense. The scatter diagram, Figure 4-8, shows one isolated point far away from the typical pattern, a loss of 22 percent. That outlier was one month out of 120, less than 1 percent of the data. Statistically, that is small. In reality, it means that on average, after you have traded successfully for 5 years, you will lose all your investment. That does not sound as good as "less than a 1 percent chance of losing."

The outlier in Figure 4-8 was the stock market plunge of 1987. Stocks plummeted and traders ran to buy bonds. There was also the invasion of Kuwait and Gorbachev's abduction a few years later. All of these are price "shocks" that can cause extreme, highly correlated moves when statistics have ruled them out for all practical purposes. These infrequent but important events are discussed in Chapter 7.

Business Risk

Common sense allows us to create a worst-case scenario. It is a necessary step for trading survival. It is not just traders that need to do this, brokerage firms have done it for years. For example, a brokerage firm has 10,000 clients trading stocks, options, bonds, foreign exchange, and a variety of commodity markets. That would seem highly diversified and very safe for the brokerage firm, which must use its own capital to cover underfunded trading losses while it tries to collect money from customers. But Kuwait is invaded. Investors run to the U.S. dollar, bond prices soar, commodity prices rise, and the stock market moves up on a combination of economic stimulation and lower interest rates. Newspapers cover the financial stories, showing individuals who have profited, and more follow. Soon the 10,000 individual investors are all holding positions that would benefit from the continuing war. The brokerage firm is faced with the situation that its total customer assets will be very volatile. If the war ends, customer losses could be huge, and all at the same time. Completely unrelated investments are liquidated to cover losses in other markets. Those customers trading on margin may not meet the calls for new money, placing the brokerage firm's capitalization at risk.

This situation actually happened in early 1980, when silver and gold rallied to all-time highs. The publicity given to the Hunt's silver position was so extensive that the general public was heavily committed to holding long positions.

Brokerage firms will deal with this by monitoring the aggregate customer positions. When a percentage of correlated holdings exceed a safe level, they recommend other positions, raise the house margin levels, and generally try whatever is needed to get clients out of current, high-risk positions and add diversification. They save the clients and they serve themselves.

Institutions that hold large house trading positions have the same problem. What appears to be diversified under normal market conditions may not provide the risk protection under extreme cases—and those are the most important. A sharp loss once every three to five years is just as bad as high volatility in daily performance. For many risk situations, there is no statistical evaluation. It is simply necessary for someone to reason out what might happen under varying circumstances.

Correlations and Time

The correlation matrix of monthly returns in Table 4-3 shows how the choice of time periods affects the measurement of similarity between assets or systems. Using only the past 10 years of data, the correlations drop significantly when monthly values replace annual data. Those values already near zero may be slightly higher without contradicting the principle. This phenomenon is not surprising. The annual, long-term relationship between interest rates and Producer Price Index may be predictable, but month-to-month reactions can vary. If interest rates overreact to an anticipated increase in prices, then daily or monthly values may move somewhat apart, while the economic relationship remains steady. As you reduce the time period, the smaller price changes become more important. Noise becomes a bigger factor in the overall pattern, and the correlation drops.

Using daily data to measure correlation is likely to give you an answer near zero for most combinations. But results over a full year could be very similar, and a poor choice if you are looking for portfolio diversification.

Table 4-3. Correlation Matrices for
Annual and Monthly Returns
(1983–1992)

	Correlation of Monthly Returns				
	S&P500	Bonds	PPI	FX	CTA
S&P500	1.00	0.12	0.03	0.01	0.00
Bonds		1.00	0.03	0.03	0.02
PPI			1.00	0.00	0.00
FX				1.00	0.00
CTA					1.00

	Correlation of Annual Returns				
	S&P500	Bonds	PPI	FX	CTA
S&P500	1.00	0.34	0.16	0.00	0.13
Bonds		1.00	0.43	0.00	0.16
PPI			1.00	0.04	0.15
FX				1.00	0.15
CTA					1.00

The two correlation matrices in Table 4-3 compare the similarity in price movement of passive portfolios of the S&P 500, Lehman Brothers Bond Index, the Producer Price Index, a Forex group, and the MAR dollar-weighted Commodity Trading Advisor Index. The monthly figures show much smaller correlations than the annual returns. As shorter time periods are used for evaluation, the noise of short-term movement interferes with the direction of the long-term trend. This makes the correlations seem lower, yet severe, volatile moves may prove that many of these markets move in the same direction.

Forecasting Correlations

Another essential step in evaluating diversification is to *forecast* the correlations. Markets change, and more so in these times of globalization. World equity markets are becoming interrelated. A severe drop in the Japanese, German, or U.S. stock markets is likely to cause similar drops in other markets, resulting in correlated performance. This tendency can be seen by calculating individual annual correlations (using monthly data) and looking at the trend of r. If the correlation coefficient is moving toward +1, then you will want to decrease the use of these markets for diversification.

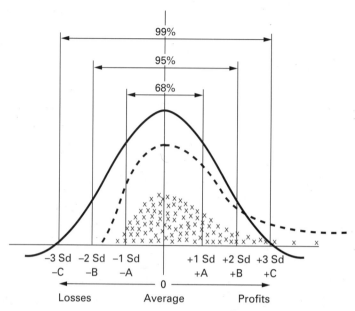

Figure 4-9. Normal versus skewed distributions. The standard deviation (sd) measurement assumes that trading profit and losses will be distributed evenly around the average (at 0). But most systems have unique skewed patterns. The trades of a trend-following system, shown by the "X" marks on the chart, have clustered losses and a few very large profits. The normal distribution does not show this correctly.

Skewed Distributions

The standard deviation assumes that profits and losses fluctuate evenly above and below the equity trend, as seen in Figure 4-2, which shows evenly spaced parallel lines. That is not a realistic assumption. Many trend-following systems are *skewed* to show larger profits than losses, but more frequent smaller losses. Then a typical profit/loss trend-following distribution will show a longer "tail" to the right, indicating larger profits, and the highest point to the left of center and below zero, indicating that the most frequent trades are small losses. Figure 4-9 shows the "normal" distribution curve on the same chart as the skewed trend performance.

Frequency Distribution. A practical way to display trading performance is by using a *frequency distribution*, or "histogram." This looks the same as a spreadsheet bar graph, except that the bars have different widths. For example, Figure 4-10 shows that each of the 10 bars represents

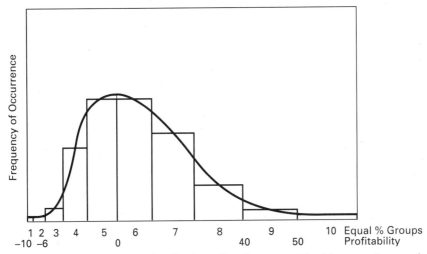

Figure 4-10. A frequency distribution of performance. The 10 uneven bars each represent 10% of the trades. The highest 10% profits are spread out while the losses are clustered together. A small tail to the left represents larger losses due to unavoidable price gaps.

10 percent of the trades, when sorted from greatest loss to largest profit. The wide bar at the right indicates that there is a large variance between the largest profits. The narrowest bar near the left shows that losses are clustered because of cutting losses short.

By looking at the chart, we can say there is a 10 percent chance that profits on any one trade will be greater than 50 percent or less than −10 percent. There is also a 20 percent chance that profits will be greater than 40 percent or less than −6 percent.

Semivariance. A useful way of measuring risk for equity distributions is with *semivariance*. This simply divides the equity into separate sets of continuous profits and losses. For example, if a trading program had the following sequence of profits and losses:

$$2.5\%, (1.0\%), 4.1\%, 3.5\%, (.6\%), (1.1\%), (.7\%), 1.5\%$$

it would be regrouped to show alternating, cumulative profits and losses:

$$2.5\%, (1.0\%), 7.6\%, (2.4\%), 1.5\%$$

The losses can be evaluated separately, giving the probability of a drawdown based on sequences of trades, rather than the probability of a loss on a single trade. This is a practical approach to evaluating risk.

Risk of Ruin

Another valuable measurement is *risk of ruin*. It is the chance of losing so much that you must stop trading. The formula that follows allows us to specify the maximum amount that we are willing to lose, constituting ruin. Before looking at the calculations, consider these premises:

- In real trading, once profits accumulate, the chance of ruin decreases. The greatest risk is at the beginning.
- If we plan to withdraw profits, thereby maintaining the same relative commitment to the market, then the risk of ruin must be greater than if we accumulate profits and keep the trading position the same.

The probability of risk of ruin is expressed as:

Risk_of_Ruin = ((1 − Edge)/(1 + Edge))^Units_Capital

where Edge = 2*Probability_of_Win − 1, the "trader's advantage"
     Units_Capital allows risk to be given relative to the size of the investment

Example 1.   A typical trend-following system will have larger profits than losses and more losing trades than winning ones. If

Probability_of_Win = 40% and
Units_Capital = 1 for a $10,000 investment

Risk_of_Ruin = ((1 − .40)/(1 + .40))^1
           = (.60/1.40)^1
           = .42857 or 42.8%

If the investment is increased to $20,000, or 2 units of capital,

Risk_of_Ruin = ((1 − .40)/(1+.40))^2
           = (.60/1.40)^2
           = .18367 or 18.3%

By doubling the investment, the risk of ruin decreases by 57 percent.

Profit Goals

Taking profits will reduce the risk of ruin. The closer the profit goal, the less chance of ruin:

Risk_of_Ruin_2 = $((((1 + \text{Edge})/(1 - \text{Edge}))^{\wedge}\text{Goal}) - 1)/(((1 + \text{Edge})/(1 - \text{Edge}))^{\wedge}(\text{Units\_Capital} + \text{Goal}) - 1)$

where all the terms are the same as the previous calculation, except Goal is the profit objective in units of trading capital (profit objective divided by one unit of trading capital).

Example 2.   If you traded the same trend-following system as example 1, with a 2-unit investment, but had a profit goal of half of one capital unit (or $5,000), then

Risk_of_Ruin_2 = $((((1 + .40)/(1 - .40))^{\wedge}.5) - 1)/(((1 + .40)/(1 - .40))^{\wedge}(2 + .5) - 1)$

$= (((1.40/.60)^{\wedge}.5) - 1)/(((1.40/.60)^{\wedge}2.5) - 1)$

$= .5275/7.3165$

$= .0721$ or 7.21%

Specifying Wins, Losses, and Risk

To be practical, a risk evaluation must use the performance profile of the system being traded. That includes the size of the profits and losses, as well as the amount of risk the investor is willing to accept. The following formula, from Ralph Vince's *Portfolio Management Formulas* (New York: Wiley, 1990), is a clear summary of P. Griffin's work, *The Theory of Blackjack* (Las Vegas: Gamblers Press, 1981), and gives a "fair approximation" of risk:

Risk of Ruin = $((1 - P)/P)^{\wedge}(\text{MaxRisk}/A)$

where the following terms are defined in the order needed for calculation:

AvgWin is the average winning trade (e.g., $400)

AvgLoss is the average losing trade (e.g., $200)

Investment is the amount invested (e.g., $10,000)

ProbWin is the probability (percentage) of a winning trade (e.g., .40)

ProbLoss is the probability (percentage) of a losing trade (e.g., .60)

MaxRisk is the maximum part of the investment that can be lost, in percent (e.g., .25)

AvgWin% is @ABS(AvgWin/Investment)

AvgLoss% is @ABS(AvgLoss/Investment)

Z is the sum of possible events,
    ProbWin*AvgWin% − ProbLoss*AvgLoss%

A is the square root of the sum of the squares of possible events,
    (ProbWin*AvgWin%^2 + ProbLoss*AvgLoss%^2)^(1/2)

P is .5*(1+(Z/A))

Example 3. Using the values given after the definitions, we get

AvgWin% = @ABS(400/10000) = .04

AvgLoss% = @ABS(200/10000) = .02

Z = .40*.04 − .60*.02 = .016 − .012 = .004

A = (.40*(.04^2)+.60*(.02^2))^(1/2) = (.00064+.00024)^(1/2)
    = .02966

P = .5*(1+.004/.02966) = .5674

Risk_of_Ruin = ((1 − .5674)/.5674)^(.25/.02966)

= .7634^8.4288

= .1016 or 10.16%

There is a 10% chance of losing $2,500 of a $10,000 investment when there is a 60% probability of a $200 loss and a 40% probability of a $400 profit. If everything remains the same and we lower the per trade profit to $350, the chance of ruin jumps to 25%. If the average profit falls to $300 per trade there is a 100% chance of losing the maximum $2,500.

Summary

Risk is important, but it does not have to be complex. The simplest risk-adjusted measure of trading performance is the return/risk ratio, which allows a fair comparison of values that are determined during different time intervals. It only requires that you use the same measure of risk and reward for all the information being evaluated.

Time periods can be deceptive. All time periods smooth performance, eliminating interim equity fluctuations that could have been large. To offset part of this problem, the maximum drawdown is needed, which puts an absolute value on the expected loss. Over time, even the maximum loss will be replaced by a larger loss. The longer the tested history, the less likely it will occur, but inevitably, all programs see larger profits and larger losses than those on record.

Diversification is the best approach to risk reduction. Deciding how much safety is gained by combining assets has been a very mathematical process; however, a simple spreadsheet program now allows anyone to combine performance history and evaluate the return/risk ratio of the proposed portfolios.

Trading cannot be successful without adding common sense. Changing volatility and fundamental relationships are seen faster by a person than by a computer. Therefore, trading requires constant watching. Risks also change; assets and trading strategies that once offered diversification can move together. It is not as important that they offer some risk reduction on a daily basis as it is that they do not mimic each other during a price shock.

PART 2

Using Old and New Trading Tools to Achieve Reasonable Objectives

5
Profit-Taking

Ask a trend follower, "How do you trade successfully?" The answer will be, "Let your profits run and cut your losses short." That seems to express the underlying philosophy behind trend-following programs. One of the most stunning examples is gold, rising from $100/oz to peak at $850/oz in January 1980. There were good opportunities to take profits at $250/oz and $400/oz, but neither of these would have been close to the profits that were possible if you had simply held a long-term position using nearly *any* trend-following method. In Figure 5-1(a), the same pattern can be seen in silver; and Figure 5-1(b) shows an S&P move in October 1987 that is difficult to forget.

Large profits represent what "might have been" in one price move. This chapter will show that waiting for the exception is not as good as

---

PROFIT-TAKING

Disadvantages

- Miss *big* profits

Advantages

- More frequent profitable trades
- Less slippage closing out trades
- Less slippage than reversing a trade (e.g., long to short)
- Better *reward/risk* ratio

When deciding to use profit-taking, the only disadvantage is the fear of "missing the *big* move." Instead, trading can be improved.

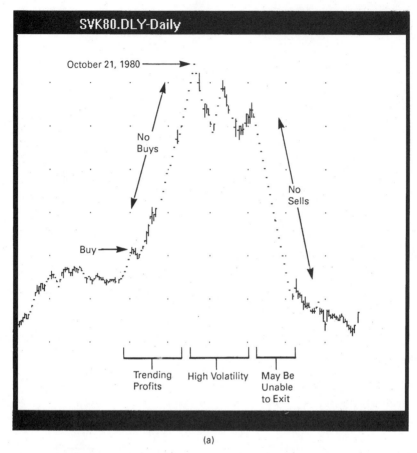

(a)

Figure 5-1. Exceptional market moves. (a) *May 1980 Comex Silver, peaking on January 21, 1980.* Exceptionally large trend-following profits could have been captured had you been able to exit near the top. By waiting, much of the profit would have disappeared. The high volatility near the top may have also reduced those returns due to slippage.

returning more frequent profits. Spectacular price moves do not occur often enough to be worth sacrificing a good, everyday plan. In addition, the great risk associated with a major move requires a constant investment that is too big to be reasonable for the few times it will serve to protect an infrequent occurrence.

A Test for Profit-Taking

This chapter will show that *a simple rule for taking profits is better than waiting until the trend changes,* which also means that profits will be taken before the "big" moves reach their peak. This will be done by testing a moving

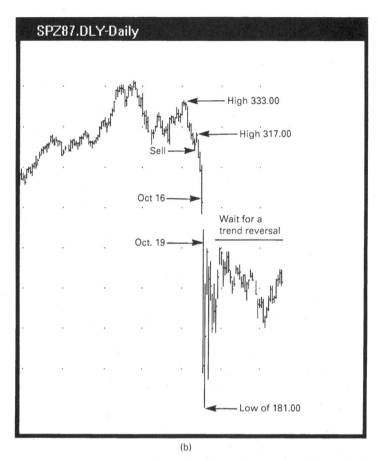

(b)

Figure 5-1. (*Continued*) Exceptional market moves. (b) *The S&P drop of October 1987.* Trend followers should have been short before the sharp drop, but the volatility of the following day would have made it difficult to justify holding a trend position. Looking back, it is clear that the trend was over on October 19. After that, a trend follower was just giving back profits waiting for a reversal.

average system with profit-taking measured as a percentage of price. Other more complicated tests could look at different trading strategies as well as different profit-taking measurements, some based on volatility. First it is important to see that the idea of taking profits is sound.

How It Was Tested

A simple exponential moving average system was tested using Telerate's *TeleTrac*, and the results were compared and plotted using a spreadsheet. The formula for the trend was

@exp_ma(price,period) = ema[1] + sc*(price − ema[1])

where @exp_ma is the exponential moving average function, saved as exp

period is the number of days over which @exp_ma is calculated
ema[1] is yesterday's exponential trend value
price is today's closing price
sc is the smoothing constant, sc = 2/(period + 1)

Six trend speeds were tested: 5, 10, 15, 25, 50, and 75 days. This distribution was selected to even out the percentage changes between the time periods in each test.

The trading and profit-taking rules were:

1. *Buy* on the close when the exponential moving average turns up; *sell* when it turns down.

2. *Close out* the trade if the unrealized (open) profits, as of the closing price, are greater than a preset profit level, PT = p × close, where p is a percentage. Exit the trade at the closing price of the day.

3. Do not reset a trade in the same direction once profits have been taken.

If the daily high and low prices had been used, profits could have been taken *at the moment the profit was reached*, instead of at the close. This could have improved results for many trades. But in this basic approach, all trades were exited at the close. If you use the interbank market, intraday data, or any 24-hour price stream, you will want to take profits as soon as they reach the target level. Here, we will only look at decisions made on the daily close of trading.

Profit-Taking Levels

To be certain that all levels of profit-taking were included in only a few tests, profit levels began at 100 percent of the trade entry price, then were divided by 2 until performance deteriorated. Because prices never doubled, no profits were taken at the 100 percent level, and those results will be used as a control to measure improvement. Profit-taking levels were:

100%, 50%, 25%, 12.5%, 6.0%, 3.0%, 1.5%

For the serious technician, this method is also convenient for comparing the *frequency* of profit-taking events with a normally distributed sample.

Measuring the Results

Although many traders judge success by the size of profits, these tests compare profits with risk. The goal is to find the greatest returns for the lowest risk. Portfolio managers would recognize this as "risk-adjusted" returns, discussed in Chapter 4. A better risk-adjusted return can be converted to higher profits simply by increasing the leverage, or reducing investment reserves, because of the lower relative risk. Expressing results in this way also allows investors to judge clearly how much risk they are willing to accept.

In this example, normal commissions and slippage were applied to trades, but analysts must be careful to use *realistic* values for transaction costs to get correct results for their own trading. Profits, losses, and risk are shown in points. Risk is measured as one standard deviation of the daily accumulated profits and losses.

The following three markets were tested:

	From	To
Hang Seng Index	January 1988	February 1993
Deutsche Mark Index	February 1988	February 1993
Unilever	November 1987	November 1992

Coding the Tests

The *TeleTrac* code is shown in Box 5-1. This can also be done using a spreadsheet; however, it is important not to reenter a trade in the same direction once a profit is taken. You can solve this problem by keeping one spreadsheet column for the underlying trend direction (e.g., +1 for long and −1 for short), and another column to show whether that position is active (+1 if holding the trade, 0 if closed out using profit-taking). It is tricky, but it can be done. Strategy testing programs, such as Omega's *TradeStation* or *TeleTrac* make it much easier.

The Results

The raw values (in points) of the test results are shown in Table 5-1 (a)–(c). The trend speed is the far left column and the profit-taking level is given along the top. The profit and risk in the "100%" column represent the trend system performance with *no* profit-taking. In each row of each of the three tables, there are tests that show increased profits; however,

Box 5-1. TELERATE *TeleTrac* CODE (USING THE CLOSE ONLY)

```
 1  item      "DMX                               Data used is the D-mark
 2  date      "DATA(date,880201,930226,item)    (indexed as a %)
 3  close     "DATA(close,item)
 4  speed     40                                Speed of the moving average
 5  exp       Exp_ma(close,speed)               Exponential MA calculation
 6  buy       exp−exp[1]>0&exp[1]−exp[2]<0      Buy signal rule
 7  sell      exp−exp[1]<0& exp[1]−exp[2]>0     Sell signal rule
 8  buysell   Trade(buy,sell,sell,buy)          Trade strategy rules
 9  openbs    Open_PL(buysell,close,0,0)        Open trade profit or loss
10  ptlevel   3.0                               Profit-taking level in %
11  ptrule    openbs*100/close>ptlevel          Profit-taking rule
12  strategy  Trade(buy,sell | ptrule,sell,buy | ptrule) Final strategy rules
13  realized  Clos_PL(strategy,close,0.001,0.001) Realized PL with trans costs
14  openpl    Open_PL(strategy,close,0,0)       Open trade PL on new strategy
15  netpl     realized + openpl                 Net PL
16  risk      Std_dv(netpl,1200)                Risk = 1200 day standard dev
17  ratio     netpl/risk                        Reward/risk ratio
```

The code shows the calculation for the exponential moving average using the "study" Exp_ma. The code first tests the simple trend change logic without profit-taking and calculates the open-trade profit, openbs. It compares the open-trade profits with the profit-taking level, then creates a new buy-sell rule named strategy.

If the high and low prices are used to take profits on longs and shorts, lines 11 and 12 are replaced by the following three lines:

```
ptlong    (openbs[1]+high−close[1])*100/close>ptlevel
ptshort   (openbs[1]+close[1]−low)*100/close>ptlevel
strategy  Trade(buy,sell | ptlong,sell,buy | ptshort)
```

these are also accompanied by increased risk. Table 5-2 presents the Hang Seng results as the return/risk ratio, making it easy to see whether the combination of risk and return gives better performance.

Generalizing the Profit-Taking Patterns

The values for the Hang Seng Index given in Table 5-1 are plotted in Figure 5-2. The slowest trend (75 days) showed best performance at the profit-taking level of 12.5 percent, the 50- and 25-day trends were best

Table 5-1. Test Results

a. Hang Seng Results in Points

HANG SENG INDEX, January 1, 1988, to February 16, 1993 (in Hang Seng points)

MA Days	100% Profits	Risk	50% Profits	Risk	25% Profits	Risk	12.5% Profits	Risk	6% Profits	Risk	3% Profits	Risk	1.5% Profits	Risk
5	4603	1109	4603	1109	4865	1186	4494	1010	4284	1099	3174	770	1652	325
10	5833	1221	5833	1221	6493	1335	4846	940	3437	710	1869	328	1666	328
15	4105	984	4105	984	4362	1063	3069	657	2103	397	1565	319	1358	244
25	2645	744	2645	744	2991	861	2626	655	1436	335	1106	359	59	222
50	1298	397	1298	397	1776	432	2181	423	1813	268	341	257	69	258
75	743	524	743	524	907	442	951	338	328	175	−33	190	−256	231

b. Deutsche Mark Results in Percent

DEUTCHE MARK IMM INDEX, February 1, 1988, to February 26, 1993 (in percent)

MA Days	100% Profits	Risk	50% Profits	Risk	25% Profits	Risk	12.5% Profits	Risk	6% Profits	Risk	3% Profits	Risk	1.5% Profits	Risk
5	9.83	4.09	9.83	4.09	9.83	4.09	10.47	4.04	5.79	4.63	10.88	4.98		
10	8.79	6.34	8.79	6.34	8.79	6.34	9.96	6.57	11.00	7.36	10.15	7.58		
15	23.47	8.04	23.47	8.04	23.47	8.04	26.73	8.59	26.58	9.49	25.90	9.90		
25	37.76	12.01	37.76	12.01	37.76	12.01	37.92	11.91	30.93	9.97	22.79	8.68		
50	39.61	12.75	39.61	12.75	39.61	12.75	50.24	14.49	26.00	8.00	21.59	7.35		
75	18.53	7.17	18.53	7.17	18.53	7.17	34.00	10.42	5.87	2.98	1.80	2.35		

c. Unilever Results in Points

UNILEVER, November 4, 1987, to November 23, 1992 (in points)

MA Days	100% Profits	Risk	50% Profits	Risk	25% Profits	Risk	12.5% Profits	Risk	6% Profits	Risk	3% Profits	Risk	1.5% Profits	Risk
5	240	1387	240	1387	240	1387	240	1387	4 330	1576	6350	1801	5620	1417
10	−1040	1313	−1040	1313	−1040	1313	−890	1313	300	1377	3530	1260	4960	1108
15	−3420	1630	−3420	1630	−3420	1630	−2440	1630	−2480	1645	1200	1214	1010	1232
25	−3360	1149	−3360	1149	−3360	1149	−2010	1149	−940	1107	6430	841	4640	676
50	−3620	967	−3620	967	−3620	967	−368 0	943	−3260	857	310	366	2940	431
75	−10060	1190	−10060	1190	−9710	1190	−11560	1092	−8080	1313	−2200	610	−2600	921

at 6 percent, the 15-day was best at 3 percent, and the faster speeds were still improving at 1.5 percent. Because slower trends allow larger profits to accumulate, it makes sense that profit-taking levels will also be greater. Fast trends need comparably smaller targets.

The consistency of the results is also reassuring. We can have more confidence in a method that begins with a logical premise and is confirmed by testing.

Table 5-2. Hang Seng Reward/Risk Ratio

Because risk declines faster than profits, the reward/risk ratio improves. By using leverage, a better ratio can be turned into higher profits for lower risk.

MA Days	Reward/Risk Ratio						
	100%	50%	25%	12.5%	6%	3%	1.5%
5	4.15	4.15	4.10	4.45	3.90	4.12	5.08
10	4.78	4.78	4.86	5.16	4.84	5.70	5.08
15	4.17	4.17	4.10	4.67	5.30	4.91	5.57
25	3.56	3.56	3.47	4.01	4.29	3.08	0.27
50	3.27	3.27	4.11	5.16	6.76	1.33	0.27
75	1.42	1.42	2.05	2.81	1.87	0.17	−1.11

Reasons for Profit-Taking

The following are strong arguments for profit-taking:

- Profit-taking has smaller slippage, because trades are closed out when prices are moving in the profitable direction.

- It is not necessary to reverse a position from long or short, or short to long, in many cases. Smaller orders mean a better execution price.

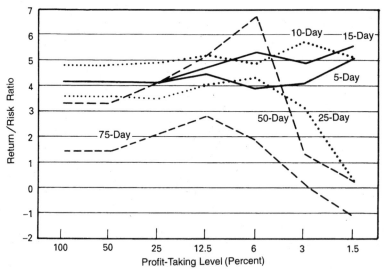

Figure 5-2. Hang Seng reward/risk chart. No profit-taking occurred at the 50% or 100% levels, but improvements can be seen in a predictable pattern at lower percentages. Longer-term trends were improved with larger profit-taking objectives, while faster trends were consistently better using smaller targets.

- The more profit-taking, the less exposure to market uncertainty and fewer equity swings. The risk declines because you are not in the market as much, thus avoiding unnecessary volatility and an occasional price shock.

- The extra profits that may be gained at the end of a move tend to have much higher volatility associated with marginal returns.

- The larger investment needed to wait for and then hold a longer, more volatile trade downgrades the total performance. Because risk is lower using profit-taking, your investment can be smaller.

- Setting a smaller profit-taking level means that the system does not depend on a few large profits, but on regular price movement.

Closing out a trade with profits is not only personally satisfying but is sensible. As with other rules, it must be done properly. In a trend-following program, there are more losses than profits; therefore, the profits must be larger than the losses. Liquidating a trade as soon as you see a profit will not result in a successful trading program. You must first test your system for a selection of profit-taking levels to see how the return/risk ratio changes. Then you have the basis for adding profit-taking to your plan.

Profit Objectives versus Time

The first part of this chapter showed that taking profits improves trend-following systems of all speeds. Longer trends develop larger profits; therefore they were helped by larger profit-taking objectives. Faster trends needed smaller goals. Using a small profit-taking objective in a long-term system causes small profits and relatively larger losses; a large profit objective in a fast trending system was rarely reached.

The relationship between the time interval (the speed of the trend or the length of the trade) and the size of the profit-taking objective is similar to the pattern of volatility over time (see Figure 5-3). As the period of evaluation becomes longer, the potential for profits levels off. This is the result of the maximum price move that would normally occur during that time period.

Taking Profits at Only One Point

It is easiest to think of taking profits at one price for each trade. This is often a fixed value or a percentage of the entry price. For example, buying

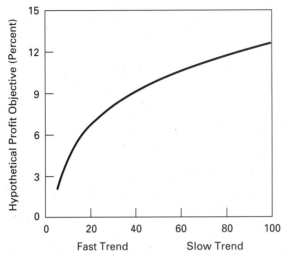

Figure 5-3. Size of profit-taking objectives for varying trend speeds. Profit-taking objectives increase in size as the trend period increases. This pattern is very similar to risk or volatility over time.

IBM shares at $60 using a medium-speed trend might have a profit-taking goal of $5 (about 8.3 percent). A foreign exchange trader might look for a profit of .0075 in the British pound, equal to .5 percent (one-half of 1 percent). Using a percentage to specify the size of profits is a little more adaptable than using fixed values.

Simple profit-taking goals are easy to test and simple to trade. The entire position goes on and off at the same time. But it is not as good as using multiple exit points, which give you more chances to succeed and reduce risk.

Problems of Using One Profit-Taking Objective

Single price objectives are impractical and often frustrating. If GM is bought at 30, with an objective of 33, what do you do if prices stop at $32\frac{3}{4}$, or at $32\frac{7}{8}$? When are you close enough to your objective so that the few extra points are not important?

A single profit-taking level is usually a number that worked "on average" over some historic period, whether it was a few weeks or many years. "On average" may have been very good in 1990 and very bad in 1994. Even clever profit-taking schemes, which adjust to volatility, may be out-of-phase for long time periods.

Benefits of Using More Than One Profit Objective

The greatest benefit of profit-taking is the reduced risk gained by being out of the market. It follows that *the sooner you begin to take profits, the faster your risk exposure will drop.* To make this work, you need to trade a position large enough to close it out in at least two parts, but preferably four parts. Two basic profit-taking strategies are shown in Figures 5-4 and 5-5. In both cases, a long position is taken at the same point—50.00—and a move of 2 percent is expected.

Because price movement looks very similar to a random distribution, prices will move back and forth by 1 percent more than twice as often as they will reach 2 percent, and they will move 0.5 percent more than four times as often as they move 2 percent. This is important information when setting profit objectives. If, for every ten trades, you capture a profit of 2 percent only once, then you should have reached a 1 percent profit twice, and a profit of 0.5 percent four times. If the market was more volatile and you captured profits of 2 percent twice in ten trades, then you should have reached a 1 percent profit four times and a 0.5 percent profit eight times.

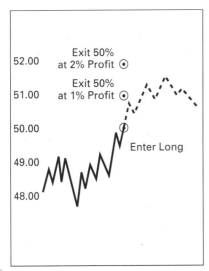

Figure 5-4. Two equally spaced profit objectives. Using two profit objectives, each for an equal part of the trade, greatly increases your chances of reaching one of the goals. Once part of the trade has been removed successfully, half the risk is gone.

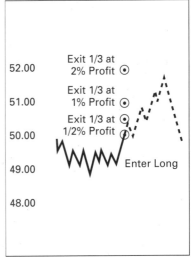

Figure 5-5. Three or four profit objectives are ideal. They should be spaced farther apart as profits get larger. This pattern takes advantage of market noise. The average profit, if all objects are reached, should be the same as the result of a single profit objective used for the entire position.

It is important that we start by *knowing* how many times you reached the profit goal in your trading strategy. That gives us a way to know how often smaller profit objectives would be reached. This approach separates theory from reality. Look again at the number of times the profit levels would have been reached:

If a profit goal of 2% was reached twice in ten trades, then:

Number Times Reached	Profit Level	Total Profits	
2	2%	4%	(known from testing)
4	1%	4%	(2 extra)
8	0.5%	4%	(4 extra)

First, we see that the *total profits remain the same.* When you divide the profit objective by 2, you double the number of times you will reach that level. That is an important feature of a normal distribution. Of course, when profit-taking objectives are small and frequent, the transaction costs will be proportionately larger. That makes very small, frequent profit-taking unrealistic for real trading.

Second, the four times that the 1 percent objective was reached *include* the two times that the price also reached the 2 percent level. Then there are only two additional times that prices reached the 1 percent level and did not reach the 2 percent level. Similarly, there were only four times that prices reached the 0.5 percent level without reaching the 1 percent level. Remember that the disadvantage is the added transaction costs due to more trades.

Example. Two Profit Levels.   Let us apply this to trading. Instead of taking a position with only 1 contract, 100 shares, or $1 million, take a position of 2 contracts, 200 shares, or $2 million. Compare the result of using a single profit objective of 2 percent with two different objectives of 2 percent and 1 percent, each for half of the position. At first we will look only at the profits that are taken:

Case 1. Profit-Taking with One and Two Targets

Units	No. of Times	Each Profit	Unit Total	Total
With one profit-taking level of 2%:				
2	2	2%	8%	8%
With two profit-taking levels (2% and 1%):				
1	2	2%	4%	
1	4	1%	4%	8%

From this, it would appear that setting more than one profit objective is the same as setting a single larger one, therefore, *why not use the smallest ones?* For two reasons:

1. *You must still achieve an average profit of about the same size.* Because the size of the losses remain the same, the average profit objective must also be similar. If you have not increased the number of system trades, you will get worse performance when you replace big profits with small ones and keep the same losses.

2. *The transaction costs become too high.* The size of the profits can become too small to make up for the transaction costs, which remain about the same. Every trade pays a combination of brokerage fees and slippage. These transaction costs are relatively fixed, that is, they are based on position size rather than frequency of trading. Taking profits at smaller levels makes these fixed transaction costs reduce profits by a larger percentage, while adding the same amount to losses.

As long as you can be profitable using smaller profit-taking levels, you have the following advantages:

- *The execution price is better.*

- *More (unit) trades are profitable.* For example, you will have taken *some* profits on 8 out of 10 trades, rather than *all* profits on 2 of 10 trades.

- *Results are more consistent.* Because market noise helps price reach some profit levels, you are out of the market more and not as subject to random market patterns.

- *You don't have to worry as much about missing the profit-taking level by a few points.*

- *Overall risk is lower.* Most important is that risk is reduced by being out of the market. The more profits taken, the less you are subject to unexpected and unpleasant price moves. The only restriction is that transaction costs eat up small profits.

Adding Risk to the Picture

We have discussed how the normal distribution of prices causes a clear pattern of how many times you can reach a preset target. Now let's look at the risk.

It is safe to say that when prices move up 0.5 percent, they also move down 0.5 percent during the same time period. It would be especially correct if we did not have a very good timing strategy, or we selected an arbitrary period of price movement. In our 10-trade example, we assumed that, for each profit level reached, there was an equal risk. Looking at the trading profile for a trend-following system, there are 10 losses and only 2 profits:

Case 2. No Profit-Taking

Units	No. of Times	Profit (Loss)	Unit Total	Total
With one profit-taking level of 2%:				
Profits generated:				
2	2	2%	8%	8%
Risk taken:				
2	10	(2%)	(40%)	(40%)
Return/risk ratio: 8/40 = .20				

Note that the 10 trades each have a risk of 2 percent, because no profit-taking is used. In the next case, where profits are taken at two levels, the risk is always 2 percent unless profits are taken at a lower level, then the risk is equal to that level. For two profit-taking levels, the results are:

Case 3. Two Profit-Taking Levels

Units	No. of Times	Profit (Loss)	Unit Total	Total
With two profit-taking levels (2% and 1%):				
Profits generated:				
1	2	2%	4%	
1	4	1%	4%	8%
Risk taken:				
1	10	(2%)	(20%)	
1	4⎤	(1%)	(4%)	
1	6⎦	(2%)	(12%)	(36%)
Return/risk ratio: 8/36 = .22				

Note that the bracket shows the 4 trades where profits were taken at the 1 percent level, and the remaining 6 trades where profits were not taken (where a full 2 percent loss is posted). This is the worst possible case, yet the return/risk ratio improved by 10 percent. This gain is the result of reducing the risk to 1 percent on a few units, rather than being exposed to a 2 percent risk on all trades.

A 10 percent improvement in the reward/risk ratio is the same as adding 10 percent to your profits (with the same investment and same risk), or reducing the risk by 10 percent.

With a Better Trading Strategy...

What we have done is to look at profit-taking based on the number of profit levels reached in your current trading strategy. We have assumed that, when profits were not reached, prices were just as volatile in the wrong direction.

A good trading strategy may only hold a trade for a short time. If profits are not reached within a preset number of days, the trade is ended. Therefore, if the market becomes less volatile and does not reach the 1 percent profit level, the trade can be closed out with a small profit or loss—and never show a 2 percent risk. This would improve the reward/risk ratio significantly.

Stop-Losses

A stop-loss that is smaller than the largest profit-taking level (e.g., 2 percent) can prevent you from reaching that profit level in 50 percent of the situations. Stops that are half the size of the largest profit level will cause the trade to be stopped out 75 percent of the time. This is simply based on the equal chance of a price move caused by market noise.

Stop-losses must be used carefully, otherwise they interfere with performance. If your trading strategy is good, prices move in a profitable direction more often and do not reach the stop. If the entry timing is not as good, the stop-loss will be hit and prevent you from reaching your goal.

More Profit-Taking

If your trading program was able to take profits 4 times out of 10 trades, rather than the 2 times used in the example, the results of using profit-taking would be even better:

Case 4. Using Profit-Taking with a Better System Performance

Units	No. of Units Reached	Profit (Loss)	Unit Total	Total
With one profit-taking of 2%:				
Profits generated:				
2	4	2%	16%	16%
Risk taken:				
2	10	(2%)	(48%)	(48%)
Return/risk ratio: 16/48 = .33				
With two profit-taking levels of 2% and 1%:				
Profits generated:				
1	4	2%	8%	
1	8	1%	8%	16%
Risk taken:				
1	10	(2%)	(20%)	
1	8	(1%)	(8%)	
1	2	(2%)	(4%)	(32%)
Return/risk ratio: 16/32 = .50				

The ratio improved 50 percent from .33 to .50 using a strategy that was able to take profits 4 out of 10 trades. That is a substantial improvement, but it can only be realized by frequent profit-taking. It would be limited to a professional trading group with the ability to watch the market closely.

Summary

Profit-taking reduces risk, and more frequent profit-taking at different levels reduces risk more. In addition:

- Transaction costs limit small profits.

- Spreading profit levels over a broad range gives the most improvement; grouping them closely together allows only a small improvement.

- Using a stop-loss that is smaller than the biggest profit-taking level will prevent prices from reaching the profit objectives.

- Limiting the time that you hold a trade reduces the trading risk by being out of the market; therefore, the more often you take profits, the lower your risk.

To find out how to get the profit-taking levels, you first need to test your own strategy assuming one profit point. That gives you the average of all profit objectives. You can then combine profit levels and position size to identify a simple pattern in the way profits should be taken. The most common plan is to have more targets at lower profit levels and spread them out further as profit targets become larger. The reduction in risk due to being out of the market may allow profit goals to be set much lower and still net very good returns with a better trading profile.

6

The Mixed Role of Stops for Controlling Risk

Keeping losses small, which can mean using a closely placed Stop order, has always been considered sensible risk control, but it may present more problems than it solves. A series of losses from short-term trades can be greater than a single, large loss caused by a longer-term position. In addition, when you get stopped out but the trend remains unchanged, how do you decide when to reenter the market?

A stop-loss order is a mixed blessing. It is not the order itself, because the act of monitoring the market and using Limit orders to carefully liquidate a trade has the same result. Large stop-losses offer some protection against catastrophic events and price shocks; however, attempts to keep risk very small causes larger losses and a worse risk profile. Small risk limits are often activated by market noise; there is little relationship between getting stopped out and the direction—or change of direction—of price movement.

Historically, there is some level of risk protection that would have benefited a portfolio. Close inspection of lengthy test results show that the reason for improved performance is a single, adverse price jump that would have been reduced by using a stop-loss. But it is not clear that such a situation would occur again, and if it occurred, that the stop-loss order could have been executed profitably.

In some cases, a poor trading strategy is improved by using stops. But then, it would also be improved by not trading. There are occasional improvements in the return/risk ratio of performance using systematic risk control. When the program has no position, after the risk limit has been reached, the equity is not subject to the ups and downs of price movement. If a large loss is averted during this time, overall performance improves. The alternative which is to trade a smaller portfolio, is often the better choice for risk reduction.

Need for Risk Control

Ideally, a Stop order that has been entered into the market is expected to automatically get you out of a position when prices move against you. It forces you to decide, in advance, how much you can afford to lose, so that your trading risk is under control. It avoids last-minute decisions and the temptation to hold a losing position with the hope that prices will recover.

Stops are normally "resting orders" held by the floor broker to be executed when the price is reached. For our purpose, we will include any trader who intends to limit losses to a fixed amount, whether or not the order is placed in advance as a Stop order.

Risk Protection or False Hope?

The use of stops, or the intent to limit losses to a predetermined fixed amount, may give a false sense of security (shown in Table 6-1). For example, a Stop order that is reached during an illiquid or quiet market will result in large slippage; during a fast market, or a price jump, it will often get the worst fill. Large traders cannot enter stops because they move the market and cause substantial slippage.

Setting Stops Based on What You Can Afford to Lose

Stops are set for two main reasons:

- They can trigger a change in market direction, or
- They can limit losses to a preset amount.

Table 6-1. Using a Stop-Loss

Expectations	Reality
Limits losses to preset levels	Slippage and price shocks increase the size of the loss substantially
Losses will be much smaller than profits	Individual losses may be smaller, but a series of losses can be very large
There can still be more frequent profitable trades than losing ones	Market noise causes more losses than profits unless the trader has a very good strategy

Stops that react to market direction are not primarily intended to limit market risk, but do so as a secondary benefit. A foreign exchange trader who gets a moving average trend signal to be long the dollar against the yen at 100.50 places a stop at 99.50, assuming that new lows in the dollar mean renewed weakness. The stop-loss combines an acceptable risk level with a perceived change of direction.

Stops placed to limit the size of losses are more common and more difficult to evaluate. The use of a small risk control can be intended to produce a particular performance profile, as in Case 1.

Case 1. A different foreign exchange trader buying 10 million $/marks expects to hold the trade for a US$20,000, or 0.20 percent profit, based on a 1-day volatility strategy. To show proper risk control, the trader would like to keep losses under US$10,000, giving a 2:1 ratio of average profits to average losses. The trader would also like to have at least half of the trades profitable over a long-term performance record. The total picture would show a steady profitability and reasonably small losses—a very pleasing performance.

But the market does not work this way. It is not possible to control both the return/risk ratio *and* the number of profitable trades.

Interference from Market Noise

"Noise" is the term given to unpredictable price movements. Normally noise is associated with small price changes, but in reality it includes large price shocks. Noise is caused by traders entering and exiting the market with different objectives and different time frames. An institution adds positions because of new investment funds; Russia sells gold to pay for a wheat purchase; or an auto company liquidates part of its stock portfolio to cover foreign exchange losses. Although each event is unique, the total picture of this noise creates a very predictable *random distribution* with some very special properties. Figure 6-1 shows the general rule that *erratic prices (noise) which are twice as large occur half as often.*

The S&P price changes appear to fall exactly on the random distribution line in Figure 6-1(a), while the bonds and Deutsche marks have about twice as many moves of 1 percent and 4 percent than a random occurrence. It is important to note, however, that the number of occurrences of bonds and Deutsche marks still decline by 50 percent as the size of the move increases in steps of 0.5 percent.

When we look closely at the larger moves (called the "tail" of the distribution) in Figure 6-1(b), the S&P has more extreme changes than either of the other markets and much more than if it were a random distribution. These large moves are caused by price shocks.

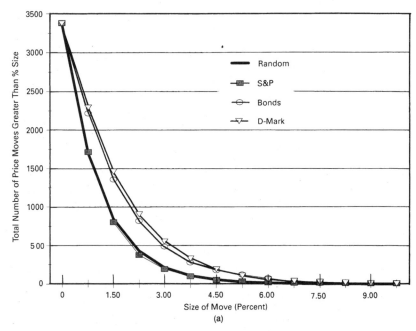

Figure 6-1. Random distribution of noise. (a) *The frequency of price movements is plotted against the size of those movements.* A random distribution has a unique property: doubling the size of the price moves reduces the number of occurrences by half. For every increment of 0.5%, the frequency drops by one-half. More than 10 years of data, totaling 3,375 days, were used to compare the S&P, U.S. Treasury bonds, and Deutsche marks against a random distribution (shown as the heavy solid line). The extent to which prices do not keep to this pattern is the way its *nonrandom* pattern is measured.

Total Losses Are the Same

The interesting phenomenon concerning the size and frequency of erratic price noise is that *the number of occurrences times the size of the move is always the same.* Although the bonds and Deutsche marks varied from a random distribution, they still conformed very closely to the same rule.

Specifying the Performance Profile.   Based on the normal distribution of prices shown in Figure 6-1 and Table 6-2, the foreign exchange trading example, Case 1, could not work. If a trader targets a US$20,000 profit with losses one-half the size, then there should be twice as many losses. As the size of the profits increases compared with the average loss, the number of small losses must also increase. If a naive trading model gives four profits averaging US$20,000 and eight losses of US$10,000, then a good strategy must capture higher profits, reduce the losses, or turn one or two losses into small profits.

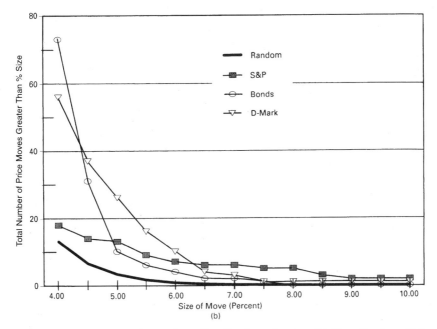

Figure 6-1. (*Continued*) Random distribution of noise. (b) *Magnification of (a) at the extreme right of the distribution.* All three markets have much larger price moves than the comparable random curve. These could occur because of price shocks.

Expectations

In these cases, the real prices are so similar to random movement that you could not tell the difference without a careful mathematical study. We can assume that decreasing the size of a stop-loss will cause a predictable additional number of trades to be stopped out, always conforming to Table 6-2, with the possible exception of large stops.

Our expectations of improved performance using a small stop should be low. As the stop-loss gets smaller, the number of trades that are stopped out gets larger. Each time a stop-loss is activated, there is addi-

Table 6-2. Size versus Frequency of Stop (If Random Price Movement)

Size of Stop	No. of Occurrences	Size of Loss
5 points	20	100 points + slippage
10 points	10	100 points + slippage
20 points	5	100 points + slippage

tional slippage because the order forces an execution in the direction of market movement.

The larger stops may be different. If prices are exceptionally volatile, then a stop-loss might save some of that loss. If you plan to get out when a price shock hits, then a stop-loss could not make things worse—and might make it better by acting as a major risk control. Large stops only work with longer-term trading; a fast trend will always give a reversal at the same time a larger stop would have been reached. Therefore, small stops will generally be ineffective, but larger stops will sometimes improve performance.

Capitalizing on Distribution. A successful system will need to capture larger than normal profits, or cut losses. The use of a stop-loss is the place to start. If a few of the unusually large price moves shown in Figure 6-1(b) can be controlled when they generate losses and captured when they produced profits, the overall system performance will improve.

Testing a System with a Stop-Loss

A simple trend-following system was tested on daily data using stop-losses to see whether they helped profits and controlled risk. The system included the following main features:

- An exponential moving average, @Exp_MA, was used for the trend.
- A buy signal was given when the trendline turned up,
  @Exp_MA > @Exp_MA[1].
- A sell signal was given when the trendline turned down,
  @Exp_MA < @Exp_MA[1].
- The trade was exited if the loss, at the close, exceeded a preset percentage level (the stop-loss), or when a reverse buy or sell signal occurred.
- All orders were executed on the close of the local trading day.
- There were no commissions or slippage charged to any trade.
- Risk was defined as 1 standard deviation of equity.

In actual trading, the more active systems will show additional losses due to relatively larger transaction costs. Because all trades are executed in the direction of the price movement, individual estimates of cost can be subtracted from the profits per trade. Without costs, the results of this test will still give a reasonable comparison of the use of different stop-loss limits.

Test Results

Table 6-3 shows a 10-year optimization of trend speed versus percentage stop-loss for Chrysler, Siemens (for only 5 years), the Deutsche mark, and Eurodollars, ending June 1993. Only the adjusted rate of return is shown to allow comparisons (see in Chapter 4, "Choosing Between the Currency and Bond Portfolios," for an explanation of adjusted rate of return). The far right column in Table 6-3, marked "None," shows the results of the trend system without any stop-loss. The far left column, marked ".02," shows a very small .02 percent stop-loss.

The conclusion is that improvements are inconsistent. The best results for this test set seem to be Siemens, which has higher adjusted returns for trends below 100 days, and scattered improvement in the middle of the table, centered near a stop-loss of .50 percent.

Because the major currencies are said to have more trends, we expected a stop-loss in the Deutsche mark to produce better results. Prices that reach the stop-loss level in the D-mark should continue in the same direction until it activates a new, reverse trend signal. That did not happen. The results from the smallest stops were uniformly worse than the use of no stops in the 10-year test. Improvement occurs in a small area in the center of the table.

Larger stops, or no stop, show a more uniform result. When using an optimization test to select the best trading rules, it is preferable to see smooth, consistent results, rather than alternating profits and losses. Both Chrysler and the D-mark have poor returns in the bottom left corner of the tables.

Another View with a Shorter Test Period

Table 6-4 compares the cash returns with risk-adjusted returns for the Deutsche mark and Eurodollars over the 4 years ending November 1992, using comparable stops. The Deutsche mark cash returns appear much better than Eurodollars but have higher, inconsistent risk. When adjusted for risk, the Eurodollar returns are clearly better.

Contour Map of Eurodollar Stop-Loss Tests. Figure 6-2 shows a contour map of the Eurodollar tests. The white areas have the highest profits and the black parts the worst losses. As in the 10-year tests, the use of small stops, seen at the left edge of the figure, is inconsistent, alternating between light and dark, with neither the best or worst results. As stops become larger toward the right, performance is more uniform and predictable. We can conclude that small stops are sensitive to specific price patterns and noise; therefore they are erratic.

Table 6-3. Stop-Losses: Results of Longer Term Tests

Values are annualized rate of return, adjusted to a 25% maximum drawdown.

a. Chrysler Motors: 2329 Days (1/05/84 to 3/18/93)

				Stop-Loss in Whole Percent								
Days	.02	.05	.10	.15	.25	.50	1.00	2.00	4.00	7.00	10.00	NONE
5	−2.8	−2.8	−2.7	−2.7	−2.7	−2.8	−2.8	−2.7	−2.8	−2.8	−2.8	−2.8
10	−2.8	−2.8	−2.8	−2.8	−2.8	−2.8	−2.8	−2.8	−2.8	−2.8	−2.8	−2.8
25	−2.8	−2.8	−2.8	−2.7	−2.8	−2.8	−2.6	−2.6	−2.6	−2.6	−2.6	−2.6
50	−2.6	−2.6	−2.6	−2.6	−2.6	−2.6	−2.2	−2.3	−2.2	−2.2	−2.2	−2.2
75	−1.2	−1.2	−1.2	−1.4	−1.4	−1.5	−1.5	−1.6	−1.4	−1.5	−1.5	−1.5
100	−1.5	−1.5	−1.5	−1.6	−1.7	−1.9	−.6	−.7	−.5	−.6	−.6	−.6
150	5.8	5.7	5.7	5.3	5.4	4.9	4.5	4.0	3.6	3.5	3.5	3.5
200	2.2	2.2	2.2	1.9	1.7	1.6	1.4	2.8	2.7	2.7	2.7	2.7
250	−2.5	−2.5	−2.5	−2.5	−2.5	−2.5	−2.5	−.4	−.1	2.0	2.0	2.0
300	3.6	3.6	3.4	3.4	3.2	3.1	3.0	2.5	2.4	2.4	2.4	2.4

b. Siemens: 1452 Days (2/3/87 to 11/23/92)

Days	.02	.05	.10	.15	.25	.50	1.00	2.00	4.00	7.00	10.00	NONE
5	1.5	1.5	2.1	1.6	.9	1.4	1.9	1.5	1.2	1.2	1.2	1.2
10	11.8	11.7	12.0	11.4	10.6	8.5	8.2	7.5	6.7	6.0	6.0	6.0
25	10.1	10.1	9.4	8.8	7.4	6.8	5.0	3.7	3.5	3.0	3.0	3.0
50	6.3	6.3	6.1	5.6	8.9	6.7	6.7	8.4	8.8	7.7	7.7	7.7
75	9.8	9.4	11.4	11.6	12.1	11.1	8.3	10.0	9.7	8.7	8.7	8.7
100	5.2	5.2	4.8	4.9	4.1	3.1	4.8	5.9	5.9	5.3	5.3	5.3
150	5.0	4.9	4.9	5.0	5.0	4.2	3.0	4.7	7.8	7.7	7.0	7.0
200	3.6	3.6	3.6	3.2	2.9	2.2	2.9	1.8	2.9	2.8	2.8	2.8
250	4.5	4.4	4.4	4.3	3.9	3.3	4.4	5.2	4.9	4.9	4.9	4.9
300	4.4	4.4	4.4	4.2	5.4	4.9	4.1	2.7	2.4	2.4	2.4	2.4

Pattern of Results.   The size of the stop-loss must be based on the speed of the trend. A small stop with a slow system will usually be hit and rarely allows the trade to reach a profit. A large stop with a fast system will never be reached before the trend signal reverses the position. It should not be surprising that only a narrow band of stops applies to one trend speed.

Intraday Stops with a Daily System

It is tempting to react quickly to an adverse price move to keep losses small. Although the trend may be determined using daily closing prices, a stop could be activated when prices move badly during the

Table 6-3. Stop-Losses: Results of Longer Term Tests
(*Continued*)

Values are annualized rate of return, adjusted to a 25% maximum
drawdown.

c. Deutsche Mark: 2570 Days (11/24/82 to 11/23/92)

Days	.02	.05	.10	.15	.25	.50	1.00	2.00	4.00	7.00	10.00	NONE
5	−1.9	−1.9	−1.9	−1.9	−1.9	−1.8	−1.8	−1.8	−1.8	−1.8	−1.8	−1.8
10	−1.4	−1.1	−1.0	−1.0	−1.1	−.7	−.6	−.6	−.6	−.6	−.6	−.6
25	1.7	2.6	3.6	2.9	3.8	3.8	5.5	5.7	5.3	5.2	4.9	5.4
50	5.2	6.9	6.8	6.4	3.7	12.8	11.0	11.5	10.8	10.8	10.8	10.8
75	3.4	4.8	6.1	5.6	8.5	13.4	10.0	8.7	7.8	7.6	7.6	7.6
100	5.3	7.2	8.5	8.3	4.5	10.8	11.5	7.4	9.1	7.5	7.5	7.5
150	.5	.3	.0	−.4	1.6	8.1	6.8	7.7	5.3	3.6	3.6	3.6
200	.7	2.0	1.7	1.1	10.1	11.7	7.7	9.6	6.9	7.6	7.0	7.0
250	8.0	9.1	8.1	8.1	6.5	5.5	7.2	8.8	5.4	11.0	9.1	10.4
300	.7	.4	.2	−.1	.5	5.1	5.1	5.6	4.3	1 2.3	10.7	10.4

d. Eurodollars: 2556 Days (1/03/83 to 12/14/92)

	Stop-Loss in Whole Percent											
Day	.02	.05	.10	.15	.25	.50	1.00	2.00	4.00	7.00	10.00	NONE
5	1.2	1.3	1.4	1.0	1.0	1.0	1.1	1.1	1.1	1. 1	1.1	1.1
10	1.8	2.1	3.1	2.7	2.7	2.6	2.7	2.7	2.7	2 .7	2.7	2.7
25	3.8	3.0	6.7	6.1	8.2	7.4	7.4	7.4	7.4	7 .4	7.4	7.4
50	4.0	8.5	10.5	7.7	8.1	7.8	7.7	7.7	7.7	7.7	7.7	7.7
75	6.5	10.2	8.1	9.2	10.8	10.0	9.9	9.9	9.9	9.9	9.9	9.9
100	7.1	4.8	8.9	6.3	6.4	7.2	7.8	7.8	7.8	7.8	7.8	7.8
150	4.1	1.8	2.9	2.6	6.4	5.0	7.6	7.6	7.6	7.6	7.6	7.6
200	7.3	5.4	.8	.4	2.9	5.9	6.5	6.5	6.5	6. 5	6.5	6.5
250	1.1	−.8	−.8	.1	4.1	3.8	6.9	5.6	5. 6	5.6	5.6	5.6
300	.2	−.1	−.6	−.8	.3	6.7	5.6	5.4	5.4	5.4	5.4	5.4

Results of Longer Term Tests: The table shows the risk-adjusted test results of a trending system. All annualized rates of return are based on a maximum drawdown adjusted to 25% of the initial investment, allowing results to be compared fairly. The far right column, marked "NONE," had no stop-loss and therefore the largest risk. Results of using the smallest stops (.02%) are in the far left column. Although stops improve performance in specific cases, there does not seem to be a consistent pattern. Smaller stops are especially erratic as the trends increase in length, often showing alternating better and worse performance.

trading session. Unfortunately, the market noise will cause many more stops to be reached. At the end of the day, you will have captured losses that would have disappeared had you waited for the closing price. The accumulation of intraday losses and the increased number of trades will be far worse than basing the stop-loss on the same daily data as the system trend calculations.

Table 6-4. Stop-Losses: 4-Year Test Results

Comparison of cash returns vs. risk-adjusting returns.
Deutsche Mark: 1030 Days (11/22/88 to 11/23/92)

Annualized Rate of Return (On Cash, in Percent)

					Stop-Loss in Whole Percent							
Days	.02	.05	.10	.15	.25	.50	1.00	2.00	4.00	7.00	10.00	NONE
5	−7.5	−7.1	−7.3	−8.3	−9.9	−8.5	−7.1	−7.1	−7.1	−7.1	−7.1	−7.1
10	−6.8	−5.0	−5.3	−6.2	−7.6	−7.0	−4.4	−4.3	− 4.3	− 4.3	−4.3	−4.3
25	2.8	5.5	5.4	5.4	5.4	4.2	6.5	7.4	7.4	7.4	7.4	7.4
50	5.6	10.2	9.9	10.1	9.6	8.3	8.3	8.7	8.0	8.0	8.0	8.0
75	2.8	2.2	1.6	1.6	5.0	7.0	5.1	5.0	3.6	3.4	3.4	3.4
100	1.3	4.2	3.6	3.5	7.4	5.4	8.7	8.6	9.3	9.1	9.1	9.1
150	1.2	.9	.7	.7	− 1.1	7.6	9.3	11.2	8.8	7.5	7.2	7.2
200	5.3	9.1	8.9	8.7	8.2	6.4	7.9	9.7	7.0	5.2	4.6	4.6
250	5.9	8.3	8.1	8.0	7.7	6.7	6.1	7.9	5.2	5.6	4.9	4.7
300	2.0	1.8	1.5	1.2	.9	4.5	6.4	8.1	5.4	6 .6	5.9	5.5

Annualized Rate of Return (Adjusted to a 25% Drawdown)

Days	.02	.05	.10	.15	.25	.50	1.00	2.00	4.00	7.00	10.00	NONE
5	−3.7	−3.6	−3.6	−3.8	−4.2	−4.0	−3.6	−3.6	−3.6	−3.6	−3.6	−3.6
10	−3.9	−2.8	−2.9	−3.2	−3.6	−3.5	−2.5	−2.4	−2.4	−2.4	−2.4	−2.4
25	2.7	4.8	4.6	4.6	4.6	3.3	7.1	10.9	10.9	10.9	10.9	10.9
50	12.7	23.3	22.5	25.2	21.7	17.3	16.0	16.8	15.5	15.5	15.5	15.5
75	4.4	3.6	2.2	2.2	7.8	14.5	7.5	6.6	4.4	4.2	4.2	4.2
100	2.8	8.7	7.0	6.8	18.1	9.5	18.1	11.3	19.1	18.6	18.6	18.6
150	3.7	2.4	1.7	1.7	−1.7	12.1	12.0	14.6	10.8	8.3	8.0	8.0
200	14.0	22.0	19.3	19.2	17.1	13.4	13.2	15.1	9.1	5.9	5.3	5.3
250	14.7	18.8	17.6	16.7	16.0	12.8	9.9	12.9	7.4	8.2	7.2	6.9
300	5.7	4.5	3.4	2.8	1.9	8.3	9.8	12.8	7.0	10.3	9.2	8.7

Benefits of Being Out of the Market

Being out of the market may reduce equity fluctuation, even though a smaller profit is taken at the end of the trade. If the use of a stop-loss neither helps or hurts profitability, then the time spent out of the market will avoid some erratic price movement and improve the reward/risk ratio of trading performance. Holding a position that alternates from a profit to a loss without ultimately ending up profitable does not benefit your trading.

Table 6-4. Stop-Losses: 4-Year Test Results (*Continued*)

Eurodollars: 1042 Days (11/22/88 to 12/14/92)

Annualized Rate of Return (On Cash, in Percent)

					Stop-loss in Whole Percent						
Days	.02	.05	.10	.15	.25	.50	1.00	2.00	4.00	7.00	10.00	NONE
5	.3	.3	.3	.3	.3	.3	.3	.3	.3	.3	.3	.3
10	.9	.9	1.0	1.1	1.0	1.0	1.0	1.0	1.0	1.0	1.0	1.0
25	.3	.4	.9	1.2	1.3	1.3	1.3	1.3	1.3	1.3	1.3	1.3
50	.3	.5	1.0	1.3	1.6	1.6	1.6	1.6	1.6	1.6	1.6	1.6
75	.7	.8	1.1	1.1	1.3	1.3	1.3	1.3	1.3	1.3	1.3	1.3
100	.9	.8	1.0	1.0	1.1	1.0	1.0	1.0	1.0	1.0	1.0	1.0
150	.0	.1	−.1	−.1	.6	.9	.9	.9	.9	.9	.9	.9
200	.1	.1	.1	.1	.7	1.1	1.1	1.1	1.1	1.1	1.1	1.1
250	.2	.2	.2	.2	.9	1.2	1.2	1.2	1.2	1.2	1.2	1.2
300	.2	.3	.2	−.3	.4	.6	.6	.6	.6	.6	.6	.6

Annualized Rate of Return (Adjusted to a 25% Drawdown)

					Stop-loss in Whole Percent						
Days	.02	.05	.10	.15	.25	.50	1.00	2.00	4.00	7.00	10.00	NONE
5	2.9	2.4	2.4	2.4	2.4	2.4	2.4	2.4	2.4	2. 4	2.4	2.4
10	21.9	22.4	25.7	19.5	25.9	25.9	25.9	25.9	25.9	25.9	25.9	25.9
25	2.9	4.6	11.3	28.6	32.9	32.9	32.9	32.9	32 .9	32.9	32.9	32.9
50	7.6	12.6	23.8	33.0	38.8	38.8	38.8	38.8	3 8.8	38.8	38.8	38.8
75	18.5	20.7	27.4	27.1	32.6	32.0	32.0	32.0	32.0	32.0	32.0	32.0
100	22.1	18.3	25.9	25.6	28.5	25.6	25.6	25.6	25.6	25.6	25.6	25.6
150	.7	1.4	−1.3	−1.3	7.3	11.4	10.9	10.9	10.9	10.9	10.9	10.9
200	3.5	1.7	1.2	1.0	9.1	13.8	14.1	14.1	14.1	14.1	14.1	14.1
250	4.4	5.9	4.9	4.4	16.8	14.8	15.1	15.1	15. 1	15.1	15.1	15.1
300	4.3	6.5	5.6	−3.4	4.1	5.2	5.4	5.4	5.4	5.4	5.4	5.4

Comparison of 4-Year Results: The pattern in the "NONE" column (indicating no stops) shows that the risk-adjusted results are, in general, more consistent than unadjusted returns. Risk-adjusted returns show some large improvements due to the use of stops, but the total picture is very inconsistent. The variation is especially apparent by comparing the smallest .02% stops in the far left column with no stops in the far right column. Large stops affect the longer-term trends first (seen along the bottom of the table) and slowly work their way to the faster trends as the size of the stop gets smaller. Deutsche mark returns are uniformly better with 2% stops but inconsistent when stops become small. Eurodollar returns are best with no stops, which confirms their strong trnding character.

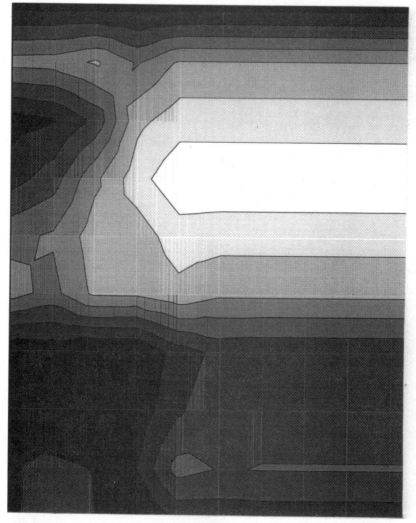

Figure 6-2. Contour map presentation of Eurodollar performance. Results using small stops, along the left part of the chart, are much more inconsistent than larger stops, or no stops, seen at the right.

Figure 6-3(a) shows the contour map test results of the 10-year Deutsche mark adjusted rate of return. The best performance is the small peak in the center bottom of the map. This corresponds to a slow trend and relatively large stop-loss of .50 percent. The darkening area as we move toward the top and left of the chart shows faster trends and smaller stops.

(a)

Figure 6-3. Contour map of 10-year Deutsche mark stop-loss tests. (a) *Adjusted rate of return.* Large stops and slower trends produce the best results, indicated by the peak at the center bottom of the map. A system must be finely tuned to capture this.

Figure 6-3(b) is the contour map of the return/risk ratio (annualized return divided by 1 standard deviation of equity changes) over the same 10-year period. The white area, showing the best performance, is larger than in the previous map and includes areas in the bottom left. This means that the use of a small stop with a slow trend *does* improve Deutsche mark performance by exiting trades that become volatile and unprofitable. The far left edge remains inconsistent, and the right side is very uniform.

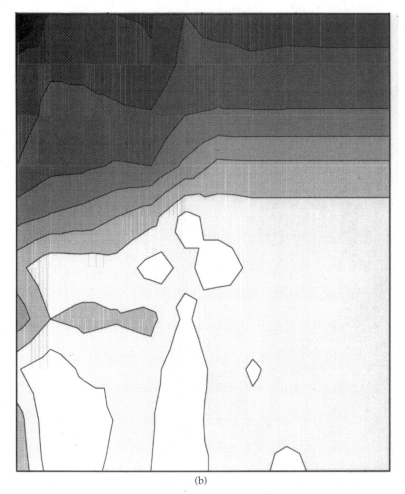

(b)

Figure 6-3. (*Continued*) Contour map of 10-year Deutsche mark stop-loss tests. (b) *Return/risk ratio.* Smaller stops may not improve profits but can improve the return/risk ratio of longer-term trends in this contour map. A better return/risk ratio can be converted to a higher rate of return using leverage.

Viewing the results as a return/risk ratio shows a much clearer picture. For the Deutsche mark, considered a "trending" market, stops should improve performance by reducing risk more than it reduces profits for longer-term trends and for most stops except those that are very small. The noisier index markets and most stocks do not show this result.

A Stop-Loss May Conflict with the Strategy

The nature of a stop-loss order is often contrary to the system with which it is used; it may "fight" with a trend-following program. The purpose of a trend is to smooth out and ignore market noise; the trend-line is substituted for prices to represent a better approximation of price direction. A stop-loss that is too close will be reached by an erratic price move, offsetting the value of the trend.

Trend Systems

When a stop is reached, the trend has not yet reversed. The system is saying that the trend is still intact. If that is true the trend will continue and the loss will turn into a profit, but you would not have a position because you were stopped out. If the stop works most of the time, then the trend changes whenever the stop is triggered. That is the same as saying the trend is too slow. A faster trend would catch the change of direction sooner. In either case, the solution does not seem to lie with the use of a stop-loss.

Countertrend Systems

Trading against the trend requires frequent small profits. To get more profits, it is necessary to hold larger losses, waiting for prices to move your way whether because of noise or good forecasting. A stop-loss will cause more frequent losses and prevent profits from developing. The two will not work together.

Apparent Improvement

Tests show that stop-losses improve results, either outright profits or reward/risk ratios. Usually, that is not the case. Tests of short intervals may not be representative of the long-term picture. The use of intraday stops can easily misrepresent the fill that is received from a stop. The lack of liquidity, or a price shock during the trading session cannot be seen by most computerized testing packages.

One event can appear to make the use of a stop-loss worthwhile. Reducing the loss from a major price shock to a reasonable level may be a good exchange for small give-ups. A trader must realistically assess whether a resting stop or visual stop would have offered the protection needed. It is difficult to design a system that continually gives up profits in expectation of possibly reducing risk in a single case.

Reentering a Stopped-Out Position

Once a trade has been stopped out, but the underlying trend or counter-trend position does not reverse or exit naturally, the trader faces another problem. Do you reenter the market and chance another loss in the same trade? Then the compounded risk would be much larger for each trade. If the decision is to reenter, what criteria should be used? Because the trend-following signal remains the same, there is no new signal to buy or sell; therefore, the trader must have additional rules for reentering the market. That makes the system much more complicated.

Managing Risk with and without Stops

If small stop-losses are not predictable, then the best choice for controlling risk is to deleverage, reducing the risk to acceptable levels. Deleveraging is always the safe alternative. It can be achieved with the following simple procedure:

1. Find the long-term risk level of the trading program, using a combination of maximum drawdown and standard deviation of equity changes (see Chapter 4).

2. Adjust the system risk to your acceptable level. You probably want less than a 1 percent chance of losing more than 10 percent of the invested capital during any year; therefore, set 3 standard deviations of the annualized risk equal to 10 percent of your investment.

3. Determine the investment size or the amount of capital to be traded, based on the adjusted risk in step 2.

4. To give protection from major price shocks, use a larger stop-loss that will not be easily reached due to noise.

For example, you have a trading program that returns 40 percent per year with a 95 percent chance that losses will be under 15 percent during the 10-year test period (1 standard deviation of the equity changes is equal to 7.5 percent). However, you want to keep the risk under 10 percent, which is two-thirds of the current level. If the required capitalization is US$1 million, then increase the investment by one-third to US$1.33 million.

Because control of risk is more important than higher profits, we accept a 20 percent expected return to keep the risk at 7.5 percent. By using a large stop-loss, the returns on the test optimization are more consistent, and we have greater confidence that the stop-loss will not interfere with the expected returns.

The Dilemma of
Professional Traders

Institutions allocate their professional traders a specific amount of trading capital on which their performance will be judged. To maximize profits and minimize risk, they tend to use high leverage and small stop-losses. The result is often modest profits and larger risk.

As discussed earlier, the amount of noise in foreign exchange markets causes small stops to be triggered frequently, preventing traders from reaching their profit objectives. But small stops are seen to be necessary because of the high leverage and potential risk. Most foreign exchange traders would be under pressure to explain losses in excess of 10 percent of capital.

Therefore, the best performance profile is not achieved by using small stops. It is best when the program is deleveraged and only larger stops, or no stops are used. But deleveraging means using a smaller amount of capital. As was pointed out in Chapter 4, if you achieve better profits trading a smaller amount (which can be seen from the size of the positions taken in the market), the head of the Foreign Exchange Trading Division might say, "If you can produce 20 percent return using only half the money, then use all of it so that you can get a 40 percent profit!" Unfortunately, the reserve capital is needed for a period of unusually high risk. It does not occur often, but you must be prepared for it anyway.

What do you do? If you *don't trade more* of the capital, it might be taken away. If you *do trade more* and the market is hit with a price shock, you can lose an unacceptably large part of the capital. The answer is *don't trade more*. You must be able to explain that deleveraging to achieve risk control is safer for the investment portfolio and for the company. Artificial risk controls are counterproductive over the long term and often over the short term. It is a corporate problem that must be resolved. The trader must only produce returns with the best return/risk ratio.

Summary

It is difficult to trade without a clear idea of risk, and a stop-loss, or fixed-value limit, is the most agreeable to traders. A stop-loss based on the number of points you are willing to lose is not a good choice. But performance using a stop-loss is inconsistent and, during a fast market or a price shock, when risk protection is most important, a resting stop-loss could result in the worst fill. Stops based on logical price levels, such as support and resistance, or volatility, are much more likely to improve performance. Tests confirm that larger stops give better performance than small stops.

If a relatively small stop-loss consistently improves a trend-following system, the trader should see if a faster trend might work even better. If a larger stop-loss improves performance, it may have been the result of a single event—it would be difficult to build a system around one situation.

Reducing risk by increasing the investment size, or lowering leverage, is the safest method of all. With smaller exposure, risk is always proportionally less. If you increase the leverage of your system because of the perceived safety of a stop-loss, one price shock is enough to cause serious damage. A stop-loss does not *guarantee* risk protection. If you need to deleverage to avoid occasional large risk, then a stop-loss may no longer benefit performance.

7

Understanding
Price Shocks

A price shock is the ultimate risk. It is an entirely unpredictable, large jump in price that is too fast to trade. Price shocks cause the ruin of more traders than any other problem. A price shock can be seen as a large opening gap, or a very volatile trading range, often three or four times the average size, sometimes bigger by a factor of 10. Because they occur infrequently but are so dramatic, price shocks are treated very differently by many analysts when they develop a trading system. Some analysts will make up special rules to be applied for specific past events; others will include shocks as a part of the normal price phenomena, to be resolved by strategy testing.

Trading Risk Is Higher
Than Expectations

This chapter will show that price shocks, which are frequently small and only occasionally extreme, are the reason the risk of trading is always greater than expected. When you look back at historic price moves, especially with a computer charting or a test program, such as *System Writer, TeleTrac,* or *MetaStock,* it is easy to identify a price shock. The clear ones are seen as highly volatile days or large gaps.

How do you handle them? When you are testing or developing a strategy, you look for a trend or pattern that would have had the right position to take advantage of any major move. But is that really possible? Could you have known which direction the price would have moved? And what about all the small shocks? Many small price shocks are not obvious. Although they do not attract attention if their size does

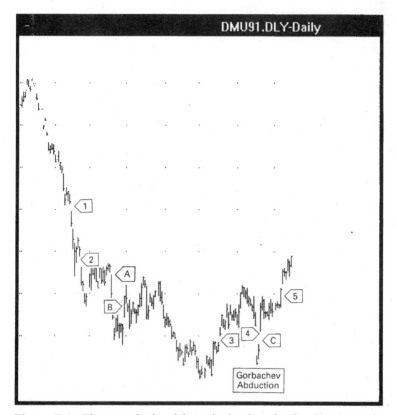

Figure 7-1. Chart analysis with typical price shocks. The Deutsche mark chart shows eight clear price shocks. Those marked 1-5 are expected to have generated profits for a trend system; those marked A-C are most likely to have produced losses. The Gorbachev abduction first appears to be the obvious price shock, but closer study shows that there are surprisingly many gaps and volatile days. Unfortunately, some analysts choose their strategy by its ability to profit from these past moves.

not cause any serious problems, they are just as unpredictable as large shocks.

Figure 7-1 is a chart of the September 1991 Deutsche mark, traded on the IMM. It shows the Gorbachev abduction on August 19, which produced a large profit for many traders. Those profits disappeared two days later when the market abruptly reversed. A closer look at the chart shows that other shocks were nearly as large. The point marked A indicates an unexpected change of direction ending two days later and 300 points lower. The Moscow coup spanned only 250 points.

Other shocks can be seen by the gaps or the high volatility in a direction opposite to the previous day. The points marked 1 through 5 are price shocks that were likely to be profitable for a trend-follower; those marked A through C would probably have caused losses. We can see that there are many sudden changes and gaps in price movement, each representing an unexpected event and all adding risk.

If you assume that you could have profited from a large price shock, you have mistakenly reduced your assessment of market risk. You can eliminate a price shock from a chart analysis or computer test, but you cannot remove it from real trading. *A price shock is not predictable.* That means you cannot assume that you would have profited from the price move, nor do you have to say that all price shocks would have caused losses. You can assume that half the shocks will be in your favor, and the other half will be against you.

Types of Price Shocks

Price shocks have no rules or patterns that can be applied in advance. Because they are always unexpected, they can occur any time and during any market environment. However, there is a distinction between a price shock that is the result of a structural change and one that is temporary or ambiguous in its effects (see Figure 7-2).

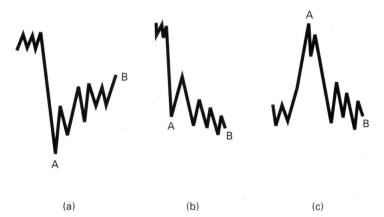

(a) (b) (c)

Figure 7-2. Three patterns associated with price shocks. (a) A sudden drop to A has a sound basis but was exaggerated. Prices partially correct to B. (b) A structural shock will continue in the same direction (B) after the initial move (A). (c) A "false" shock (A), without basis, reversed as news corrected the situation. After 3 days, the effect had disappeared.

A price jump based on an assassination or abduction, such as the Gorbachev coup on Sunday, August 18, 1991, is entirely speculative. How do you assess the importance of the death of a leader in terms of Swiss francs? Whether temporary, as in the case of Gorbachev, or permanent, as with the Kennedy assassination, the economy of a country often shows little long-term effect.

In general, wars, rumors, assassinations, and political coups have temporary effects on price (see Box 7-1). Weather could cause a structural change in supply but rarely does; it always results in an immediate overreaction. Lack of rain, too much rain at the wrong time, freezes, and monsoons all cause a nervous reaction. By harvest, it is clear that corn and soybeans are exceptionally healthy crops, and that Brazil is more than happy to supply the U.S. consumers with any orange juice shortfall at an agreeable price.

Price shocks based on surprise economic news are often structural; prices try to jump to a level that is a fair assessment of the news. The market may push prices a little too far, but overall a trader cannot expect to profit from a price reaction. When the Central Bank announces a rate cut of 0.5 percent, prices must move to the level dictated by that change. If a 0.25 percent cut was anticipated, then prices move down; if a 1 percent reduction was expected, then prices move up. With periodic economic and statistical releases, the difference between the news and the anticipation determines price reaction.

Many long, fast price moves are not price shocks. Weather-related news is often anticipated by the market. A freeze or hurricane does not occur without warning. As cold weather moves south to Florida, traders and growers become concerned about the increasing likelihood of a freeze. They start hedging by buying futures, or covering their shorts. The result is a market that starts drifting higher in advance of a freeze. A speculator using a simple moving average system may get a buy signal ahead of severe weather, the result of informed reaction to anticipated weather.

Similarly, a change of regulation that affects industry often has warning. A vote before Congress to change pollution control or standards has clear, sometimes measurable effects on a group of companies. A bill likely to pass finds its results already discounted in the stock price.

Impact of a Price Shock on an Investment

A price shock can cause a severe equity fluctuation in a fully funded account, but many traders use leverage whenever possible. Shocks can vary from 3 percent to 30 percent of the value of the asset. If you hold a conservative portfolio with 50 percent cash reserves and the rest allocated to unleveraged stocks, or 50 percent cash and the rest leveraged at 5 percent margin in futures, then the impact of a price shock will be:

Portfolio Portion Allocated to This Position	Size of Price Shock (Not Leveraged)	Corresponding Drop in Stock Portfolio	Corresponding Drop in Futures Portfolio (5% Margin)
50%	3%	1.5%	30%
(Maximum exposure)	30%	15.0%	300%
10%	3%	.3%	6%
	30%	3.0%	60%

The stock portfolio has no problem absorbing a 3 percent equity drop in a worst-case scenario when only 10 percent, or $\frac{1}{5}$ the available trading capital, is exposed to one correlated group. Even the 15 percent loss is unpleasant but not fatal. Futures is another story. Mostly traded with high leverage, a portfolio is rarely prepared for a large adverse price move. The most conservative futures portfolio, with 5 assets allocated 10 percent each, and 50 percent in reserves, still lost 6 percent on a 3 percent price drop.

Eliminating Price Shocks from System Performance

During the testing of a new strategy, most traders and analysts eliminate the losses due to price shocks, or gain from their moves, without being aware of it. They can

- Select the most profitable system from an optimization test.
- Luckily miss being in the market during a shock.
- Test data that did not have significant shocks.

In the enthusiastic search for a great trading system, traders would select the system that performed best over historic tests. They are not critical of a system when there are profits. If a 25-day moving average had resulted in a long S&P position on the Friday before Gorbachev was abducted, it had large back-to-back losses over 3 days. A 5-day trend might have just entered a new short or closed out a long that day, and would have benefited from the shock.

Selection of the wrong system parameter can happen when you choose only the best results (i.e., as is automatically entered using a *TeleTrac* optimization). If the slower system netted a 5 percent return

Box 7-1. THREE CLASSIC PRICE SHOCKS

1. The Kuwait invasion in August 1990 found most traders long
   (Figure 7-3(a)). The possibility of sustained oil shortages moved
   prices steadily higher. The U.S. retaliation in January was still an
   unknown, and the sharp reversal proved that the market's reaction was a surprise to traders (see Figure 7-3(b)).

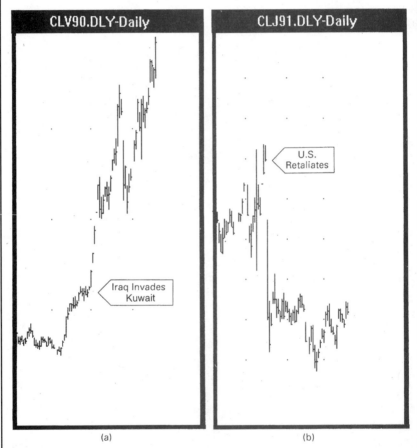

Figure 7-3. Kuwait price shock. (a) Iraq invades Kuwait. (b) The U.S. retali-
ates with Desert Storm.

Box 7-1. (*Continued*)

2. The markets were not expecting the conservatives to win the British election in January 1992 and posted large gains for the Sterling as a result (see Figure 7-4).

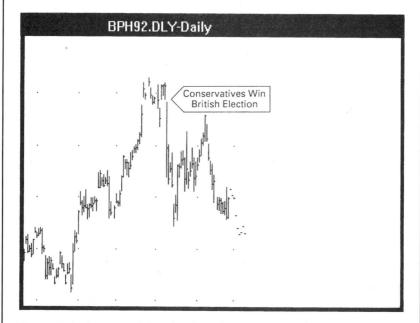

Figure 7-4. Conservatives win the British election.

---

with 20 percent risk, while the faster program returned 4 percent with a 6 percent risk (due to large losses during the Moscow coup), the numbers make clear that the faster program is more desirable. No one would immediately pick the system with lower profits and higher risk.

What really has happened? By picking the system that profited from the coup, you have unconsciously assumed that you could predict a price shock. But that's impossible. Therefore, your conclusion is not valid. That is not to say that the slower system was better. At this point, we really do not have enough information to tell, because the test results are too distorted by incorrect assumptions.

Box 7-1. (*Continued*)

3. The political coup in Russia on Sunday, August 16, caused a uniform pattern in Forex, oil, and equity markets. The S&P (Figure 7-5(a)) moved opposite to a trend position, crude oil would have caused new longs to be set (Figure 7-5(b)), and the Deutsche mark (Figure 7-1) would have profited. However, they all would have posted large losses when markets reversed two days later, after Gorbachev's release.

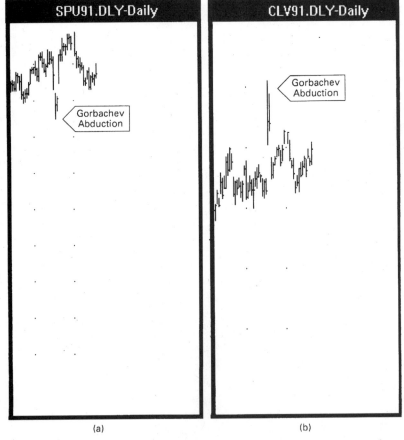

(a)   (b)

Figure 7-5. Political coup in Russia. (a) The Moscow coup causes a sharp drop in the S&P. (b) Oil prices rally on expected supply interruption in Russia.

Short Tests May Not See Shocks

Some systems are evaluated over recent data because older prices do not seem representative of current market conditions. The European Monetary System (EMS) has changed the spread relationship between the exchange rates of member currencies. By creating limits, prices are supported and patterns are different from pre-EMS data. Short amounts of data have the disadvantage of not having enough price patterns to develop a robust trading model. They may show only a bull market, or a few small price jumps. It would be unusual to see a large price shock in a small data sample.

Frequency of Price Shocks

You might think of every price change based on news as a price shock. Markets are filled with little jumps because of unexpected events such as periodic reports on unemployment claims, corporate earnings, an unexpected charge, Federal Reserve or Central Bank shifts in monetary policy (never announced in advance), trade balance, announcements of new government policy, crop estimates, daily marketing of livestock, amount of rain in the Midwest, or cold in the northern hemisphere. The difference between the market's anticipated assessment of a piece of information and the reality of the event causes a price shock.

Most price shocks are small. Often, the relative accuracy of market anticipation to the released information obviates a change in price. Sometimes, the difference between actual and expected is unimportant in light of other effects attracting the public's eye. After three years of prolonged recession (beginning in 1991) and steadily lower interest rates, a worse unemployment number is not as important to the market as a Consumer Price Index that signals possible inflation.

Only the bigger price shocks attract our attention, even though smaller jumps occur frequently. Being unpredictable and frequent, shocks occur in a pattern (or lack of pattern) very similar to a random distribution. There are many small shocks and a rapidly decreasing number of large shocks.

Gaps and Ranges. Figure 7-6 shows the frequency of opening gaps and daily trading ranges and compares the S&P with the Deutsche mark for the 10 years ending with 1993. The inset chart begins with gaps and ranges of 0.5 percent; however, the frequency drops off quickly and the smaller number of large percentage moves cannot be seen. The larger chart shows only those 1-day gaps and ranges above 3 percent of the current price. These values can be seen exactly in Table 7-1.

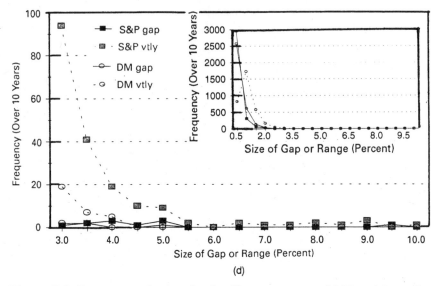

Figure 7-6. Frequency of price shocks. The comparison of S&P and Deutsche mark price shocks shows that the Deutsche mark has many more gap openings, while the S&P has much larger daily price ranges. The frequency of these larger gaps and ranges points out that price shocks and uncontrolled risk occur more often than we would expect.

Table 7-1. Frequency of Price Shocks (January 1983–June 1993)

Size of Move (%)	S&P No. of Gaps	S&P No. of Ranges	DM No. of Gaps	DM No. of Ranges
0.5	2963	118	2572	824
1.0	307	1273	622	1728
1.5	64	1069	133	581
2.0	24	510	34	164
2.5	6	219	10	48
3.0	1	94	2	19
3.5	2	41	2	7
4.0	3	19	0	5
4.5	1	10	0	0
5.0	3	9	1	0
5.5	0	2	0	0
6.0	0	0	0	0
6.5	0	2	0	0
7.0	0	1	0	0
7.5	0	1	0	0
8.0	0	2	0	0
8.5	0	1	0	0
9.0	0	3	0	0
9.5	1	0	0	0
10.0	0	1	0	0
Total	3375	3375	3376	3376

The patterns in Figure 7-6 are different for the two markets. The S&P, a U.S. domestic market, shows very few opening gaps compared with the Deutsche mark, which is actively traded 24 hours a day. (This is discussed in Chapter 11 in the section "Overnight Risk.") The S&P also shows much larger risk, with one gap of 9.5 percent and 51 daily ranges above 4 percent; the Deutsche mark had only 5 for the same period. *The S&P was 10 times more likely than the Deutsche mark to have a price shock greater than 4 percent.*

The implications of this are important. There are 51 of 3375 days (on average, 4 days each year), in which a price shock in the S&P will occur. From experience, we know that these are likely to be clustered together; therefore, we can assume that once each year there will be a volatile period of 4 days. One year, that move might be profitable, and the next year it might generate a loss. In either case, a 4 percent range is a 40 percent swing in equity for futures traders, based on margin.

The chart shows that large gaps and ranges will occur periodically and will be large enough to represent a problem. Individually, the risks might be absorbed within a well-diversified portfolio, but in reality, price shocks often affect a broad range of markets and assets at the same time.

Why All the Fuss?

During testing, many trading program do not distinguish a price shock from other moves. By applying special combinations of rules, and selecting the best trend speed, the trading program can successfully be on the right side of the market whenever a major price jump occurs. It would be easy for a computer to scan stock market historic prices and identify a pattern of extreme drops. A system that sold stocks on every Friday, during the last half of October (from 1929 through 1993), covering the position on Monday afternoon, would have made a fortune. Although most trades produced a small profit or loss, a few major plunges overwhelmed the result.

What is wrong with this approach? You are collecting, classifying, and creating rules to take advantage of price shocks that are unpredictable. You are attributing special traits to events that, by definition, have no traits. In general, if you have developed a system that did not show a large loss, you have done something wrong.

Using Stops for Risk Protection

In addition to a reduction in expected profits, the inability to identify a historic price shock affects risk control. You cannot assume that a price shock would produce a profit, and you cannot assume that a stop-loss would have saved even part of a loss. Resting stop-loss orders tend to be filled at the worst place, and visual stops are too slow to be effective.

- A stop cannot get you out of a short position that is limit bid, or a stock that moves quickly after a news release.

- A stop will get you out at the worst price when the market begins to trade.

- In historic testing, a stop cannot tell that an intraday shock caused prices to jump through the risk level and that the order was at the high of that interval. (It is always safe to assume that you were filled on a buy at the high of a 15-minute range, or sold at the low of a 15-minute range.) A computer system that assumes a fill during an intraday shock presents unachievably good results.

- A "fast market" exists during a price shock and price quotes run late on the screen. A visual stop could never cut losses because the event could be over before it appears on the screen.

It would be comforting to place the stop in advance and expect that execution price, but an occasional shock is nasty, and a stop-loss rarely improves risk control.

Key Price Shock Concepts

Risk is always higher than expectations because historic testing (either computerized or manual) does not distinguish between data that can be used to forecast profits and price shocks that cannot be predicted:

- You cannot know which shocks would have been in your favor, or which would have resulted in losses.

- You cannot know which days contained intraday price moves that would not have allowed a stop-loss or a new trade entry to be executed at a reasonable price level.

- Many small price shocks that result in bad executions are much more difficult to recognize when only historic price data is available.

Handling Price Shocks

So far, price shocks paint a dismal picture. They cannot be predicted, many of them cannot be seen afterward, and they can generate devastating losses. The comforting thought is that, when you accept the uncertainty of price shocks and do not assume profit opportunities, you know the worst case of risk. This is not necessarily good, but it is a safe way to evaluate trading and investment returns. Believing that a system has less risk will lead to more serious problems.

Guidelines for Assessing Risk

The following guidelines will help you avoid mistakes and assess risk more accurately. These points will not identify every price shock, nor is it likely that the final risk level will be as great as the real risk of trading, but it should be very close:

- *More test data gives more realistic results.* Larger periods of test data contain a greater variety of price patterns and more price shocks. Parameter selection based on longer tests tends toward the longer-term forecasts and slower trends. These can better absorb the effects of price shocks. Faster trading strategies must show profits from price shocks, in order to prevent losses from appearing disproportionately large. The expected profits of a longer-term system may be lower, and the risk higher, than a faster trading method, but the real trading results are more likely to be similar to the slower system, and may vary far from expectations of a fast system.

- *Use less data for parameter selection and more data for risk evaluation.* If older data is not representative of current market conditions, it may be more reasonable to select parameters based on a short test period. Once those parameters are fixed, test a longer set of old data to get a better evaluation of risk. It is not possible to find all the risk from a small test sample. Use the old data to show more patterns of volatility and risk, and recent data for trend timing and profit patterns.

- *Find a worst case scenario in past prices.* It is not difficult to look at past charts to see obvious price shocks. Look for the largest price moves, then consider a worst-case scenario to evaluate the risk. It is safe to assume that what has happened before will happen again.

Creating an Artificial Data Series

A valuable transformation of data can give realistic system test results. It will be necessary to use a computer to do the following:

1. *Scan the historic daily data* and remove the data for the day a price shock occurred, plus the next two days of data. The day of the shock can be identified by a large opening gap or an unusually large trading range. You can select different size shocks by requiring the opening gap or trading range to be 3, 5, or even 10 times larger than the average gap or range.

2. *Create an index* of prices without the 3 days of data associated with the price shock. This will close any gap created by the elimination of data and change all the prices to percentage changes.

3. *Test the trading strategy* using the gap-adjusted series. This will result in parameter selection that does not try to profit from price shocks, or assume that it could be stopped out at unrealistic levels. It will produce a system that works in a "pseudo-normal" market (although "normal" must really contain price shocks).

4. *Run the trading strategy* with the selected parameters through the original data series, including all price shocks. The results should be similar profits, but much larger risk. Half of the shocks should have generated profits, and the other half large losses. If you find that there were no shocks that caused losses, then use the profitable shocks to indicate the magnitude of the potential losses. It should be considered simply good fortune that a few shocks occurred in the direction of the current position; in real trading it could be reversed. You should manually evaluate the size of the past price shocks and assume that it represents future risk.

You now have a realistic set of return and risk values to decide the merits of the system and the investment necessary to trade it successfully. The parameters selected for "normal" markets should return more consistent profits, and the final risk figures will give a realistic idea of the effects and frequency of price shocks. By removing the price shock data, the optimization process will never be able to fit parameters so that they profit from an unpredictable price shock.

The clear identification of price shocks which was used to create a gap-adjusted series also allows you to automatically recognize the same shock as the system during actual trading. When the shock occurs, you can change rules and treat the situation as a special case. Box 7-2 gives the FORTRAN code for creating this series. More on adjusting data can be found in Chapter 10.

Managing a Price Shock

You are going to take a big profit or a big loss from a price shock. Because you cannot predict when it will happen, you must assume that you will be holding a position, either long or short. We have discussed the use of a stop-loss to reduce risk and believe that a resting Stop order is more likely to capture the worst possible price. Then what are the choices?

You could hold a trade or exit it after the shock with a large profit or loss, whichever occurs. Because you can automatically identify a price shock on a computer, you can also test special strategies. For example, if the price shock is up, set a long or short position on the close, depending on the type of shock, then exit one or two days later (see Table 7-2). You can determine which shocks tend to continue and which reverse. If there are enough cases you can develop a clear price shock strategy.

Qualifying the Shock

There is a logical, accepted strategy to managing a price shock even without computerized testing. First, you must qualify the situation. If the price shock was caused by a fundamental, structural change, then only a small reversal should be expected. An announcement to raise interest rates $\frac{1}{4}$ percent by the Central Bank means that bond prices will fall to the new level. If a $\frac{1}{2}$ percent increase was expected, prices will rise. It is not an issue of anticipation, but of fact. Interest rates are more definitive than most other news. Putting a price on the Gorbachev coup, planting intentions, retail drug prices, or a new national health program is not as simple. While most price shocks move further than necessary, a structural change means a permanent price shift. Some correction is normal, but a continuation of the new direction is also possible. Opportunities for recovering losses from a structural change are small.

Political news, natural disasters, and rumors dominate most other prices shocks. Assassinations are tragic but do not necessarily affect the safety or economy of a nation. Hurricanes, droughts, floods, and freezes devastate small countries and regions but rarely cause a substantial change in total supply. In the past, a freeze in Florida caused orange juice prices to soar; now, any shortfall in supply is happily filled by Brazil. Price shocks that cannot be confirmed or cannot be translated clearly into a price change are likely to move too far, too fast. These moves allow traders to recover a substantial part of their losses.

The Shock Is in Your Favor

When a price shock gives you a windfall profit, the position should be closed out immediately. Even though a structural change is likely to show additional profits, the increase in risk is greater than the potential for further profits. If the shock causes a loss, the position can be managed to recover part of the loss.

Figure 7-7(a) shows a price shock with some fundamental basis. Prices move sharply higher, then start a volatile, erratic decline. A short-term and long-term trend are shown as (1) and (2). Because prices move fast, system (1) cannot exit. The short trend would have been stopped out at the high, reversed to long and been stopped out again in a few

Box 7-2. CREATING A "SHOCK-ADJUSTED" PRICE SERIES

The following code to create a gap-adjusted and shock-adjusted series cannot be done using *TeleTrac, Easy Language,* or spreadsheets because the new data series is shorter than the old one. The following code in FORTRAN reads the original data series OLD and creates an adjusted series NEW.

```
SUBROUTINE GAPADJ(PERIOD,GFACT,TRFACT,RDAYS)
C---- "GAPADJ"    subprogram for removing price shocks
C---- PERIOD      the number of days to determine normal price movement
C---- GFACT       the relative size of the overnight shock versus normal
C---- TRFACT      the relative size of the intraday shock versus normal
C---- RDAYS       the number of days to remove including the day of shock

      PARAMETER      (max$ = 500)
      INTEGER    DATE(max$),RDAYS
      REAL       OPEN(max$),HIGH(max$),LOW(max$),CLOSE(max$),
     +           TRANGE(max$),GAP(max$),INDEX

      IF(RDAYS.LT.1)RDAYS = 1
C---- Open input and output files
      OPEN(10,FILE = 'IN')
      OPEN(11,FILE = 'OUT')
C---- Initialize output count
      N = 1
C---- Read original input data
   10 READ(10,1000,END=50)DATE(N),OPEN(N),HIGH(N),LOW(N),CLOSE(N)
 1000 FORMAT(I6,4F8.2)
C---- Start output file on day of full period
      IF(N.EQ.1)THEN
        NX = 1
        INDEX(NX) = 1000.
        WRITE(11,1100)DATE(N),INDEX(NX)
 1100   FORMAT(I6,F8.2)
      ENDIF
      IF(N.GT.1)THEN
        NX = NX + 1
        INDEX(NX) = INDEX(NX) + ABS(CLOSE(N)-CLOSE(N-1)/CLOSE(N-1)
C---- True range
        TOP = HIGH(N)
        BOT = LOW(N)
        IF(CLOSE(N-1).GT.TOP)TOP = CLOSE(N-1)
```

```
            IF(CLOSE(N-1).LT.BOT)BOT = CLOSE(N-1)
            TRANGE(N) = TOP - BOT
C---- Gaps
            GAP(N) = ABS(INDEX(N) - INDEX(N-1))
            ENDIF
C---- Test for a price shock
         IF(N.GT.PERIOD + 1.AND.
        +(GAP(N).GT.AVGGAP*GFACT.OR.TRANGE(N).GT.AVGTR*TRFACT))THEN
C---- Skip RDAYS + 1
         DO 30 I = 1,RDAYS
            PRIOR = CLOSE(N)
            READ(10,1000,END = 50)DATE(N),OPEN(N),HIGH(N),LOW(N),CLOSE(N)
  30     CONTINUE
         INDEX(NX) = INDEX(NX) + (CLOSE(N) - PRIOR)/PRIOR
         WRITE(11,1100)DATE(N),INDEX(NX)
C---- If enough data, calculate average range and gap
         IF(N.GT.PERIOD)THEN
         SUMTR = 0
         SUMGAP = 0
         DO 20 I = N,N-PERIOD+1,-1
            SUMTR = SUMTR + TRANGE(I)
  20        SUMGAP = SUMGAP + GAP(I)
         AVGTR = SUMTR/PERIOD
         AVGGAP = SUMGAP/PERIOD
         IF(N.LT.max$)THEN
           N = N + 1
           GOTO 10
           ENDIF
         STOP 'Data too big for array. Increase max$ and rerun.'
  50 CLOSE(10)
         CLOSE(11)
         RETURN
         END
```

Identification of a price shock once the factor has been determined:

```
IF (open > @AVERAGE((@ABS(open-close[1])/close[1]),period)*GapFactor
OR @TrueRange > @Average(@TrueRange,period)*RangeFactor) THEN
```

Table 7-2. Price Shock Characteristics

	Structural Change	Temporary Panic
Pattern	■ Volatile, quieting quickly	■ Continued volatile
	■ Likely to produce more profits, but incremental risk greater than profits	■ Likely to reverse
	■ Small reversal	■ Large reversal
If a profit	Close out the trade	Close out the trade
If a loss	Wait for a small reversal to exit	Wait for a 25% to 50% reversal or add to the position to recover more than 50% of the loss

days. The slower trend gets a windfall profit but gives back one-third before getting a trend reversal signal.

After the price shock, both fast and slow trends are catching up to the price jump while in Figure 7-7(a) prices have actually *reversed* direction. It is difficult to say that we are "following the trend" when the trend ended with the shock. This was exactly the situation following the 1987 stock market drop. Sensible management requires that trend positions be closed out after a windfall profit. If the change is structural, the position may be reset, but in most cases it is best to wait for a new trend signal to re-enter.

Figure 7-7(b) depicts a structural change. Although prices continue higher, the faster trend system is stopped in and out because of higher volatility. The slower trend would have increased profits before encountering the same sideways period. Both strategies, however, would have been improved by taking profits immediately after the price shock.

Risk Reduction

Price shocks are accompanied by high volatility. By taking profits as soon as possible, you would not be holding a position during the period of increased risk following the first price peak. Even though a structural change produced more profits when the trade was held, the risk (measured by the volatility) was far greater than the marginal profit gained. Once this equity fluctuation is part of performance, it cannot be erased. Focusing on low risk translates into higher leverage and greater profits.

The Shock Produces a Large Loss

Once the price shock hits, and you are on the wrong side, risk is no longer an issue. The most important concern is to find the best chance for

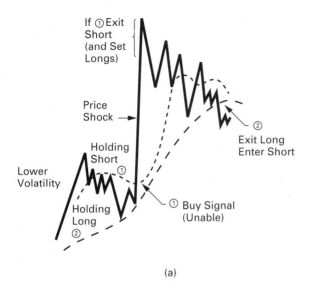

(a)

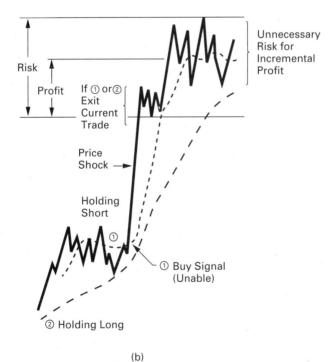

(b)

Figure 7-7. Trading price shocks. (1) Trend-following where the shock is a loss, and (2) Trend-following where the shock is a profit.

recovering part of the loss. If the change is structural, you can expect only a small recovery, and the risk of further loss may be just as high. Timing is important. A professional trader can monitor the market, waiting for a sign that trading is quieting and the surge of orders has been filled. Whatever correction is likely will come at this time. Afterward, prices may again move in the direction of the shock. A longer-term trader, who may have seen the shock only after the close, would do best to get out as soon as possible, as long as the market is actively trading.

A temporary event that is likely to reverse can be managed in two ways. A conservative trader may hold the original position and wait for a reversal to exit, expecting a 10 percent to 30 percent recovery. It may be closed out after one day if proved wrong and prices reach new ground, or if the reason for the shock appears to become structural. A more aggressive trader may double the original position, looking to recover 20 percent to 60 percent of the losses. In neither case should you expect to turn a loss into a profit. This is entirely a defensive management strategy.

Management Obligations

Traders often feel that they have an obligation to follow their system no matter what the circumstances. It is true that, if the rules are strictly followed, it is easy to explain why things went wrong. Deviating from the plan, and subsequently losing more, will be embarrassing to explain.

Offsetting the rigid systematic approach is the concern that it is not reasonable to follow a "trend" when prices are moving in the opposite direction after a price shock. To resolve this dilemma, record the following list of clear rules to use when a "price shock day" is identified:

1. *Identify the shock.* A price shock occurs when a gap or trading range is greater than a threshold value.

2. *If profitable,* then take profits and wait for a new trend signal.

3. *If losing,* then hold losses for one day after market trades. Exit if a new extreme price, a 50 percent reversal, or a contrary trend signal occurs.

Using two clear sets of rules, a manager can justify the proper response to a price shock.

Long-Term Systems Are More Predictable Than Short-Term Systems

When choosing a trading strategy, remember that the longer-term, slower systems are more likely have returns similar to their historic testing and expectation. Because the tests cover a long time period, they include more price shocks, more patterns, and more risk. They generate larger profits by holding the trade for longer periods; therefore, a price shock does not seem as important or disruptive to performance. The relative size gives it a chance to absorb the shocks. It is difficult to add a short-term rule to a long-term system for the purpose of eliminating a price shock. Short-term rules tend to change a slow trading system to a fast one, including large periods of being out of the market.

Summary

We prefer to trade a system which we perceive as having low risk, but we often create larger risks by unrealistically assuming that we can profit from price shocks. This leads to undercapitalized accounts and unpleasant results. A price shock affects all trading the same way, whether you are a short-term or long-term trader, a trend-follower or a countertrend trader. If a government report causes the yen to jump 300 points, all trades will be affected. It only matters whether you are long or short when the price shock hits. However, in the total performance profile or in a fully diversified portfolio, the effects of a shock on a longer-term view will be less dramatic.

By accepting the uncertainty of price shocks, you can implement alternate trading rules to limit further risk and possibly recover some loss. Once the price shock hits, it triggers a new plan. Trend-following systems do not apply to a market that has just experienced a structural change, no matter which direction prices move.

Understanding the real risk of trading is the most important part of system testing and performance evaluation. The business of trading is expected to return a profit for an acceptance of risk. Without clearly understanding the risks of each strategy, you cannot intelligently choose the best system and decide how much capital will be required to trade.

8

Smarter Trend-Following

If you could achieve only one goal in price analysis, it should be identifying the price direction, or *trend*. If you take positions in the direction of the trend, then you should capture the biggest price moves and have reasonable control over risk. When you use a trend to select trades or set hedge positions by confirming the correct trend direction, your trading performance must improve.

Forecasting and Following

Finding the Trend

There are two ways to find the trend. By analyzing major economic factors, you can conclude that prices should go higher. Greater demand, good management, better technology, and cheaper money may all contribute to long-term growth, higher dividends, and higher share prices. Energy prices may be pushed up by greater consumption, a unified OPEC position to cut production, or supply disruption in Siberia. But basic fundamental evaluation is difficult and dependent on reliable information. The conclusion may change if new factors are introduced. Changes must be constantly monitored and weighed.

Many traders supplement or substitute a *moving average* to identify the trend. There may seem to be no relationship between a simple mathematical formula and the result of events that drive prices, but that is not the case. A moving average creates a trend by smoothing erratic price movement. Because it is an average of past prices, it reduces the effects of outliers that appear to have been extreme reactions to news.

a third way is to objectively define trend based on price actions

Averaging longer periods of data gives smoother trends. The result is often a good representation of long-term market direction, and a valid parallel to government monetary or interest rate policy. Moving averages are also used in econometrics to remove known seasonal or cyclic effects. For many years, stock market analysts have used a 200-day moving average as their benchmark.

A *moving average* is exactly what it seems to be: the average value of a prior data period. A 3-day moving average is simply

average = (price + price[1] + price[2])/3

Most computer trading software, even spreadsheets, will have the moving average formulas preprogrammed, so that it is only necessary to enter

@average(price,n)

where price is the data to be averaged, and n is the number of periods (e.g., days or hours). There are many variations on a moving average:

- A *weighted average* may assign different importance to each data item. A 3-day weighted average typically values 60 percent of the most recent price and 30 percent of each prior day:

  @weighted_average(price,3) = .60 × price + .30 × price[1] + .30 × price[2]

- An *exponential moving average* (called an "exponential") is a special type of weighted average, in which each data item is reduced in value by a constant percentage as it becomes older:

  exponential = exponential[1] + percentage × (price − exponential[1])

  which may also be entered

  @exp_ma(price,smoothing_constant)

  where smoothing_constant is the percentage weighting.

In most of this book, whenever a moving average is needed, an exponential moving average ("exponential") will be used. It is the simplest calculation because it does not require all the past data, and the results are nearly identical to other moving averages.

Fundamental Analysis and Trend Following

Economic or fundamental analysis *forecasts*, and trend evaluation *follows*. Fundamental analysis attempts to anticipate events by assessing the reaction to current factors and weighing the impact of probable events. Trend calculations look at past data, reduce price movement to a net direction, and assume that prices will continue to do the same as in the past. Trend-following systems *respond* to events, rather than anticipate them.

Both fundamental analysis and trend following are good methods, but neither are simple nor are they foolproof. This chapter is concerned with trend-following methods and computer applications. New, high-powered graphics equipment has made looking backward much easier, and computerized strategy testing packages have made searching for successful systems painless. But it is not that easy. What worked in the past does not seem to work in the future—at least not as well, or not all the time.

Trend Trading

Noise

Trading in the direction of the trend is a safe, conservative approach. An important feature of trending systems is that they let profits run and cut losses short. Financial analysts call this "conservation of capital." The most reliable trends are slower ones, capturing the long-term direction of interest rates or the decline of the U.S. dollar. Long-term trends should reflect the same direction as government policy.

Trend systems should not be expected to work with data periods shorter than 1 hour. As you look at prices over intervals such as 5 minutes, you see mostly "noise." Noise is caused by buy and sell orders from all over the world entering the market for different reasons. Liquidation of stocks for personal reasons, trading objectives that focus on different time periods, currency transactions that hedge international business exposure, all come in a steady flow into the marketplace. Orders vary in size, and some larger orders find periods of low volume. This results in price gaps and short, fast moves that may appear to be a new price direction.

The level of volatility that occurs during a sustained sideways, directionless period is a convenient measure of *intrinsic noise*. A price trend will be unreliable if it is signaled by a move that is no greater than the intrinsic level of market noise (see Figure 8-1).

Slow Trends and Lags

Although longer-term trends are the most dependable, they respond very slowly to changing market conditions. A 200-day moving average

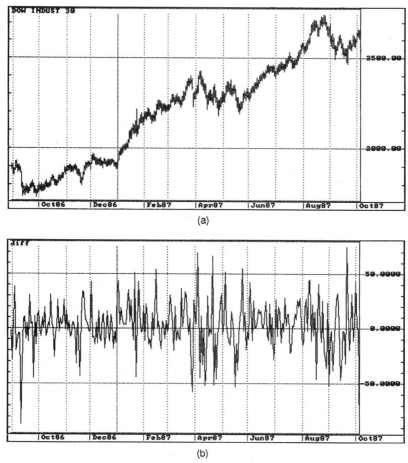

(a)

(b)

Figure 8-1. Intrinsic noise in the Dow Jones Industrial Average. (a) *Intrinsic noise can be seen as the lowest normal level of volatility.* In the year before the October 1987 plunge, the DOW showed remarkably uniform volatility. The daily trading range of about 25 points makes a stop-loss of 25 points likely to be executed without any expectation that prices would continue in one direction. (b) *Because of noise, small changes in the daily closing price cannot be considered important.* Price changes, from close to close, show that over 2 to 3 days, prices could move up or down 30 points. A trend system that buys when prices move up by only 20 DOW points will be unreliable. (Charts courtesy *TeleTrac.*)

barely reacts to a 10-day burst of energy in a stock issue. If the price of IBM ran from $50 to $70 per share in 20 days, a 200-day moving average would have moved up by no more than $2. It is difficult to consider a method as "trend-following" when a moving average is catching up to a price move that is already over.

Adaptive Approach

To avoid false signals due to noise, yet eliminate some of the lag inherent in long-term trends, an *adaptive* method is needed—a moving average that will speed up when markets move and do nothing when there is no direction. "Adaptive" is the term given to techniques that self-adjust to market conditions. But again, it is not always clear what patterns will signal the moving average to change speeds.

The Traditional Solution

The most popular way of finding the "best" moving average speed is simply to test all possible trend speeds using historical data. The answer given by the computer depends on the amount of data tested. If you use a long data history, the best choice will be a very slow moving average. If short time periods are tested, the computer will find a number of highly profitable fast and slow solutions; often it will hone in on a single large price move to capture all its profits. Because these patterns do not continue, faster trends rarely succeed.

Typically, the more data tested, the more likely the results will be a very slow trend-following system. And that solution is correct. Short-term price bursts are erratic and unpredictable, but the long-term trend is stable. Unfortunately, large equity swings are associated with holding a trade for weeks or months. Everyone wants a short-term, fast-trading trend that works without large losses. That combination does not exist.

Another popular solution is using a computer frequently to retest the speed of the trend. By including the most recent data, the trend speed is always expected to be the best. This still requires decisions such as how often to retest and how much data to use for retesting. Jumping from one fast trend speed to another creates two additional problems. The computer may want you to get into a trade that it entered some time ago and is already highly profitable. That should worry you. It may also result in "overfitting," isolating a very short-term pattern that does not work anymore. If the "best" choice changes frequently, it is because the last choice was not the best.

Adapting to Different Market Traits

A trend-following method is needed that adapts to different market conditions. It must be slow when prices are drifting aimlessly and fast when it is necessary to capture profits. Frequent retesting cannot find this trend because an emerging pattern is only a small piece of the total data.

A solution can be found by remembering how certain market patterns affect trends. To begin, what do we know about price movement that would help an analysis?

- Fast-moving averages are best when the market is moving quickly in one direction.

- Slow-moving averages are best when prices are going nowhere in choppy markets.

Therefore, the system would be "smart" if it changed speeds according to a combination of market direction and speed. Figure 8-2 shows four cases that explain the transition.

Another important principle to remember is that analyzing a lot of data produces robust results. It may give less profitable solutions, but these tend to be more dependable. Analyzing small amounts of data results in many solutions that appear to be good but rarely work.

Moving from Specific Cases to a General Solution

The best choice for a moving average will be the fastest one that can be used for a situation. What, then, do these four cases have in common? Each one shows that the fastest trend that can be used is limited by the amount of noise, or unpredictable price movements. As the market pattern goes from ideally smooth to very noisy (from (a) to (c) in Figure 8-3) the trend speed must get slower to avoid whipsaw losses.

When prices move faster in one direction, the market speed makes the noise less important. Therefore, the choice of a trend speed is based on both noise and direction. A price move that is either cleaner or faster can use a faster trend. What is needed is a mechanism to sense market speed and choppiness; this information can then be fed back into the moving average to adjust the speed of its smoothing.

The *Efficiency Ratio* combines these features. This ratio divides the net price movement by the total price movement (the sum of each of the individual moves taken as a positive number). It can also be considered a ratio of the price direction to its volatility. The more *efficient*, the faster the trend. A safety factor is built in to the selection of the right trend. If there is any uncertainty, a slower trend is picked. Some readers will recognize the Efficiency Ratio as being what has been recently named *generalized fractal efficiency*.

(a) Runaway markets: Very fast.
Markets that break out and never look back can be traded using the fastest practical speed.

(b) Fast markets: Fast speeds.
Fast markets may have some sharp reversals within a prolonged directional move. A moving average must lag enough to avoid getting caught by the short reversals. The faster the market is rising (falling), the less impact the reversals have on the speed of the trend.

(c) Congested markets: Very slow.
Markets that enter, or are already in, a sideways pattern, cannot be actively traded. A slow trend speed with a large trend change criteria will hold the same position, therefore it will avoid getting whipsawed.

(d) Middle-trends with some volatility: Slightly faster sometimes.
As markets start to trend after a sideways period, the speed of the trend can increase. This only works if the level of noise declines; otherwise, a slow speed is still necessary.

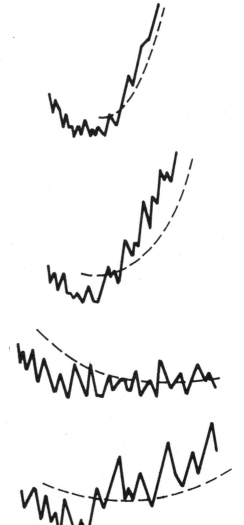

Figure 8-2. Observing price patterns and trends.

The Efficiency Ratio has values ranging from 0, when markets are very noisy for the current amount of direction, to +1 when prices are highly directional. This notation is convenient because it fits perfectly as an exponential smoothing constant. A small transformation scales the value and increases stability (see Box 8-1).

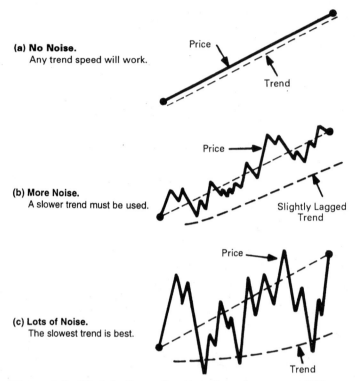

(a) No Noise.
   Any trend speed will work.

Price

Trend

(b) More Noise.
   A slower trend must be used.

Price

Slightly Lagged
Trend

(c) Lots of Noise.
   The slowest trend is best.

Price

Trend

Figure 8-3. What do these situations have in common? Figure 8-2 shows two characteristics in common: the speed of the price change and the amount of noise associated with that move. Look at the same price change with different amounts of noise.

Defining the Range of Trend Speeds

The range of the Efficiency Ratio (ER), from 0 to 1, can be *mapped* onto a range of trend speeds using a simple formula. Let ER = 0 be the slowest speed and let ER = 1 be the fastest speed. Then the ratio itself can be used as a percentage that moves between the slowest and the fastest. If the trend speed, in days, is converted to a smoothing constant approximation using sc = 2/(N + 1), then the slowest speeds have the smallest values. The formula for scaling the smoothing constant becomes

Scaled smoothing constant = ER × (fast sc − slow sc) + slow sc

The range of fast to slow is selected as 2 to 30 days, which is the same as the smoothing constants .6667 and .0645. The scaled speed formula is then

Box 8-1. VOLATILITY MEASUREMENT

There are three popular ways to measure volatility. The method chosen may differ for specific applications. Figure 8-4 (a)–(c) shows the three approaches. The first (a) is simply the *net change* in price from the first to the last point. This tends to be the most conservative measurement, because it smooths any price movement that occurs between the beginning and end. The *high-low* range (b) is more descriptive of any extremes that might have occurred within the period. The *sum of all changes* (c) is the most encompassing measurement because it distinguishes the number of times a price moves from high to low. The *Efficiency Ratio* uses the last method because a low value of this sum is consistent with the strictest idea of "efficiency."

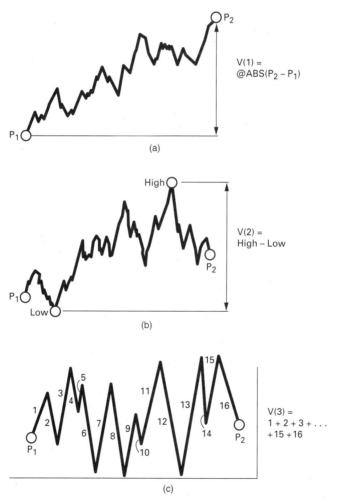

Figure 8-4. Volatility measurement. (a) *Positive change in price.* (b) *High-low range.* (c) *Sum of all positive changes.*

Scaled smoothing constant: sc = ER × (.6667 − .0645) + .0645

$$= ER × .6022 + .0645$$

One last step is necessary because the longer-term 30-day moving average will still move slowly up and down, even in a sideways market. The Adaptive Moving Average will be best if it can *stop* moving when the direction of the market is uncertain. To accomplish this, the final speed is the result of squaring the scaled speed value.

c = sc × sc = sc^2

The Adaptive Moving Average

The smoothing constant c is calculated every day and used in the exponential moving average formula. This becomes an *Adaptive Moving Average:*

Adaptive Moving Average:

AMA = AMA[1] + smoothing_constant × (price − AMA[1])

The complete calculation of the AMA can be found in Box 8-2. This trendline has special features:

- It uses a small number of days (always fixed at 10 in this book) to assign a trend range from very fast to very slow.
- The AMA trendline appears to stop when markets have no direction.
- When prices make a significant move, the AMA trendline catches up, resulting in a very small lag.
- Only one parameter may be changed. The Efficiency Ratio can be based on a 10-day calculation, and that time period may be used for all markets. The filter size (discussed later) allows some flexibility for different trading speeds.
- The AMA was based on analysis rather than testing.

Stock and Forex Examples

Castrol is used to compare the Adaptive Moving Average with a 30-day standard and a 30-day exponential moving average. Comments on trading are also included. The Deutsche mark is used to show how the AMA can produce a smooth trendline through a period of changing market patterns and speed. They also show the adaptability of the AMA, independent of the market selected.

Castrol

The Castrol chart (Figure 8-5) shows that the three trendlines come together at key points. The AMA does not necessarily turn up or down ahead of the others, but it shows much less lag. Notice the two periods, December 1992 and March 1993. In the first case, the AMA moves up in a few days, then sideways for the next 1½ months until the other trendlines catch up. A similar situation occurs in March, although the AMA continues to move slowly lower, based on a slightly directional market.

Trending versus Lagging. During December 1992, the Castrol chart shows that the standard trendlines successfully stayed in the upward move until after the peak near the end of February. But during the month of December, there was no trend. December was highly volatile. Had the market continued lower in mid-December, the standard and exponential moving averages would have lost all their profits.

A serious problem with any trend that is fixed at one speed is that it spends most of the time catching up to a price move that has ended. In December and March, the price moves took only a few days, but the trendlines needed another month to catch up. When a trending indicator tells you that the trend is down, it really means that the trendline is going down, even though prices may be going up.

Profit-Taking. The selection of the fastest AMA trend speeds, seen during the sharp rise and fall of the trendline in December and March, precede the end of a significant price move. For reasons discussed in detail in Chapter 5, this becomes an excellent point to exit the position. The December peak above 1000, and the first March low at 800 are near, or better, than the exit price that would have been achieved by waiting for the end of the trend. Combined with better executions and lower volatility, covered later, profit-taking is strongly recommended based on a high value of the Efficiency Ratio.

Deutsche Mark: Efficiency Ratio and AMA Trendline

Figure 8-6 uses an arbitrary period for the Deutsche mark to show the Efficiency Ratio and the corresponding AMA trendline. In the middle of November 1992, the Efficency Ratio declines to 0, indicating a period of

---

Box 8-2. A SMARTER MOVING AVERAGE USING THE EFFICIENCY RATIO

To create the *Adaptive Moving Average,* it is first necessary to calculate an *Efficiency Ratio,* then convert that ratio to a trend speed.

Step 1: Price Direction

Price direction is expressed as the *net price change over time.* For example, using the time interval of *n*-days (or *n*-hours):

    direction = price − price[n]

or

    direction = @momentum(price,n)

where direction is the current price difference, or directional value
        price is current price (daily close or hourly price)
        price[n] is the close *n*-days ago (or *n*-periods ago)

Step 2: Volatility

Volatility is the amount of market "noise." It can be defined a number of different ways, but this calculation uses the sum of all the day-to-day or hour-to-hour price changes (each taken as a positive number), over the same n periods. It is expressed as

    volatility = @sum(@abs(price − price[1]),n)

where volatility is today's volatility value
        @abs is the absolute value (positive value of any number)
        @sum(value,n) is the sum of "value" over n periods

Step 3: Efficiency Ratio

These two components are combined to express the ratio of directional movement to noise, called the *Efficiency Ratio,* ER:

    Efficiency_Ratio = direction/volatility

By dividing the directionality by the noise, the ratio varies from 0 to 1. When the market moves in the same direction for all *n*-days, then direction = volatility and Efficiency_Ratio = 1. If volatility increases for the same price move, volatility gets larger and the ratio ER moves away from 1. If prices go nowhere, then direction = 0 and ER = 0.

This result is convenient as an exponential smoothing constant, which changes the trendline by a percentage each day. ER = 1 is equivalent to 100 percent, the fastest moving average, which should work because prices moved in one direction without a retracement. When ER = 0, a very slow moving average is best to avoid getting stopped out while the market goes nowhere.

Step 4: Transforming the Ratio into the Trend Speed

The ratio will be changed into a smoothing constant c, for use in an exponential moving average. By using this formula, the trend speed can change each day by simply changing the smoothing constant. It becomes *adaptive*. The formula for this is

@exp_ma = @exp_ma[1] + c × (price − @exp_ma[1])

which shows that the exponential moving average gets closer to today's close by a percentage, c, of yesterday's gap. The constant c relates closely to the number of days in a standard moving average by the relationship 2/(n − 1), where n is the number of days.

Tests show that squaring the value of the smoothing constant greatly improves the results by virtually stopping the trendline from moving during a sideways market. This process selects very slow trends during sideways markets, and speeds up to a very fast trend (but not 100%) during highly trending periods. The smoothing constant is then

$$fastest = 2/(N + 1) = 2/(2 + 1) = .6667$$

$$slowest = 2/(N + 1) = 2/(30 + 1) = .0645$$

$$smooth = ER × (fastest − slowest) + slowest$$

$$c = smooth × smooth = smooth^2$$

Squaring smooth forces the value of c toward zero. This means that slower moving averages will be used more often than fast ones. That is the same as being more conservative when you are uncertain.

AMA = AMA[1] + c × (price − AMA[1])

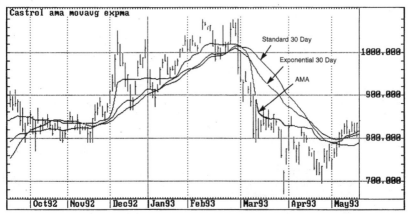

Figure 8-5. Castrol chart. Three trends are shown: a standard 30-day moving average, a 30-day exponential, and the 10-day adaptive moving average. (Chart courtesy *TeleTrac.*)

more noise relative to trend direction. The AMA trendline becomes nearly horizontal for this period (see Figure 8-6(a)), indicating a sideways period and allowing the system to hold its long position, or to stand aside, depending on your rules.

During the months of October 1992 and June 1993, clear trends cause the AMA trendline to begin slowly, then increase its speed as the trend develops. In both cases, the Efficiency Ratio peaks over .80 (see Figure 8-6(b)). The Efficiency Ratio may vary from 0 to .40 without the speed of the trendline changing by much. The period from March through May

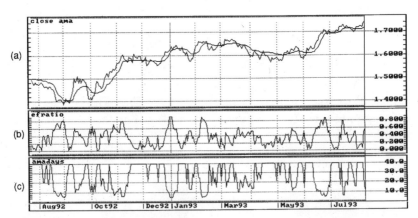

Figure 8-6. Deutsche mark on TeleTrac. (a) Deutsche mark prices with AMA trendline. (b) Efficiency ratio. (c) Moving average days corresponding to the changing AMA smoothing constant. (Charts courtesy *TeleTrac.*)

1993 shows a relatively noisy but low level for the Efficiency Ratio, resulting in a very slow trend for the AMA.

Figure 8-6(c) shows the moving average days corresponding to the smoothing constant. The days appear upside down relative to the Efficiency Ratio because the trendline slows as the days increase. The days also move in a more extreme manner than the Efficiency Ratio, remaining at its peak level (the program cuts the tops off at 40 days) longer but moving from fast to slow quickly. This is due to the squaring of the smoothing constant after all other calculations are done.

Trading Rules

A basic trend-following system should not be confused with a complete trading strategy. There are no subtleties in the selection of entry and exit timing, nor are there special techniques for entering multiple positions, taking profits, or using other risk controls. Those features must be analyzed separately to maintain their integrity in a lateral solution. To know if one trend-following method is better than another, it is necessary to simply enter and hold a long position when the trendline moves up, and reverse to a short position when the trendline turns down.

Basic Buy and Sell Signals

The trading rules for the Adaptive Moving Average are:

- Buy when the Adaptive Moving Average turns up.
- Sell when the Adaptive Moving Average turns down.

Because the trendline is the result of netting all the price moves, it should represent the best evaluation of the trend. Therefore, the buy and sell signals are based on the direction of the trendline, rather than the price penetration of the trendline.

When exponential smoothing is used, the trendline always turns up and down at the same time the price penetrates the line. The benefit of using the trendline for the Adaptive Moving Average signal is that the formula limits the amount of change in the trendline, making it easy to increase reliability by using a small entry filter.

A Filter for False Signals

A filter is needed for any trending system to avoid false signals caused by noise when prices are moving sideways. During a nondirectional period, prices will move back and forth through the smoothed trendline value. This affects all moving average systems in the same way, but it is more obvious with faster trends. The trendline must move higher or lower by the amount of the filter to qualify for a trading signal.

The Adaptive Moving Average produces a very slow trend during noisy market periods. The 30-day maximum, or .0645 smoothing constant, becomes .0041 when squared, equivalent to a 486-day moving average. When prices move through the AMA, the trendline makes only a very small change. Therefore, only a small filter is needed to avoid most whipsaws.

Self-Adjusting Filter.   To be consistent with the adaptive nature of the system, the filter will be also get larger and smaller when prices become more or less volatile. To accomplish this, the filter is defined as a small percentage of the changes in the AMA trendline:

filter = percentage $\times$ @std_dev(AMA $-$ AMA[1],n)

where percentage is the percentage of 1 standard deviation,
@std_dev(series,n) is the standard deviation of series
over n periods, and
AMA $-$ is the 1-day change in the AMA trendline.

The smallest filter percentages of .01 can be used for faster trading, while the larger percentages of 1.0 select those trades that have had a more significant price move. Typically, forex and futures markets trade faster, stock and interest rate markets trade slower. Normally, the filter is calculated over a period of 20 days.

Adding the Filter to the Rules.   Using the filter, the one-period change in the AMA trendline must be bigger or smaller than the filter size to get a buy or sell signal. This works well for selecting trades and eliminating false signals. One problem occurs, however, when the trendline very gradually changes direction. The change in the AMA trendline may not be greater than the filter on the first or the second or the third day. That may be good, because a slow trend change may reverse to be a continuation of the opposite trend direction. But if those small changes continue, the trend could have reversed without giving a new trading signal.

If the new buy and sell signals are based on comparing the one-period changes in the AMA trendline with the filter, a signal could occur well after the new trend begins. To eliminate this possibility, the most recent lowest and highest points on the AMA are recorded. Instead of comparing the one-period changes with the filter, the total change in the AMA since its recent high and low is compared against the filter.

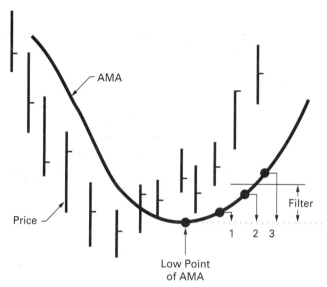

Figure 8-7. Filtering a slow trend change. Because a slow trend change may result in a series of days which fail to penetrate the filter, the net change over 1 to 3 days is substituted for a single day.

The first day of the trend change, marked "1" in Figure 8-7, is very small, therefore no buy signal occurs. The changes on days 2 and 3, taken separately, are also smaller than the filter. Instead, on day 2 the total change from the 2nd day of the trend change to the recent low is compared with the filter, but that is still too small. A signal occurs on the third day, when the total difference from the low is greater than the filter, AMA(low + 3 days) > Filter.

The new rules for trading signals are

Buy when AMA − @lowest(AMA,n) > filter

Sell when @highest(AMA,n) − AMA > filter

When programming a computer, the sell signal may also be written

Sell when AMA − @highest(AMA,n) < −filter

Alternate Buy and Sell Rules. It is difficult to record the recent high and low trend points on some computers and programmable trading machines. A simple, practical substitute is to compare the last three accumulated trend changes against the filter to generate a buy or sell signal.

This approach should work as well in all cases. For example,

Buy when AMA − AMA[1] > filter

or

Buy when AMA − AMA[2] > filter

or

Buy when AMA − AMA[3] > filter

Testing the AMA

Before using the Adaptive Moving Average, it will be necessary to test each market. The following points should help:

1. The primary parameter is the number of days used to calculate the Efficiency Ratio. This will be near 10 for the fast trader. Using a value below 5 will cause the ratio to jump from 0 to 1 quickly. Using a much larger value will cause the ratio to be more stable noise relationship that can be very attractive to the position trader.

2. The filter value is expressed as a percentage of the standard deviation of the trend changes; therefore, it is independent of price. However, a larger or smaller filter percentage is used to change the length of a trade. A small value allows an entry sooner, while a larger percentage will delay entry.

3. The number of days in the standard deviation, which determines the filter, could be fixed at 20. A statistical measure requires at least 20 days to have some stability.

Testing for short-term trading could fix the AMA days at 10 and the standard deviation days at 20, and test only the filter. Fewer parameters mean a more dependable solution. Longer-term positions are not affected by the filter; therefore it can be fixed at some value under 1.0.

Profit-Taking.   Another look at Figure 8-6 shows that the Efficiency Ratio peaks over .80 (panel b) and the moving average days drops under 10 (in panel c) at points that would be good for taking profits. It is a characteristic of the Adaptive Moving Average that a high value for the Efficiency Ratio cannot be sustained and will be followed by a reversal. It would be best simply to take profits whenever the value exceeds a preset level. That threshold will vary based on the intrinsic noise of the market.

Programming the Adaptive Moving Average

The Adaptive Moving Average can be programmed into any spreadsheet or strategy-testing software. The following examples show the codes for *Quattro Pro* (very similar to *Lotus*), Telerate's *TeleTrac,* and Omega's *TradeStation.* Signals should not begin for 25 days, because the filter requires 20 days of AMA trendline changes, and the AMA needs an additional 5 days to start up.

Spreadsheet Instructions

Box 8-3 and Table 8-1 give the spreadsheet instructions and sample results. All constants have been placed in row 2. The recent AMA highs and lows are recorded in columns *L* and *M.*

Telerate's *TeleTrac*

The *TeleTrac* code (Box 8-4) uses the alternate buy and sell signal calculation, comparing 3 days of AMA changes separately. It also uses the *MACD* study (*"SIGNAL"*) to calculate an exponential moving average with a changing smoothing constant. This code can be used to trade live data. Realized profits and losses are shown in the last line.

Omega's *Easy Language*

The *TradeStation* code is the same for both *System Writer* and other Omega products (Box 8-5). Figure 8-8 shows the *TradeStation* display using the "AMA" system (Part 1) to give signals, the "AMA" indicator (Part 2), scaled to price, to plot the AMA trendline with the price chart, and "AMA smooth" (Part 3) to place the smoothing constant along the bottom of the graph.

Box 8-3. CALCULATING THE ADAPTIVE MOVING AVERAGE USING A SPREADSHEET

The Adaptive Moving Average can be easily calculated using a spreadsheet. In Table 8-1, columns *B* and *C* are input and the rest are calculated. Values begin in row 5. Repeated calculations are shown for row 15 (row 5 is for initialization). The AMA calculations (*E-H*) begin in row 15, because they require 10 days of data for the first value.

Cell	Title	Description	Formula
Constants:			
C2		2-day smoothing constant	=2/(2+1)
D2		30-day smoothing constant	=2/(30+1)
J2		Filter percentage factor	.10
Initial Values:			
B5	Date	Daily date	[Input data]
C5	DMZ92	Deutsche mark price	[Input data]
I5	AMA(t)	(Use price C5* until row I5)	[Input data]
L5	Lows	Recent AMA lows	+I5
M5	Highs	Recent AMA highs	+I5
Repeated Formulas:			
D15*	D(t)	10-day momentum	+C15-C5
E6*	1DP	Positive 1-day volatility	@ABS(C6-C5)
F15*	V(t)	10-day volatility	@SUM(E6..E15)
G15*	ER(t)	Efficiency Ratio	@ABS(D15/F15)
H15*	C(t)	Smoothing constant	(G15*(C2−D2)+D2)^2
I15*	AMA(t)	Adaptive Moving Average	+I14+H15*(C15−I14)
J6*	DAMA	Difference in AMA	+I6−I5
K15*	Filter	Entry/exit filter	@STD(J15..J6)*J2
L6*	Lows	Recent AMA low	@IF(I6<I5,I6,L5)
M6*	High	Recent AMA high	@IF(I6>I5,I6,M5)
N15*	Buy	New buy signal	@IF(I15−L15>K15,'BUY',")
O15*	Sell	New sell signal	@IF(M15−I15>K15,'SELL',")

*Indicates to copy the contents of the cell down.

@ Indicates a *Quattro* function.

Table 8-1. Spreadsheet Values for the Adaptive Moving Average

	B	C	D	E	F	G	H	I	J	K	L	M	N
Line		0.66667	0.0645						0.15				
3			10-Day	Abs	10-Day	10-Day	Smooth		1st Diff	E/X	AMA(t)	AMA(t)	Trade
4	DATE	DMZ92	D(t)	1DP	V(t)	ER(t)	C(t)	AMA(t)	DAMA	Filter	Lows	Highs	Signal
5	920601	6063						6063				6063.0	6063.0
6	920602	6041		22				6041	−22			6041.0	6063.0
7	920603	6065		24				6065	24			6041.0	6065.0
8	920604	6078		13				6078	13			6041.0	6078.0
9	920605	6114		36				6114	36			6041.0	6114.0
10	920608	6121		7				6121	7			6041.0	6121.0
11	920609	6106		15				6106	−15			6106.0	6121.0
12	920610	6101		5				6101	−5			6101.0	6121.0
13	920611	6166		65				6166	65			6101.0	6166.0
14	920612	6169		3				6169	3			6101.0	6169.0
15	920615	6195	132.0	26	216	0.61	0.187	6173.9	4.9	3.6	6101.0	6173.9	6195
16	920616	6222	181.0	27	221	0.82	0.311	6188.8	15.0	3.2	6101.0	6188.8	
17	920617	6186	121.0	36	233	0.52	0.142	6188.4	−0.4	3.3	6188.4	6188.8	
18	920618	6214	136.0	28	248	0.55	0.156	6192.4	4.0	3.3	6188.4	6192.4	
19	920619	6185	71.0	29	241	0.29	0.059	6192.0	−0.4	3.1	6192.0	6192.4	
20	920622	6209	88.0	24	258	0.34	0.073	6193.2	1.2	3.1	6192.0	6193.2	
21	920623	6221	115.0	12	255	0.45	0.113	6196.4	3.1	2.9	6192.0	6196.4	
22	920624	6278	177.0	57	307	0.58	0.169	6210.2	13.8	2.8	6192.0	6210.2	
23	920625	6326	160.0	48	290	0.55	0.157	6228.4	18.2	1.0	6192.0	6228.4	
24	920626	6347	178.0	21	308	0.58	0.170	6248.6	20.2	1.1	6192.0	6248.6	
25	920629	6420	225.0	73	355	0.63	0.199	6282.7	34.1	1.6	6192.0	6282.7	
26	920630	6394	172.0	26	354	0.49	0.128	6296.9	14.2	1.6	6192.0	6296.9	
27	920701	6400	214.0	6	324	0.66	0.214	6318.9	22.0	1.6	6192.0	6318.9	
28	920702	6446	232.0	46	342	0.68	0.224	6347.4	28.4	1.6	6192.0	6347.4	
29	920706	6442	257.0	4	317	0.81	0.305	6376.3	28.9	1.5	6192.0	6376.3	
30	920707	6543	334.0	101	394	0.85	0.331	6431.4	55.1	2.0	6192.0	6431.4	
31	920708	6550	329.0	7	389	0.85	0.329	6470.4	39.1	1.8	6192.0	6470.4	
32	920709	6442	164.0	108	440	0.37	0.083	6468.1	−2.4	2.2	6468.1	6470.4	6442
33	920710	6516	190.0	74	466	0.41	0.096	6472.7	4.6	2.4	6468.1	6472.7	6516
34	920713	6597	250.0	81	526	0.48	0.123	6488.0	15.3	2.4	6468.1	6488.0	
35	920714	6568	148.0	29	482	0.31	0.062	6492.9	5.0	2.5	6468.1	6492.9	
36	920715	6580	186.0	12	468	0.40	0.092	6501.0	8.0	2.5	6468.1	6501.0	
37	920716	6610	210.0	30	492	0.43	0.103	6512.3	11.3	2.6	6468.1	6512.3	
38	920717	6682	236.0	72	518	0.46	0.115	6531.7	19.5	2.5	6468.1	6531.7	
39	920720	6537	95.0	145	659	0.14	0.023	6531.9	0.1	2.6	6468.1	6531.9	
40	920721	6552	9.0	15	573	0.02	0.005	6532.0	0.1	1.8	6468.1	6532.0	
41	920722	6563	13.0	11	577	0.02	0.006	6532.2	0.2	1.0	6468.1	6532.2	
42	920723	6573	131.0	10	479	0.27	0.053	6534.3	2.1	1.0	6468.1	6534.3	
43	920724	6498	218.0	75	480	0.04	0.008	6534.0	−0.3	1.0	6534.0	6534.3	
44	920727	6593	24.0	95	494	0.01	0.005	6534.3	0.3	0.9	6534.0	6534.3	

Box 8-4. *TELETRAC* CODE FOR THE ADAPTIVE MOVING AVERAGE

```
item      "DEUTSCHMRK_3/93
date      "DATA(date,first,last,item)
open      "DATA(open,item)
high      "DATA(high,item)
low       "DATA(low,item)
close     "DATA(close,item)
vol       "DATA(vol,item)
oi        "DATA(oi,item)
period    10
diff      Abs_val(close-close[1])
noise     Sum(diff,period)
signal    close-close[period]
efratio   Abs_val(signal)/noise
smooth    Power(efratio*(.666-.0645)+.0645,2)
macd      close
ama       Signal(macd,smooth)
dama      ama-ama[1]
dama2     ama-ama[2]
dama3     ama-ama[3]
sdays     20
filter    .10
sdama     Std_dv(dama,sdays)*filter
buyif     dama>sdamaldama2>sdamaldama3>sdama
buy       dama>=0&buyif
sellif    dama<-sdamaldama2<-sdamaldama3<-sdama
sell      dama<0&sellif
strategy  Trade(buy,sell,sell,buy)
realized  Clos_PL(strategy,close,.0001,.0002)
```

The *TeleTrac* code uses a special function, Signal, to calculate a trendline based on a changing exponential smoothing constant. This code also compares three days of accumulated trend changes to avoid a gradual change that might not give a new signal. Period, filter, and sdays are entered as "coefficients" to allow for optimization.

Box 8-5. OMEGA EASY LANGUAGE CODE FOR THE ADAPTIVE MOVING AVERAGE*

Part 1: Enter as a "system."

```
inputs: period(10), filter(.1);
vars: noise(0), signal(0), diff(0), efratio(0), extlow(0), exthigh(0),
      smooth(1), fastend(.666), slowend(.0645), AMA(0);

{ CALCULATE EFFICIENCY RATIO }
diff = @AbsValue(close - close[1]);
if(currentbar < = period) then AMA = close;
if(currentbar > period) then begin
    signal = @AbsValue(close - close[period]);
    noise = @Summation(diff,period);
    efratio = signal/noise;
    smooth = @Power(efratio*(fastend - slowend) + slowend,2);

{ ADAPTIVE MOVING AVERAGE }
    AMA = AMA[1] + smooth*(close - AMA[1]);

{ TREND CHANGE FILTER FROM LAST TURN }
    if(AMA > AMA[1] and AMA[1] < AMA[2]) then extlow = AMA[1];
    if(AMA < AMA[1] and AMA[1] > AMA[2]) then exthigh = AMA[1];

{ TRADING SIGNALS }
    if(currentbar > period + 5) then begin
        if(AMA > AMA[1] and AMA - extlow > filter) then buy on close;
        if(AMA < AMA[1] and exthigh - AMA.> filter) then sell on close;
        end;
    end;
```

Note that this code saves the most recent trend turning points as **extlow** and **exthigh**. It can then use those points to compare the accumulated change of direction against the filter and avoid missing a signal due to a very slow trend change.

Box 8-5. (*Continued*)

Part 2: Enter as an "indicator" to see the trendline on the chart page.

```
inputs: period(10);
vars: noise(0), signal(0), diff(0), efratio(0),
     smooth(1), fastend(.666), slowend(.0645), AMA(0);

{ CALCULATE EFFICIENCY RATIO }
diff = @AbsValue(close - close[1]);
if(currentbar < = period) then AMA = close;
if(currentbar > period) then begin
     signal = @AbsValue(close - close[period]);
     noise = @Summation(diff,period);
     efratio = signal/noise;
     smooth = @Power(efratio*(fastend - slowend) + slowend,2);

{ ADAPTIVE MOVING AVERAGE }
     AMA = AMA[1] + smooth*(close - AMA[1]);
     Plot1(AMA,"AMA");
     end;
```

Part 3: Enter as an "indicator" to plot the smoothing constant on the chart page.

```
inputs: period(10);
vars: noise(0), signal(0), diff(0), efratio(0),
     smooth(1), fastend(.666), slowend(.0645);

{ CALCULATE EFFICIENCY RATIO }
diff = @AbsValue(close - close[1]);
if(currentbar < = period) then AMA = close;
if(currentbar > period) then begin
     signal = @AbsValue(close - close[period]);
     noise = @Summation(diff,period);
     efratio = signal/noise;
     smooth = @Power(efratio*(fastend - slowend) + slowend,2);
     Plot1(smooth,"AMA smooth");
     end;
```

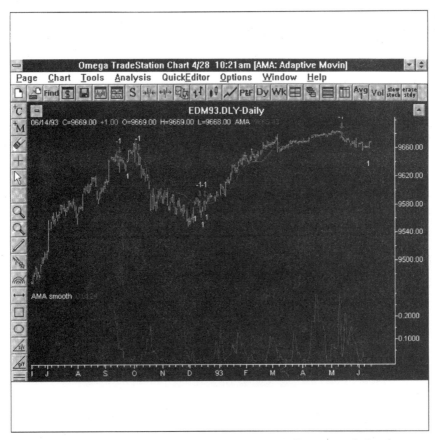

Figure 8-8. Adaptive Moving Average for the Eurodollar on *TradeStation*.

9

Computer Learning, Neural Networks, and New Technology

Using a computer develops special skills in the same sense as driving a car or learning a new language. The process is more intimidating than it is difficult. New computer applications are much more user-friendly than they were five years ago. Most programs allow you to use a "mouse," provide pop-up help screens, and explain each option on the screen whenever you point the mouse at a special icon symbol. To our relief, it is also harder to destroy a program by hitting the wrong keys. This removes some of the concerns about learning. If you press the *Enter* instead of the *Esc* key, the computer may tell you **ENTRY INVALID. TRY AGAIN.** or just ignore you.

Teaching a computer the rules for a trading strategy is a learning process for both you and the computer. Unlike the human brain, the computer cannot infer a meaning, it must be told precisely. We often think that we are very clear about giving instructions, but the section on "fuzzy logic" will show how many of our expressions are vague. The following section is intended to emphasize how exact you must be in specifying rules to get the computer to give the right answer. If you have never programmed trading rules, it will be well worth your time to follow this process through the next few pages.

The Teaching Process:
First the Trainer

Because some important new technologies "teach" the computer how to solve a problem, and strategy-testing programs allow you to define specific rules, this chapter will show how *human* this process can be. An early marvel of engineering skill, the *Erector Set,* will be used to illustrate the steps (Box 9-1).

The basic Erector Set has flat metal pieces, screws, and bolts. Our sample set uses only nine pieces, conveniently designed to fit together, as shown in Figure 9-1, with the pieces numbered for reference. It has 18 sets of bolts and nuts, exactly $\frac{1}{2}$ the number of total corners.

Your task is to build a flat, narrow 4-inch bridge long enough to cover a 33-inch span. You must write the rules for constructing the bridge clearly enough for someone else to follow them exactly. You can start with the five rules given in the first panel of Box 9-1.

Applying Prices to
the Training Game

When we apply the same process to finding a sequence of prices that results in a net move of +50 points in the DJIA, some interesting similarities and differences appear. If we think of each "piece" as a price, we can restate some of the rules:

RULE A. Begin with a partially constructed bridge of length I (the original investment).

RULE B. Decide on the length of the final bridge before starting.

RULE C. You must take the prices ("pieces") in the order they come, but you may discard them if they are too small (but only if you have decided in advance, what is "too small").

Discarding a small piece is a threshold criterion that will be used later in this chapter in the section, "Neural Networks." It allows us to decide that a very small price is not relevant for determining a new trading signal.

RULE D. Prices that exceed the threshold are always attached at the same end (of the price series).

RULE E. A price piece can either add or remove (positive or negative) length.

RULE F. The length cannot become less than $\frac{1}{2}$ the original size (maximum loss rule).

RULE G. The bridge must be constructed by a certain time using a fixed number of pieces (return on investment rule).

Some additional considerations are:

- Price changes come in more sizes. Some are exceptionally big, and others are very small and can be ignored. When a very large positive piece appears, the goal is successfully reached; when a very large negative piece appears, the game is lost. The frequency of catastrophic loss is based on the number of occurrences of large negative pieces, or price shocks. Chapter 7 shows that there is no way to avoid these events, but there are ways to survive them.

- If too many small pieces are used, the time spent is no longer cost-effective.

- You cannot reach the goal in the scheduled time if too many pieces take away from its length.

Most important, when using prices instead of playing games,

- There *may not* be a solution within the limits of the rules, time, and objectives.

Once again: *There may not be a solution.* Forcing an answer from price patterns and data is not a solution. It may be necessary to look at the problem from an entirely different perspective.

Computers do not think; they simply follow your instructions. Writing the rules requires practice. When an instruction is missing, the answer is wrong, even when the results appear to be good. The only way to know that the computer has calculated everything correctly is to check the results manually for a few different cases. The more complex the trading strategy, the longer it will take to verify.

It is easy to make mistakes when specifying rules and typing formulas. It is not likely that any system has been written that did not require careful computer debugging. The following sections on new technologies will describe a number of interesting approaches to defining rules and making decisions.

Artificial Intelligence and Pattern Recognition

The field of artificial intelligence (AI) includes many new technologies for prices forecasting, such as expert systems, neural networks, and

Box 9-1. THE ERECTOR SET PIECES

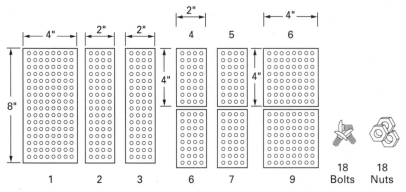

Figure 9-1. Erector set pieces.

Erector set pieces

There are nine pieces, forming four sets of plates each with an area of 4" × 8". Each plate is fully covered with holes. There are 18 bolts and 18 nuts.

Objectives

Can you construct a bridge that is 33" long and 4" wide at all points? Can you teach someone else by writing the exact rules for doing this the first time? The following five rules will get you started:

RULE 1. You must take the pieces in any order.

RULE 2. Two flat pieces can be attached by inserting a bolt through a hole in each of the two pieces, and fastening it with a nut.

RULE 3. The bridge must be 4" wide at all places.

RULE 4. All corners must be fastened except the four at the two ends of the bridge.

RULE 5. The bridge must reach across a 33" span.

Teaching Yourself

To follow the rules, you select each piece with your eyes closed. You must write an unambiguous rule for using any piece *before* you see it. This is important because, when you test stock or futures prices, you do not know what will come next.

You take the first piece and look at it. You realize immediately that the five rules do not include instructions for the first piece. The rules require *at least two pieces.* You cannot continue without adding:

RULE 6. Start with two pieces; after the first move, take one piece at a time.

Starting again, you take two pieces and fasten them together by applying Rule 2. You realize that you do not know *which* holes to fasten.

RULE 7. Fasten the shortest sides together by overlapping the edges (Figure 9-2) so that the holes nearest the edges align; if the shorter edges are the same size, then attach them so that they are aligned at the ends; if they are different lengths, attach them so that one end is aligned.

Rule 7 will prevent bolting a small piece in the middle of a big piece, and will prevent the bridge from going around in a circle.

Beginning again, we draw pieces 8 and 4 and attach them end to end, into an "L"-shaped form, as in Figure 9-3. Notice that the total length is $\frac{1}{4}$ inch less than the sum of the two pieces, because they overlap. Piece 1 comes next, but there are two choices: It can be attached to the end of piece 8 or the end of piece 4. This suggests two more problems that need rules:

RULE 8. Continue to add pieces in the same direction.

RULE 9. Before adding a piece at the very end of the ramp, first check to see if the piece fits a missing slot to finish the 4″ width.

This process of adding rules based on experience is called *learning by feedback*. By continuing, we will eventually complete a bridge that spans the 33 inches with 1 inch overlapping each end. This lengthy process is identical to "teaching" the computer.

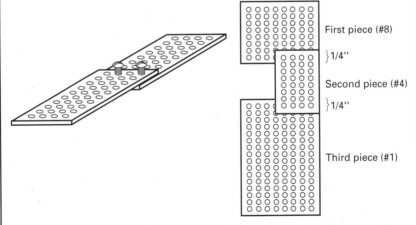

Figure 9-2. Overlapping pieces. Bolting two pieces together takes away $\frac{1}{4}$″ from the total length.

Figure 9-3. Attaching the first three pieces together. Extra rules are needed.

fuzzy logic. There is still a lot to learn from the first AI methods, which centered around basic pattern recognition.

Think about price changes as direction only:

up, up, down, up, unchanged, up, up, down,...

What comes next? If you were taking a school test, the answer would be up. If you were investing in the market, how much would you risk on the next day being up? Nothing, because the pattern was not repeated enough times, and markets are not expected to perform with such regularity.

The existence of a previous pattern that is identical to the current one is not enough to risk an investment. For example, you test 10 years of data and find 74 cases of identical 5-day patterns, either up, up, down, up, up or down, down, up, down, down. If the results are random, then this pattern will be followed by 37 up days and 37 down days. If there are 42 up days and 32 down days, would you consider buying each time this pattern appears? There may be an edge, but a very small one. Or there may not have been enough cases in the 10 years for the random distribution to have appeared.

Simple pattern recognition is a difficult tool to use in trading. Its success is entirely an issue of statistics, and must be treated in that light. The following methods of artificial intelligence are much more likely to produce good results.

Applications of Expert Systems

Applications of *artificial intelligence* are intended to have computers operate the way humans think. It may not be clear that the process is really desirable, but science considers the unachievable as a challenge, and sometimes pursues it without understanding why. The development of the following concepts began long before everyday technology could support them.

Expert systems have the very sensible goal of duplicating expert advice and decisions. This approach has had remarkable success in medical diagnosis and could be equally applicable to financial issues.

New technology tends to create terminology to express the ideas, and expert systems are no exception. Having the proper words seems to be part of the process:

- *Teaching the computer* refers to the act of entering data and rules into the machine, such as:

FACT 1: Bob's parents are George and Martha.

FACT 2: Mary's parents are George and Martha.

RULE 1: If you drive faster, you will get there sooner.

RULE 2: You can't drive faster than the speed limit.

RULE 3: If there is more traffic, you must drive slower.

- *Inference* means creating new facts from existing ones. Using facts 1 and 2, we get

INFERENCE: Bob and Mary are brother and sister.

- *Pruning* is the sorting through of all the information to find the most relevant. Because the brain and the machine are filled with data and rules, it is necessary to select the ones that apply to the current problem. You would not want to answer the question, "Why did the stock market drop?" with "Because of the earthquake in Armenia." An interesting item, but unrelated.

- An *expert system* is one that deals with a special area, such as medical diagnosis, oil spills, or stock market forecasting. By listing all the facts and rules in the specialized *domain*, the system is expected to substitute for the benefits of a team of experts.

To create an expert system to make stock market decisions, first write the relationships that are facts, in any order. For example, Table 9-1 gives a set of 10 rules.

Forward Chaining

The definitions and rules in Table 9-1 combine to form a *knowledge base*. For convenience, the shortened names referring to data are explained in the list of *variable names.* Using a process called *forward chaining*, start with an important piece of information and follow one rule to another until you find your answer. For example, *The Wall Street Journal* front page reads:

FED CUTS RATE HALF POINT TO 4¼

and you want to know how the stock market should react. Rule 1 states that, IF interest FALLS, THEN stocks RISE. Therefore, expect the stock market to rally.

If the *Journal* had said:

DOLLAR DROPS AGAINST THE YEN

Then Rule 2 gives IF dollar FALLS, THEN interest RISE. That is chained to Rule 1, which states, IF interest RISE, THEN stocks FALL.

Table 9-1. Expert System Rules for Stock Market Decisions

Rule	Statement of Rule (a)			Opposite Rule (b)		
1	IF THEN	interest stocks	FALL RISE	IF THEN	interest stocks	RISE FALL
2	IF THEN	U.S. dollar interest	FALL RISE	IF THEN	U.S. dollar interest	RISE FALL
3	IF THEN	inflation interest	RISE RISE	IF THEN	inflation interest	FALL FALL
4	IF THEN	GNP interest	FALL FALL	IF THEN	GNP interest	RISE RISE
5	IF THEN	Ger Bund rate interest	FALL FALL	IF THEN	Ger Bund rate interest	RISE RISE
6	IF THEN	p/cap spend inventories	RISE FALL	IF THEN	p/cap spend inventories	FALL RISE
7	IF THEN	unemployment p/cap spend	FALL RISE	IF THEN	unemployment p/cap spend	RISE FALL
8	IF THEN	inventories production	FALL RISE	IF THEN	inventories production	RISE FALL
9	IF THEN	production GNP	RISE RISE	IF THEN	production GNP	FALL FALL
10	IF THEN	Fed money sup interest	ADD FALL	IF THEN	Fed money sup interest	DEC RISE

Variable Name	Meaning
Interest	U.S. interest rates
Stocks	U.S. stock market
U.S. dollar	U.S. dollar exchange rate
Inflation	Rate of U.S. inflation
GNP	The Gross National Product
Ger Bund rate	German Bund interest rate
P/cap spend	Per capita spending
Inventories	U.S. manufacturers' inventories
Production	Total U.S. manufacturing production
Fed money sup	Federal Reserve money supply target

If the news is:

UNEMPLOYMENT RISES

Start at Rule 7b,	IF unemployment RISES, THEN p/cap spend FALLS,
Then to Rule 6b,	IF p/cap spend FALLS, THEN inventories RISE,
To Rule 8b,	IF inventories RISE, THEN production FALLS,
To Rule 9b,	IF production FALLS, THEN GNP FALLS,
To Rule 4a,	IF GNP FALLS, THEN interest FALLS,
Finally to Rule 1	IF interest FALLS, THEN stocks RISE.

By chaining one rule to another, the computer should reach the same conclusion as an expert. The only problem is that this answer does not make sense. In this case, although all the rules are perfectly correct, the conclusion *unemployment rises, therefore the stock market rises* is wrong.

To be fair, it is not technically wrong. What is missing is the time delay. Unemployment will cause interest rates to be lowered, which will move the stock market higher. But not on the same day. First, the market will drop on the news. Each sequence, represented by a rule, must be assigned a reaction time or completion criterion. Rule 7b should really read:

IF unemployment RISES, THEN p/cap spending FALLS
over the next 3 months.

By adding time to each rule, we come closer to an expert system.

Drawing on the Knowledge Base

Once the knowledge base has been established, many different questions can be asked: "What is the effect on the stock market when the Fed wants to increase the money supply? What is the effect of an increase in unemployment on the U.S. dollar?"

The reverse of many items in the knowledge base, but not all, may also be used: "IF interest rates DO NOT FALL and the GNP IS NOT POSITIVE, THEN the stock market WILL NOT RISE."

Resolving Conflicts of Multiple Events

As easy as it is to show sequences stemming from single events, it is not realistic. Two or more significant factors are usually present and often conflict with one another. Which is more important, if any? The following rules can be added to help determine which government statistic is most important:

W1. IF actual statistic minus expectations IS MOST EXTREME THEN most important.

W2. IF cumulative difference of last 3 statistics minus expectations IS MOST EXTREME
THEN most important.

W3. IF actual statistic minus year ago IS MOST EXTREME
THEN most important.

W4. IF statistic minus long-term mean IS MOST EXTREME
THEN most important.

But it is still not complete. Two or more events may be extreme in different ways. They may be cumulative or offsetting in their effect on the stock market. Rules must be written to resolve these factors. This conflict resolution can be the weak point of expert systems.

Validation

When it is all in the computer and an answer pops out, how do you know it is correct? Because the process is logical, the individual steps can be traced to prove the answer. But the example of "UNEMPLOYMENT RISES" gave the right answer but not the right time. In the end, the final decision is yours. The answer must seem right, and satisfy the *test of reasonableness.*

Neural Networks

Although the idea and words for a computerized *neural network* come from the biological ideal of the human brain, an *artificial* neural network is not a model of a brain, nor does it "learn" in the human sense. It is simply very good at finding patterns. In fact, it can be so good that it "overfits" the data, finding patterns that exist only by chance. In that way, nearly all methods for finding the "best" performing systems share the same problems, whether very simple or complex techniques.

A wide selection of neural network software is available for the personal computer. Many of these can be found through trade magazines such as *Technical Analysis of Stocks & Commodities* and *Futures.*

Terminology of Neural Networks

The brain is composed of cells called *neurons,* which process and store information. They are unique in the human system because they do not die, which is why we are able to remember. Neurons function in groups called *networks,* which have thousands of interconnected neurons, and those networks are connected to other neural networks.

Information is received through *dendrites* and goes directly into a neuron. The data can be passed to other neurons through an output connector called an *axon.* As the information passes from one neuron to another neuron or neural network, it may pass through a *synapse,* which can inhibit or enhance the importance of the data going in different directions. A synapse may also be considered a "selector." Figure 9-4 shows a biological neural network and its components.

The human neural network is remarkable in its ability to receive vast

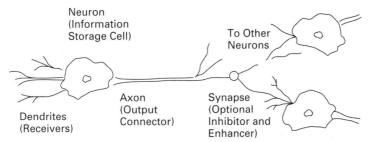

Figure 9-4. A biological neural network. Information is received through *dendrites* and passed to a *neuron* for storage. Data are shared by other cells by moving through the output connector, called an *axon*. A *synapse* may be located on the path between some individual neurons or neural networks; they select the relevant data by inhibiting or enhancing the flow.

amounts of data, store it away, and make you aware of only the most important items. This sophisticated selection process can vary for each individual and situation. For example, you may no longer hear the ticking of a clock in your bedroom but are instantly aware of the smallest unusual sound coming from a child's room. We actually hear the clock, but the sound becomes routine and our neural networks do not alert us to action. When the clock stops, an efficient human system will notice.

Artificial Neural Networks

Using the same structure as the biological neural network in Figure 9-4, we can show how economic and price information passes through a computerized, *artificial,* neural network (ANN) to produce a decision on the direction of stock prices.

The first step is shown in Figure 9-5. The system receives a wide assortment of input data, as does the human system. It must select which of these are relevant in finding the answer and assign *weighting factors* to represent their value. Because "Domestic Health" influences interest rates and subsequently stock prices, we select how each of the five inputs will be used. Two are discarded as irrelevant by giving a weighting factor of zero to their importance; however, all items remain stored in "neurons" for later use.

Unemployment, GDP, and inventories are all considered to contribute to Domestic Health. The value placed on their importance will be decided by the computer neural net program. We can expect the weighting factors for GDP and inventories to be positive, because rising GDP and inventories indicate strong economic activity. Inventories are

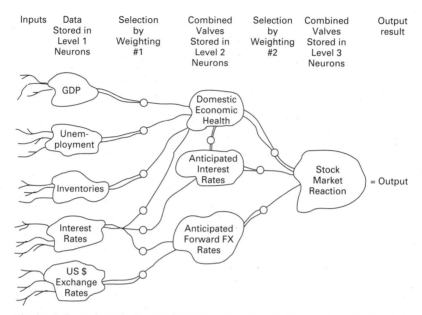

Figure 9-5. A three-layer artificial neural network. Economic and price data are received and stored in Level 1 neurons. Information is passed to Level 2 through synapses that reduce or increase the importance of each item, forming new composite values representing the economic health of the country and the anticipated direction of the U.S. dollar. These values are then combined into Level 3, an expected movement in U.S. stocks. In most artificial neural networks *each* neuron in Level 1 is connected to *all* neurons in Level 2.

not as clear and get a smaller value. Unemployment gets a negative factor. When unemployment rises, domestic health declines.

The Three-Layer System

Domestic health is only one element needed to forecast stock market prices. Current and anticipated interest rates may be the greatest factor. But interest rates are used to achieve an economic growth target, which may be measured by domestic health. Therefore, each feeds on the other. To make matters more complicated, world political events cause money to move to safety. If Eastern Europeans are buying the U.S. dollar regardless of current interest rates, then rates can go lower. On the other hand, if the United States needs to attract foreign investors to support its debt, then U.S. interest rates must rise to attract buyers, regardless of domestic health.

Each neuron in Level 2 and 3 depends on the weighting factors of each of the neurons that feed it. Unlike the expert system, it is not told the effect

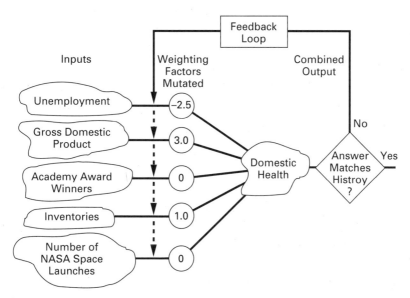

Figure 9-6. Learning by feedback. A neural network program uses the known answers as feedback to find the weighting factors that work.

of each piece of input data, but determines its use by comparing historic examples. For example, the value assigned to domestic health in Figure 9-6 is the result of many inputs, each with unique weighting factors.

The Training Process

The ANN arrives at an answer through a computer-intensive process of pattern recognition. The most popular method is called a *genetic algorithm,* because random selection in determining the importance of each input causes one solution to be better than another. This "mutation" is used in the same way that natural selection would allow a better species to survive.

The neural network uses the genetic algorithm to "learn" how to arrive at the best answer in a feedback process called *training.* This method compares the random use of input data and indicators with a known answer until it finds the combination that comes closest to being correct. Figure 9-6 shows the "feedback loop" that mutates weighting factors, using random numbers, until the answers match a large sample of historic situations.

Because this is a trial-and-error process, rather than an analytic approach, the best results could be caused by a coincidental occurrence of data, rather than cause and effect. Keep in mind the famous warning, *Post hoc ergo prompter hoc* (literally, "After this, therefore because of this"), which refers to the error in thinking which assumes that because one event followed another, the second event was caused by the first.

A Training Example

We would like to train a neural net to tell us

Should we buy or sell the stock market?

using only the five inputs shown in Table 9-2. To make it simpler:

1. Each input is given an adjusted value, from +100 to −100, indicating whether the current state is strong or weak, high or low, or neutral.
2. Buy signals are given when the total value is above 120; sell signals occur when the value is below −120.
3. Any value from +120 to −120 is considered neutral.

The initial test has only two training cases, that is, the computer is given two sets of input data and the correct answers. History tells us that, when evaluated correctly, Case 1 will give a strong signal and Case 2 a weak signal. To begin, the weighting factors are all set to 1.0. As seen in Table 9-2(a), both Case 1 and Case 2 produce neutral results, which are wrong.

Trial and Error

Through the process of random assignment of weighting factors (which was chosen as the "genetic algorithm"), the network "mutates" the pattern. When the ANN arrives at a wrong answer, by comparing it against the historic facts, an error signal is produced and the neural net is told to try again. This is the feedback process. The system then changes the weighting factors until it stumbles on the reverse sign for interest rate and unemployment values (minus instead of plus). The neural net had started by assuming that "low" meant negative and "high" meant positive. But the effect of low or high interest rates is the reverse in the stock market. By changing the weighting factor to −1.0, a correct answer is generated in Table 9-2(b).

Because there were only two cases, many combinations of weighting factors would have given the correct answers. For example, interest rates could have been assigned a factor of −5.0 while all other inputs were given a value of zero. These ambiguities are quickly removed when the number of training cases increases.

Table 9-2. Two training cases

(a) First Test with Unit Weights

Input	Case 1				Case 2			
	Relative	Value	Wgt	Net	Relative	Value	Wgt	Net
GNP	Strong	50	1.0	50	Weak	−60	1.0	−60
Unemployment	Low	−25	1.0	−25	High	40	1.0	40
Inventories	Low	−50	1.0	−50	Neutral	15	1.0	15
U.S. dollar	Vry Strg	75	1.0	75	Neutral	0	1.0	0
Interest rates	Falling	−25	1.0	−25	Rising	45	1.0	45
Total of all test values				75				40
Buy/sell threshold levels				±125				±125
Computer training answer				Neutral				Neutral
Actual answer should be				Strong				Weak

(b) Training Cases with Mutated Weighting Factors

Input	Case 1				Case 2			
	Relative	Value	Wgt	Net	Relative	Value	Wgt	Net
GNP	Strong	50	1.0	50	Weak	−60	1.0	−60
Unemployment	Low	−25	−1.0	25	High	40	−1.0	−40
Inventories	Low	−50	1.0	−50	Neutral	15	1.0	15
U.S. dollar	Vry Strg	75	1.0	75	Neutral	0	1.0	0
Interest rates	Falling	−25	−1.0	25	Rising	45	−1.0	−45
Total of all values				125				−130
Buy/sell threshold levels				±125				±125
Computer training answer				Up signal				Down signal
Actual answer should be				Strong				Weak

Relative values assigned in a range from −100 to 100. WGT is the weighting factor, set to 1.0 to start. *Actual* is the response you want to get, or the actual price change over the next 10 days.

Specifying a Neural Network Test

Training the neural network can be a very long process. Allowing the computer to assign weighting factors to countless data items, and continually comparing the answers with the correct one, can take longer than we are prepared to wait. To control the process, it is necessary to put limits on the training and help it along.

Preprocessing. Rather than giving the system all the data possible, select the most significant information. Rather than using automobile and department store sales separately, use a single retail sales figure. Eliminate similar items; each piece of information will continue to be analyzed by the computer over and over again without distinguishing whether two items are the same. Combine some items into indicators and eliminate the less important elements as redundant. If an index is more complicated than a simple weighting of its elements, then the neural network will not include it properly. Include a trend of prices; the ANN cannot create one itself.

Break the Problem into Clear Steps. Solving the problem in a single step may be overly complicated. More important, it becomes very difficult to validate the results. For example, separate forecasts into components. Before looking at the expected move in the stock market, forecast interest rates one week out, or forecast a cut or rise in the prime rate. If the stock market direction is dependent on interest rates, verifying the decision process for rate changes should be a necessary step.

Choose the Number of Decision Levels. Two or more inputs are given weights and may be combined into a single item in a new decision level. If all the inputs can be taken two at a time, combined, and then used with the combination of two other inputs, the computer creates an excessive number of "hidden layers." More hidden layers allow more combinations and increase processing time. They allow the solution to be more specific and require much more data to offset possible overfitting. A four-layer system will also take much longer to process than a three-layer one, therefore the three-layer is highly recommended.

Choosing the Smallest Number of Neurons. Although limiting the number of "hidden" layers will make the solution faster and more general, the number of neurons that hold intermediate results also can be specified. Just as fewer layers create a more general and faster solution, a small number of neurons in each layer has the same effect. Fewer neurons mean a more general solution.

Trade-Offs. As with conventional optimization, neural networks can produce a result that is overfit. Too much data, much of it irrelevant, and too many hidden layers and neurons allow the computer to find spurious patterns. Too few data items, levels, and neurons may make the result so general that it is useless. The analyst must find the proper compromise.

Forever Learning

The neural network responds to combinations of events in the manner in which it was "taught." A drop in interest rates without the associated poor economic news (e.g., a flight to the safety of the U.S. dollar) results in a signal to buy equities. The neural network learns that this situation is still good for stocks. But one day, interest rates drop sharply when investors move their money fearing a plunge in stock prices. You are a buyer of stocks because the move to lower interest rates satisfies the rules. The trade is a large loss as more stock is liquidated. The neural network adds a rule to bypass trades that begin under high volatility conditions.

The system continues to learn. There is no way to know how many different situations will be added to the list of conditions that build a complete network. A synthetic neural network is a technical achievement of large proportions. It can find patterns that cannot be identified by conventional methods (such as multiple regression used in econometrics). It can train itself to determine the importance of each input. But there are many problems it cannot resolve. It will recognize only those inputs that it expects and may not respond properly to combinations of inputs that it has not "seen" before. If there are too many inputs, the network may respond correctly, but to the wrong events. It is the best so far, but it does not guarantee the results within the limits of your investment.

Fuzzy Logic

Fuzzy logic is not a brand name, or a description of scatterbrain thinking; it is a formal area of mathematics. Along with neural nets, fuzzy logic pushes the bounds of science. The idea of "fuzziness" describes the lack of precision in normal human conversation and thought. The concept will allow human uncertainty to be introduced to artificial intelligence methods. Think about most casual conversations:

"There were a lot of people at the game."

"Most of them were tall."

"It was really cold last night."

"The market was strong yesterday."

"The dollar collapsed when the trade deficit was higher than expected."

Although these conversations do not include specific numbers, we accept and understand what the other person is saying. In fuzzy logic, all is not *true* or *false, 0* or *1, there* or *not there.* It will answer questions such as "If a half-eaten apple is still an apple, how much do you have to eat before it stops being an apple?"

The fuzziness concept includes *fuzzy numbers,* such as "small," "about 8," "close to 5," and "much larger than 10," as well as *fuzzy quantifiers,* such as "almost," "several," and "most." The phrase "Surprise government reports cause big moves" is a common fuzzy expression.

Fuzzy Reasoning

"Fuzzy events" and "fuzzy statistics" are combined into *fuzzy reasoning*. Surprisingly, answers to the following examples are remarkably clear to a brain, but not to a machine:

Example 1:   X is a small price move.

Y is much smaller than X.

How small is Y?

Example 2:   Most price moves are small.

Most small price moves are up.

How many price moves are up?

Example 3:   It is not quite true that the quarterly earnings were very bad.

It is not true that quarterly earnings were good.

How bad were the quarterly earnings?*

Practical Solutions

Fuzziness is not intended to describe the same concepts that can be explained precisely by probability (referred to a *crisp logic*.) Because fuzzy logic and possibility theory are new, mathematicians believe that practical applications will use both (fuzzy) possibilities and (crisp) probabilities. Up to now, the fuzzy part has been assigned ranges to represent commonly used values. For example, in expressing the S&P price change, we might have the following:

Description of Change	Value of an S&P Rise or Fall
unchanged	± 20 points
small	± 145 points
medium/normal	± 150 to 400 points
large	more than ± 400 points

*The answers to the examples (1) *very small*, (2) *most*, and (3) *bad*.

The advantage of being human is that we can express these ranges in a vague but sophisticated way. We have defined "unchanged" to be a close within 20 points of the previous close; yet following a few very volatile days, we might call a move of $\pm$ 50 points "unchanged." We all seem to have the same understanding of relative volatility when we speak to one another, but trying to put it on paper evokes disagreement.

Suboptimization or Deoptimization

Fuzzy logic may bring a better solution than other methods that are now being used to develop trading models. By its very nature, a fuzzy solution must be general. Writing fuzzy rules for a trading program will not have to be as precise as traditional specifications. That also means there should be fewer rules and a more robust solution. No matter how hard we try, it may be impossible to overfit the solution using fuzzy data.

State of the Art

Fuzzy systems have been combined with neural networks and expert systems, which provide a framework for "learning." Neural nets provide the behavioral structure so that correct answers are reinforced and incorrect ones are rejected. Expert systems give the program a knowledge base.

Japanese firms have led the financial industry in the application of fuzzy expert systems. It is said that programs already exist for financial dealing, especially stock market trading. These models have been based entirely on price information, but may soon include expectations, or "feelings," about political outcome. It seems that, once the idea is planted, the technology moves forward at a furious pace.

PART 3

Making a Trading Strategy Robust

10
Testing for Robustness

A trading strategy is *robust* if it is successful under many different conditions. It is especially good if it works under situations that are very different from those used in testing, for example, a more volatile move to new high prices.

Many users can blame the speed of the computer for trading systems that do not work. Combined with strategy-testing and statistical software, the computer has made it too easy to simulate thousands of trading rules and techniques. Preprogrammed strategies, countless indicators, and the ability to create your own variations often draw inexperienced users into an indiscriminating and unfocused approach to testing. In the end, the computer has tested too much and used too little as criteria for success. Often, the resulting trading programs appear to be remarkably profitable but in reality are complete failures.

Overfitting

A system that has been tailored to work on a specific period of historic data is called *overfit*. Everyone who develops a trading system will use past data to verify the results. It would be irresponsible to define a set of trading rules, open an account, and begin trading without knowing whether those rules would have worked in the past. The historic risk will give you an indication of the investment size needed to achieve your goal and survive the interim losses required to reach your objective.

A careful study of historic results will often point out an area of high risk. Sometimes a simple rule is all that is needed to reduce the risk to a comfortable level. For example,

Reduce the size of the entry position as the market increases in volatility.

Further analysis could lead to other rules:

Close out all positions if the S&P drops more than 1500 points in 3 days.

or,

Close out all long positions on Friday if the S&P has dropped more than 10% during the previous week.

These rules move from a general, logical risk control to very specific guidance intended to isolate one or two past problems. Where do these changes stop being reasonable and start being manipulative? The answer is rarely clear.

In this chapter, we will consider a system *robust* if it does not depend on a narrow set of conditions. A profitable 10-day moving average system will not be used if similar 8-day and 12-day systems generate losses. The best system is one that is profitable for a broad set of parameters, including trend speeds, risk control, profit-taking, and filters. The trader gains a more dependable program when nearly any choice of parameters is likely to give profits.

Separating Robustness from Parameter Selection

There is a clear separation between determining that a trading strategy is valid, and being able to use that method to produce profits in the future. Historic testing can verify a premise and show which sets of parameters, or variables, were successful in the past. But this does not mean the parameters that generated the most profits in the past will lead to future profits. And, when there are two tests with similar historic success, which will be the best?

Comprehensive testing, called *optimization,* results in some cases that show profits and others that have losses. The profits show that the logic behind the strategy is sound. The more cases that are profitable, the more confidence we have in the trading method. However, the parameters that gave profits in historic tests do not always generate profits during real trading. The ability to choose, *in advance,* which parameters will give future profits is a separate problem from defining robust trading rules.

Most of this chapter will focus on how to build a robust trading system; the more robust it is, the less it will depend on picking the right parameters. We can assume that an arbitrary choice of parameters will yield the average performance; therefore, we should be sure that the average is good.

Principles

The development of a trading model that is independent of parameter selection is always the ideal solution. But it is elusive. It is the opposite concept of an arbitrage, which takes advantage of distinct economic anomalies. This chapter will set down a procedure that will greatly improve the robustness of any trading model. It is not a simple process, but it can be implemented one part at a time. The more that is done, the better the results.

No model is without some limitations or restrictions. Each has a purpose that requires some definitions of its operating environment. It is certainly reasonable to exclude a 3-day moving average from a long-term trading system. Both trading frequency and risk can be narrowed to ranges that make sense for the strategy as well as for the type of business. Exploiting a price pattern is valid if the patterns can be identified in advance. It is within this framework that the program can be robust.

Some basic principles of parameter selection assure a choice that yields superior results. These include slower trends and fewer artificial risk controls. This chapter will draw on previous conclusions to suggest a set of rules and a testing approach that will give test results similar to real trading.

Example of Optimized Performance

Table 10-1 compares test results of a moving average system with a percentage stop-loss. The speed of the moving average (from 5 to 50 days) and the percentage stop-loss (from 0 percent to 2.0 percent) are the two parameters needed to trade. A *TeleTrac* optimization was used to find the returns for each combination of speed and stop for the Hang Seng Index during each of the calendar years 1991 and 1992.

If we had used the best results of the 1-year test on 1991 data to select the parameters to be traded in 1992, we would have tended toward the slower moving averages. The highest return of 17.4 percent was given by the 45-day trend. Speeds from 5 to 30 days showed erratic results and only a few small profits.

The 1992 results show nearly the opposite. Moving averages from 5 to 20 days had large returns, while speeds from 40 to 50 days had the worst results. Had we chosen the parameters that posted the highest profits in 1991, the 1992 performance would have been only 1.3 percent (if executed perfectly).

Table 10-1. Moving Average
Optimization of the Hang Seng Index

	Parameters			
Moving Avg Days	% Stop-Loss	1991 P/L	1992 P/L	Change in P/L
5	0.0	4.5	29.2	+24.7
	1.0	4.0	29.2	+25.2
	2.0	1.6	29.2	+28.0
10	0.0	−0.1	35.1	+35.2
	1.0	−0.1	35.1	+35.2
	2.0	10.2	35.1	+24.9
15	0.0	−11.3	26.9	+38.2
	1.0	−11.5	26.9	+38.4
	2.0	−11.1	26.9	+38.0
20	0.0	3.4	16.6	+13.2
	1.0	3.4	19.8	+16.4
	2.0	1.7	19.8	+18.1
25	0.0	−3.7	4.3	+8.0
	1.0	−7.0	0.9	+7.9
	2.0	−7.0	1.4	+8.4
30	0.0	−13.3	7.2	+20.5
	1.0	−16.4	5.9	+22.3
	2.0	−16.4	5.9	+22.3
35	0.0	1.0	20.7	+21.7
	1.0	1.0	20.7	+21.7
	2.0	1.0	20.7	+21.7
40	0.0	13.0	−15.9	−28.9
	1.0	12.2	−7.5	−19.7
	2.0	−2.9	−7.5	−4.6
45	0.0	17.4	1.3	−16.1
	1.0	17.4	1.3	−16.1
	2.0	17.4	1.3	−16.1
50	0.0	−3.7	1.8	+5.5
	1.0	−3.7	1.8	+5.5
	2.0	−4.6	1.8	+5.5

This simple moving average test shows the typical inconsistency in the performance of the "best" choices when a test uses only a small amount of data. The area of highest profits in 1991 produced the worst results in 1992.

The Underlying Method for Determining Robustness

We can improve the selection of parameters by focusing on systems that have the broadest success. If all test cases are profitable, we would have the perfect robust system and any selection of parameters should return profits.

To measure which strategies are better than others, we will define test procedures that measure the results using the *average and standard deviation of all tests*. The highest average alone is not enough. A smaller standard deviation shows the consistency of performance for all tests. A *Best Choice Index* combines both values by subtracting the standard deviation from the average:

Best Choice Index = Average returns − 1 Standard deviation of returns

Because one standard deviation represents a grouping of 68 percent of all data, the Best Choice Index tells us that this system gives an 84 percent chance of a return greater than or equal to the Best Choice Index value. Remember that losses are half the probability, on the left part of the distribution curve. For example, if all combinations of test returns averaged a rate of return (ROR) of 14 percent with a standard deviation of 6 percent, we have

- An 84 percent chance that any choice will yield returns greater than 8 percent (the average minus 1 standard deviation).
- A 97.5 percent chance that any choice will yield returns greater than 2 percent (the average minus 2 standard deviations).
- A 99.5 percent chance that any choice will yield returns greater than −4 percent (the average minus 3 standard deviations).

The minimum test criterion should be an 84 percent chance of success, given by the Best Choice Index.

Testing Process

The total solution is the *test process*. It begins with conceptualization. It must be followed by clear steps that lead to a well-defined result. Experience shows that if you do not control the process, the process will control you. The test procedure can be separated into five parts:

1. Deciding what to test.
2. Deciding how to test it.
3. Evaluating the results.
4. Choosing the specific parameters to trade.
5. Trading and monitoring performance.

Each of these steps is critical to the success of the program. Setting up this process for the first time will take a lot of careful work, but most of it will only need to be done once. There will be many decisions to make with regard to the data, testing software, and the method of evaluation. Because the proper development of a trading strategy is so important to its success, these issues will be discussed in detail in this chapter. Box 10-1 provides a checklist that will serve as a reminder.

Part 1: Deciding What to Test

Before you begin testing, define the system and the test plan completely. You must tell the computer what to do, not allow the computer to tell you. Do not drift from one idea to another as you reach obstacles. Try to follow the original idea to completion and learn its advantages and disadvantages.

Step 1. Is the Strategy Logical?

Did you write the rules before you began testing? Where did you get your ideas? Successful trading programs are based on sound ideas such as economic relationships (e.g., arbitrage, seasonality, and the spreading of strong and weak economies) or valid technical strategies (e.g., breakout of a support or resistance level, selling volatility with options, or use of divergence). Letting the computer uncover an obscure short-term pattern, no matter how reliable it seems, is not a sound trading approach. Price patterns can always be found, but they have doubtful predictability and often change without notice.

When you develop your program, the strategy must make sense for the market and fit your own objectives, as in the following examples:

- For the *stock market*, you might want a long-term buying strategy with no short positions.

- For the *bond market*, a long-term strategy that parallels slow-changing economic and government policy might be most conservative.

- For *foreign exchange*, a short-term method that would buy or sell in the direction of an intraday breakout with small profit-taking objectives might make more sense for tactical hedging and limited overnight positions.

Using Logical Ideas.   A logical idea does not need to be based on fundamentals. Years of watching price movement on Chicago's International Monetary Market (IMM) may give you the idea that dependable entry signals occur only during the three periods of high volume each day—at the

Box 10-1. CHECKLIST FOR ROBUST TESTING

PART 1: Deciding What to Test

- [ ] 1. Is the strategy logical?
- [ ] 2. Can you program all the rules?
- [ ] 3. Does the strategy make sense only under certain conditions?
- [ ] 4. Take a guess as to the expected results.

PART 2: Deciding How to Test

- [ ] 5. Choose the testing tools and method.
- [ ] 6. Do you have enough of the "right" data?
- [ ] 7. Have you included realistic transaction costs?
- [ ] 8. Will you test a full range of parameters?
- [ ] 9. In what order will the parameters be tested?
- [ ] 10. Are the parameters distributed properly?
- [ ] 11. Have you defined the evaluation criteria?
- [ ] 12. How will the output be presented?

PART 3: Evaluating the Results

- [ ] 13. Are the calculations correct?
- [ ] 14. Were there enough trades to be "significant?"
- [ ] 15. Does the trading system produce profits for most combinations of parameters?
- [ ] 16. Did logic changes improve overall test performance?
- [ ] 17. How did it perform on out-of-sample data?

PART 4: Choosing the Specific Parameters to Trade

- [ ] 18. Did the last test include the most recent data?
- [ ] 19. Did you choose from an area of broad success?
- [ ] 20. Are profits distributed relatively evenly over the tested history?
- [ ] 21. Are the profits per trade large enough to absorb errors?
- [ ] 22. Did the historic results show any large losses due to price shocks?
- [ ] 23. Have you risk-adjusted the returns to your acceptable risk level?

PART 5: Trading and Monitoring Performance

- [ ] 24. Are you following the same rules that were tested?
- [ ] 25. Are you trading the same data that was tested?
- [ ] 26. Are you monitoring the difference between the system and actual entries and exits?

open, close, and just after traders return from lunch. The low volume periods between give less dependable indication of direction and require a more demanding price move to enter a trade. The important rule is to *know what you want to do,* and then use the computer to *verify* your idea. *You must control the process.*

Starting with One Idea and Ending with Another.   Be sure that computer feedback does not cause you to stray from your original idea. A logical strategy can evolve into meaningless patterns. There is a natural tendency to explain why a system must be fundamentally sound, simply because you have already seen that the test results are good.

Step 2. Can You Program All the Rules?

Can all the rules in the trading strategy be entered into the computer or a spreadsheet program? Have you assumed anything that was not programmed? A strategy that cannot be tested cannot be evaluated. If you assume that you would not have been caught in a price shock because the program does not trade overnight, then you leave yourself open to unexpected losses, undercapitalization, and justifiable criticism.

Writing clear trading rules is essential to testing. You must be certain that you can account for entry and exit conditions, risk control, types of orders, time of day, and other situations that completely describe your plan. Writing the rules will tell you the type of data needed for testing (whether it is only prices, the Producer Price Index, or API statistics) the frequency and extent of the data (open, high, low, close, or 30-minute prices with tick volume). As carefully as you try, you will always need to add details later.

Intraday Breakout Example.   Start with the most basic approach, omitting risk control, profit-taking, or qualified entries. If you believe that an intraday breakout system is a sound idea, then first test only the breakout entry and the basic exit signals. You might want to close out the trade at the end of each day; or, you might exit if prices reverse and breakout in the opposite direction. It is important that you know whether the underlying idea works before adding profit-taking, risk control, and other more specialized features.

Decide which parts of the system can vary. You know that a breakout early in the day allows more time to reach bigger profits during the rest of the trading session. Therefore, you will want to test the time of the breakout. You will not want to accept an entry signal late in the day, because of the limited potential for profits before the close.

If the program is fully computerized, you will want to look at the data no more often than every 5 minutes. Although you may be able to execute an order within 60 seconds of a breakout, it is not practical to assume good executions. Using 5-minute bars for testing; rather than 1 minute, will also reduce the time needed to test the strategy.

Before you start testing, you know that an intraday breakout system depends on the period over which the breakout is measured, the time of day for entry, the size of the profit-taking objective, and some risk control.

Trend System Example. All systems have common features: entry and exit rules, risk control, and possibly profit-taking situations. A trend system requires a trend speed. This can vary significantly with your application and objectives. Equities programs, with little leverage and higher transaction costs, require a range from 50 to 500 days. A futures trader, with margins of only 5%, will favor faster trends, from 5 to 30 days.

It is a mistake to use a smoothing approach on intraday data. As the time period between data observations gets shorter, the level of noise increases. Because of illiquid periods in all markets, prices can jump in either direction without indicating a true trend change. This causes frequent false signals that cannot be eliminated by using a longer trend based on the same intraday prices. The combination of intraday noise and trend lag will be a difficult obstacle to overcome.

Step 3. Does the Strategy Make Sense Only under Certain Conditions?

Decide, in advance, whether the strategy targets certain market movement, or a specific set of conditions. The idea may only make sense for long or short time intervals. For example, a day-trading program using 15-minute data would not use a 200-period moving average, while a long-term investment program in stocks would not use a 3-day trend. By defining the range over which the trading model will operate, you reduce the chance of being diverted from your objective. Write out the most reasonable test range for each of the parameters that are considered important to the strategy. The more you can define your expectations, the better the results.

Step 4. Take a Guess as to the Expected Results

Decide the expected rate of return, the percentage of profitable trades, and the size of the losses. The objective is to compare the test results with your expectations. Whether the results are much better or worse than planned, when you have a basis for evaluation it will be easier to correct and move forward with the development of the system. To say "something is wrong" with the test results, you must first decide what you expect.

Part 2: Deciding How to Test

Step 5. Choose the Testing Tools and Method

With more sophisticated strategy-testing software, it is no longer necessary to program the trading method in FORTRAN, BASIC, or C to test its success. In a few minutes, using a strategy testing package such as *TeleTrac,* Omega's *System Writer,* or even a *Lotus* or *Quattro* spreadsheet program, you can have a good idea of the viability of the technique.

An increasing number of programmable graphics terminals and new strategy-testing software are available at very competitive prices. They all have the advantage of calculating profits and losses accurately, the flexibility of rule changes and data selection, and the ability to plot both data and profitability. In some cases, results can be read into spreadsheets for further evaluation. The time saved is well worth the price. For the more sophisticated analysts, supplementary software such as Manugistics *Statgraphics* and Mathsoft *Mathcad* are impressive tools for evaluating complex statistical relationships and expressing mathematical formulas.

Long Test, Short Test, or "Step-Forward" Test?   The pattern in Table 10-1 is not unusual. Tests using a small amount of data give results showing that many combinations of parameters will work. The shorter the test period, the more profitable the system will appear. Consider a bond market that has moved steadily up for 3 months. If there were only small retracements, then any moving average from 10 days and longer would have yielded the same results, which is the net move from the beginning to the end of the period (see Figure 10-1(a)).

When a short test interval has one or more price swings, the slower trends give back profits, while some of the faster ones are very successful. The size of the swing and the amount of market noise determine which trend speeds are best (see Figure 10-1(b)). In general, tests of small amounts of data give:

- Individual and average test results that are much higher
- Risk that is sometimes lower
- Profitable results for more models that trade faster
- Erratic forecasting ability

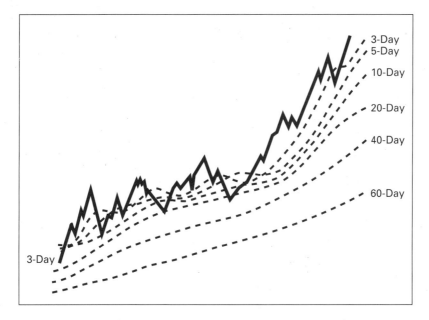

(a)

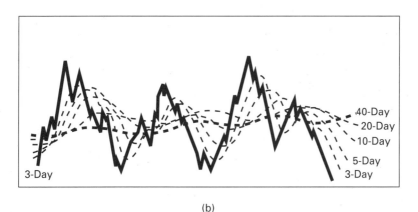

(b)

Figure 10-1. Moving average results for a short test period. (a) A short period with a strongly trending market allows most trend speeds to perform well. (b) A short period with price swings may allow fast trends to capture profits, but net losses for the longer term trends.

It is much more difficult to find a trading method that is good over longer test periods. The best tested performance (annualized rate of return) of a system tested over many years will never be as high as the rate of return of a similar system tested over a few months or a year. Using more data, you should expect:

- Much lower returns
- Larger risk when positions are held longer
- Difficulty in getting consistent profits from short-term trading
- Questions as to the relevance of older data
- Better forecasting ability

Therefore, test results using smaller amounts of data look better, but do not perform as expected; results based on longer tests look worse but perform closer to expectations. You should not be disappointed in the results of a long test period when compared with shorter tests. It is only that the shorter tests are misleading.

Select a Long, Representative Test Period.   When more data are tested, there is a greater variety of unusual situations, longer profitable price moves, sequences of losses, and price shocks. When longer periods are tested, both risk and reward increase; however, risk increases faster than returns. Testing shorter periods can give an unrealistically small risk, cause undercapitalized trading and fatal results. A good rule is to be certain that the data contain *two full cycles,* that is, there should be two clear bull markets, two bear markets and two prolonged sideways intervals.

Because results never look as good when the same strategy is tested over longer periods, you might argue that markets have changed and the old data are no longer representative; that globalization and regional alliances have changed the price relationships and patterns in many sectors, or that government controls will prevent an economic collapse. By saying that the market will continue to exhibit only the price patterns seen recently is unrealistic. It will evolve to new patterns; however, we have no way of knowing what they will be. The past contains the most accessible, practical, and realistic examples of changing situations. Box 10-2 shows that performance drops but predictability increases with the use of more data. Short test periods produce unreasonable expectations of profits.

"Step-Forward Testing" versus One Long Test.   The technique of "step-forward testing" seems to be a sensible approach to resolving some of the testing dilemmas. It works as follows:

1. Select a short data interval, called a "test window" (e.g., 2 years of data).

2. Test (optimize) a full set of parameters on the test window and select the "best."

3. Run the model on a short period of out-of-sample data, immediately following the test window (e.g., the next 3 months), using the "best" parameters (see Figure 10-2).

4. Collect performance data on the "out-of-sample" period, including a comparison with the "in-sample" test-window returns.

5. Move the test window forward and repeat steps 2 through 4 until done.

6. The parameters that perform most consistently in the out-of-sample period are considered best.

Hidden Problems.   Step-forward testing seems to duplicate the way we would operate a trading program. But there are hidden problems:

- Shorter test periods favor faster strategies that produce higher profits and more trades. But the performance of fast-trading strategies varies sharply from one test window to another, as discussed in the previous section and shown in Table 10-2. The "best" parameters are not a good choice for trading.

- Short test periods do not represent long-term trading fairly. Each short test period can have only a few long-term trades, and they may start and end in the middle of a trade. Moving the test window forward does not correct the treatment of these trades.

- Retesting the same system with modified rules means that the "out-of-sample" data is no longer new. This is called "feedback." Once used, the data is no longer "out-of-sample." You know what to expect and how to make the data patterns show more profits.

The step-forward process will usually select an inconsistent, fast-trading method over a better long-term system simply because the test window forces this result. Instead, use all the data in one long test to get continuous performance over as many changing patterns as possible.

Step 6: Do You Have Enough of the "Right" Data?

The more data you test, the more situations the program will experience. There must be at least two bull markets, two bear markets, and two sideways periods. Unless you can prove that the older data is misleading, or no longer valid, you should use as much data as possible. Put some data aside for out-of-sample validation after the final system has been selected. This is discussed further in Step 18.

Box 10-2. MORE DATA IMPROVE TEST RESULTS

Using more data produces more consistent and realistic results. Final results may show that risk is higher and profits are lower, but these figures are more likely to be achieved in trading. It is more difficult to find persistent short-term patterns in a longer data series; therefore, selections favor slower trading. Long-term solutions, in turn, include realistic equity fluctuations because they cannot be fine-tuned to avoid specific losing periods. This performance profile shows higher risk and makes it necessary to have higher capitalization.

A simple test of the MATIF CAC-40 Index (Table 10-2) shows the predictive ability of tests based on 1, 2, 3, and 5 years of data. The system tested was

1. An exponential moving average from 5 to 50 days, in increments of 5 days.

2. A trend change criterion ("filter") from 0 to 10 points, in increments of 1 point.

3. A *buy* signal that occurred when the trend turned up by the amount of the filter; a *sell* signal that was generated when the trend turned down by the amount of the filter value.

The highest profits for each test determined the trend speed and entry filter that were to be used to evaluate the next 1 year of data. The averages for each test case were compared.

Table 10-2. Tests of CAC-40 (MATIF) French Stock Index

	1-Year Test					2-Year Test			
Year(s) Tested	Best Performance			1 Year Ahead	Year(s) Tested	Best Performance			1 Year Ahead
	Speed	Filter	P/L			Speed	Filter	P/L	
1982	5	3	63	(54)					
1983	50	0	118	(70)	82–83	40	2	216	(79)
1984	10	6	81	(134)	83–84	25	1	124	(162)
1985	10	2	287	556	84–85	10	5	385	620
1986	10	7	683	4	85–86	20	3	938	362
1987	30	10	578	(600)	86–87	15	3	1242	(447)
1988	35	6	515	(427)	87–88	25	9	1160	(338)
1989	10	7	378	232	88–89	45	1	569	3
1990	35	0	708	(126)	89–90	10	8	734	(141)
1991	20	7	266	208	90–91	20	6	501	237
1992	15	6	328	—	91–92	—	—	—	—
Avg/Yr	21	5	364	(41)	Avg/Yr	23	4	326	6

Speed and filter vary.
Test is sensitive to current patterns.

Average trend slows.
In-sample profits decline.
1 year ahead improves.

Summary of results

- *1-year test.* The best trend speed and filter varied considerably from year to year. The average speed was lowest of all tests, showing that a fast trend often looks best for a short test period. Performance was inconsistent in 1-year-ahead tests, averaging a loss of 41 points. Using 1 year of data to forecast 1 year ahead does not look promising.

- *2-year test.* Overall profits per year declined and the average best choice slowed slightly, showing that more test data become harder to fit. However, results for 1 year ahead increased and became net positive.

- *3-year test.* The performance pattern continued to improve. The 1-year-ahead tests for 1988 and 1989, which show large losses, were studied to find out that those years posted new highs. Performance in the out-of-sample data seems to be better when the price movement is within the range seen in the tested period.

- *5-year test.* Improvement continued overall. Longer trends were selected and tested performance declined. These are especially good results because 1985 and 1986, which showed large profits in the 3-year test, were not part of this out-of-sample performance.

Table 10-2. Tests of CAC-40 (Matif) French Stock Index (*Continued*)

	3-Year Test					5-Year Test			
Year(s) Tested	Best Performance			1 Year Ahead	Year(s) Tested	Best Performance			1 Year Ahead
	Speed	Filter	P/L			Speed	Filter	P/L	
82–84	15	2	162	215					
83–85	20	2	472	119					
84–86	20	3	1165	362	82–86	20	2	968	355
84–87	20	3	1414	(454)	83–87	20	2	1515	(39)
86–88	25	9	1225	(388)	84–88	20	2	1327	(344)
87–89	50	1	910	362	85–89	40	0	1374	345
88–90	10	7	900	(71)	86–90	10	7	1640	(71)
89–91	30	4	832	73	87–91	25	9	1394	9
90–92	25	10	1072		88–92	30	0	1024	—
Avg/Yr	24	5	302	27	Avg/Yr	28	4	264	43

Average trend is slower.	Average trend is slowest.
In-sample profits are lower.	In-sample profits are lowest.
1 year ahead is better.	1 year ahead is best.
New highs in 1988 generated losses because it is not part of sample data.	

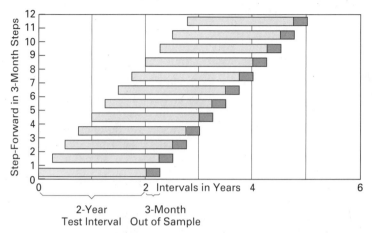

Figure 10-2. Step-forward testing. A process that follows a very appealing and strict testing approach, often jumps from fast to slow parameters because of the short test window. It may miss selecting slower, more conservative strategies.

Are You Testing the Same Data That You Will Trade?   Do not test one set of data, then trade another. Do not use a "continuation" series because either the gaps have been removed, or they cause windfall profits or losses that would not have happened in trading. A "perpetual" contract has prices that never existed and usually dampens any severe price move causing the risks to look smaller.

Did You Verify the Accuracy of the Data?   Data can be inaccurate even when prepared by a reliable vendor. Look for prices at the beginning or end of a contract that are completely different. Sometimes the data will have prices from another market that have not been erased, or an erroneous date one or two years earlier. Check for blank or zero entries. If you chart the data, you will easily see errors. The ones that are too small to see can be ignored.

Special Cases in Selecting Test Data.   It is not always possible to have enough data for testing. New markets or changing situations may render old data questionable. Or, you are looking to profit from a recent price pattern, without expectation of using the system for very long. The following sections offer some alternatives.

Selecting Similar Data Periods.   A stock that has dropped to a very low level can have a very different performance pattern from a period of high prices and high volatility. Selecting similar historic periods, such as those following a prolonged decline, or after a sell-off of 10%, may be the only way to model your strategy.

Using Cash Markets to Model Futures. Cash markets are often used to test a system that will be traded as a new futures contract; however, a new contract can be illiquid. A good model will account for similar situations in other new markets, adapting to the change between the cash and futures. Because there are many examples of changing markets, this should be a successful exercise.

Stock and Futures Markets under Special Situations. All markets go through severe changes: a corporate scandal or mismanagement, sudden new competition or government regulation; a price shock in coffee or orange juice due to a freeze. These special situations must be also studied separately, rather than absorbing them into the flow of everyday price movement. Market reaction to special situations is often similar because of the human response, rather than the fundamentals of a company or commodity. Similar cases can be found in other markets. When the special situation is a "price shock," a new set of rules can be used. This is discussed in Chapter 7.

Structural Changes and Not Enough Data. The European Monetary System (EMS) imposed a structure on participating currencies that had little precedent. A previous period, under the Bretton Woods agreement, may not provide enough similarity or adequate data for modeling a trading strategy. In this case, a fundamental analysis is the only course. Results based on small amounts of data are unreliable. A sound understanding of the fundamental interaction and the rules under which the new agreement operates may allow some confirmation by testing. To date, the EMS has proved to be unstable, therefore, a test of the 1 to 2 years of data would have led to poor results.

Creating More Data. For some markets, it is possible to create synthetic data. By studying volatility at different price levels, sequences of runs, variation in periodicity between highs and lows, and seasonality, it is possible to use random price generation to create data with the same statistical qualities as the one being evaluated. Synthetic data gives you the ability to test more situations and develop a more robust solution, but it is not the same as real data. It is best to use synthetic data first, before testing actual data.

Type of Data to Test. The data used for testing strategies should always be the same as the data to be traded. This is very straightforward for stocks, but becomes more difficult when you use foreign exchange or futures prices. The forex market will require adjustment for interest over the holding period, but the futures market presents the greatest problem. Although the nearest futures has the greatest liquidity, it may trade actively for as little as one month, and rarely more than three months. This frequent expiration makes testing inconvenient. The following sections will show how to fix this problem.

Original Data Series. For stocks, foreign exchange, interest rates, or other cash market data, a long series of original, unadjusted data is available for testing. When trading the cash market you will also need the spot interest rate to calculate a forward price. Treating the cash price as a valid entry and exit point omits the need to roll the position forward daily. Each rollover has an implied transaction cost that eats away at profits. Alternately, you can use spot prices for entry and exit, and calculate the net interest rate credit and debit when liquidating the position. Additional transaction costs must be included in testing each time the position is rolled over.

Futures Contracts. Original futures contract data can also be used for testing, without modification. Use the following steps:

1. Read the futures contract data.

2. Start the strategy calculations at the beginning of the series ("winding up the strategy"), or as soon as there is enough data.

3. Begin taking positions in the new contract on a specific date, or on the day that the previous contract stopped trading. If the previous contract had an open position when it was "rolled," then assume the same position on the same day in the new contract. Exceptions should be made for markets that do not have a high correlation between delivery months, such as livestock, or at critical seasonal periods such as the change for old to new crop for grains, or February-March in heating oil.

4. Exit any trade on a specific preset date before expiration. For interest rates, this is usually the last day of the month prior to delivery. For currencies, it is about 3 days before expiration.

This method is inconvenient because results are usually given by contract. For a 10-year test of interest rate futures, 40 separate sets of results must be accumulated. In addition, it is difficult to assess maximum drawdown unless you can treat the segments of data as a continuous equity stream.

Continuous Data Series for Futures. Many data vendors provide a constructed series that pieces together the nearest futures contract to create a new series (e.g., a 3-month price) calculated in a way that resembles the London Metal Exchange forward contracts. These choices are unacceptable for testing because they do not show the data that will be traded in a way that can duplicate a realistic trading environment. The constructed 3-month series, with interpolated carrying charges or interest, is frequently a smoothed version of prices that occurred at that time, reducing both the profit and risk.

Gap-Adjusted Series and Index Series. A *gap-adjusted* data series is a good alternative for most technical applications in futures. It puts the nearest-to-delivery segments together into a single price series by closing the gaps at the time one contract rolls into the next. By proceeding backward, the most recent futures or forward contact has today's prices, and the older contracts are adjusted up or down according to the gaps.

The gap-adjusted series works well for trend-following applications and strategies where the comparative price, rather than the actual price, is needed. It does not work for chart analysis, economic studies (supply/demand/price relationships), and similar uses. One problem with gap-adjusting, where older prices are changed, is that the very old data can take on negative or unrealistic values. Because the prices are not real, the rate of return and risk measurements must refer back to the actual prices, rather than base their values on the gap-adjusted series.

With one additional step—indexing—the gap-adjusted series becomes more useful. Indexing is simply starting with the value of 100 (or 1000, depending on convenience), then adding or subtracting successive values as a percentage change. For example,

index = index[1] + (price − price[1])/price[1]

Today's new index value, index, is yesterday's value, index[1], plus the percentage change in yesterday's price. The notation [1] means the 1-day prior value. The index price represents a percentage change and allows simple comparisons between returns of different markets. It eliminates the need to reference the original price data to calculate risk and returns.

Building a Gap-Adjusted Series. If you are working with futures contracts, a continuous series can be very useful. There are three steps to follow, (1) creating a continuous series with duplicate entries on the day of the rollover, (2) gap-adjusting the series, and (3) indexing. Figure 10-3 shows a flowchart of this process beginning with Step 2. Use the prices in Table 10-3 to follow the flowchart. For example, if the S&P 500 were being combined, *Step 1* causes the June 93 contract to stop on the last day of May, and the September 93 contract to start on that day. *Step 2* would gap-adjust the prices, working backward, whenever it identified a duplicate date. In Table 10-3 the June contract values are adjusted up by 12.00, equal to the roll-forward gap on May 31. *Step 3* would assign 100 to the first value, then calculate the percentage changes for each successive entry. *Note:* A clever analyst can eliminate Step 2 if an index is the only output.

Alternatives. The only remaining problem with gap-adjusting is that transaction costs cannot be posted at the time of the roll-forward, because that date can no longer be identified. It may be more difficult, but prefer-

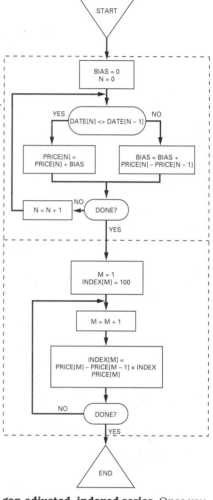

Step 2: Gap-Adjusting

1. Start at the most recent data entry and scan backward.
   Initialize BIAS, the accumulated size of the gap.
   Initialize price counter N.

2. If the prior date is not equal to current date, add BIAS and keep data, otherwise add the new gap to BIAS and skip this duplicate entry.

3. If done with data, then go to Step 3, otherwise increment N to look at next older data.

Step 3: Indexing

4. Start at oldest data, M
   Initialize index to 100.

5. Increment M to look at next sequential data item.

6. Calculate index value as the percentage change.

7. If not done, continue at (5).

Figure 10-3. Flowchart for continuous, gap-adjusted, indexed series. Once you have a continuous series built (Step 1) according to the form shown in Table 10-3, it becomes easy to scan backward and gap-adjust, the go forward to index.

able, to write program logic around the continuation file, which contains the duplicate dates and data. When a duplicate date is encountered, the old trade is closed out and the new trade entered.

Shock-Adjusted Series. A FORTRAN program for removing price shocks, then restoring the continuity of the data by indexing, can be found in Chapter 7. It is a similar program to the one in Figure 10-3 and gives coding details.

Table 10-3. Sample S&P Prices Combined before Gap-Adjusting

Contract	Date	Price	Gap-Adj Value	Index
JUN93	930528	451.50	463.50	100.000
JUN93	930529	449.25	461.25	99.502
JUN93	930530	446.50	458.50	99.388
JUN93	930531	448.00	no entry	99.225
SEP93	930531	460.00	460.00	no entry
SEP93	930601	462.50	462.50	100.005
SEP93	930604	460.75	460.75	99.622

S&P prices have been combined into a single series, and still show the original prices. A duplicate entry appears on May 31, which will be the date of the roll-forward where the gap is adjusted. The "Gap-Adj" and "Index" columns show the values after those steps have been completed.

Step 7. Have You Included Realistic Transaction Costs?

Transaction costs include brokerage and slippage. But other factors reduce performance.

Do You Expect Any Missed Trades? "Unables" have a great impact on results because they reduce only the profits and not the losses. If you over-trade the liquidity of the market, then unables become an important factor. Programs that trade intraday will face more problems than those that trade on the close. Part of a successful program is achieving actual trading results similar to expectations. A full discussion of slippage and unables can be found in Chapter 2.

Step 8. Will You Test a Full Range of Parameters?

Determine, *in advance,* the range of parameters that is sensible for this strategy. If you are trading stocks for an institutional portfolio, a moving average test range may be 50 to 400 days. Stop-losses must be equally large. However, do not prescan and remove very fast and slow ranges because they showed losses. That is the same as eliminating everything except the one set of parameters that was profitable. You cannot develop a robust model by looking at a narrow range that has been preselected to work.

Step 9. In What Order Will the Parameters Be Tested?

Test the most important variables first, the ones that cause the largest change in performance. That would be the number of days (the "period")

in a moving average, Relative Strength Index (RSI), or stochastic; the time of day or number of days in a breakout system; or, the deviation from the norm in a countertrend or arbitrage approach. These variables usually have the greatest effect on profits. Tests of other rules should follow, in order of most impact on profits or most frequently applied.

Testing the variables that are most important will speed up the test process. Rather than testing all combinations of all variables in one procedure, selecting the test range for one variable at a time can reduce the number of tests and the total time of the testing process.

In some cases, the most profitable combination of parameters occurs when the primary variable is "suboptimized." For example, profit-taking opportunities may be increased when the moving average is very fast, therefore you want high-momentum situations for very fast profit-taking objectives and a short holding time. If two features must work together, testing both the trending period and the profit-taking level simultaneously can work. It may also be that the profit-taking level is the most important variable, and the trending period is not as significant.

Step 10. Are the Parameters Distributed Properly?

Not only should the range of parameters be set in advance, but the distribution of those tests is important. Box 10-3 describes what needs to be done. This is a crucial step in preparing to see the whole test picture, which is essential for a robust system.

Because the final decision is based on the average of all tests, the distribution of parameters must not favor either the fast or slow strategies. They must be evenly distributed. When a moving average system is tested, it is generally thought that a test of 5, 10, 15, 20,... days is a reasonable choice. Equal increments, however, favor the very slowest trading.

Figure 10-4 shows how equal days have very unequal percentage changes from one test to the next. A change from a 5- to a 10-day moving average is a 100 percent change in the amount of data. A change from 10 to 15 is a 50 percent change, but a change from 95 to 100 is only a 5.2 percent shift. An equal distribution of days will skew the results toward the slower tests.

Visual Distribution.   It is not necessary to use mathematics to decide the distribution of parameters for testing. A very effective visual method can be best shown by the following example. If the fast end of the test shows 100 trades and the slow end has 10 trades, choose test periods so that 11 tests give results showing trades of 100, 90, 80,..., 20, 10. In reality, a perfect distribution is impossible, but the goal is clear. Try to find the parameters that cause the number of trades to be evenly distributed across the full range of tests.

Step 11. Have You Defined the Evaluation Criteria?

What do you measure to decide which system is better? To evaluate results, it is necessary to produce a minimum number of statistics for each test. Selecting the test with the highest profits may not be as important as finding the one with the best return/risk ratio. Decide in advance how you will select the best strategy. Most often, you need a combination of statistics, including reward/risk ratio, profits per trade, and risk-adjusted returns.

- *Return/risk ratio* is the compounded, annualized rate of return divided by one standard deviation of the annual equity changes. For practical purposes, monthly or daily values can be used for comparison testing as long as all tests are the same. This standard, set by the securities industry, allows a fast, uniform comparison of tests over different time intervals.

  Compounded annualized rate of return,
  $$CROR = (Ending\ value - Starting\ value)^{\wedge}(1/years)$$

  Standard deviation,
  $$SD = @STD(Monthly\ changes\ in\ equity)$$

  Return/risk ratio,
  $$RR = CROR/SD$$

Calculations should use returns on cash to see the raw performance before deciding on the potential use of leverage. The importance and use of these three statistics are discussed thoroughly in Chapter 4.

- *Profits per trade* show how much room you have for unexpected problems and allow you to see the impact of transaction costs. If two systems have the same percentage returns and similar equity swings, the one with the highest profits per trade is the better choice. If market volume drops when trading a new market, or when trading is at an illiquid time of day, the test showing the highest profits per trade can absorb more transaction costs. A system with less than $50 profit per trade is an unlikely candidate to succeed.

Box 10-3. DISTRIBUTION OF TRENDS FOR TESTING

The selection of which trend speeds to test will give a correct or distorted view of the potential of the system. If moving averages from 5 days to 100 days are tested, the total picture is skewed toward longer trends; that is, the results of trend periods from 55 to 100 days can be very similar, while those of 5 to 50 days may each show very different performance.

By viewing the percentage change in consecutive tests, it is evident that there should be fewer tests as the trend speed becomes longer. Table 10-4 shows (1) **Days**, equal test periods, in days, for an exponential moving average; (2) **%Change**, the percentage change in the length of the period; (3) **ExpSC**, the equivalent exponential smoothing constant; (4) **Equal**, an equal distribution of smoothing constants, calculated as

smoothing_constant = 2/(days + 1)

and (5) **Days**, the equivalent number of days corresponding to the smoothing constants in column (4). The averages are at the bottom of the columns.

Table 10-4 Distribution of Trends

(1) Days	(2) % Change	(3) ExpSC	(4) Equal	(5) Days
5.000		0.333	0.333	5.000
10.000	100.000	0.182	0.317	5.313
15.000	50.000	0.125	0.300	5.659
20.000	33.333	0.095	0.284	6.047
25.000	25.000	0.077	0.267	6.481
30.000	20.000	0.065	0.251	6.974
35.000	16.667	0.056	0.234	7.535
40.000	14.286	0.049	0.218	8.182
45.000	12.500	0.043	0.201	8.934
50.000	11.111	0.039	0.185	9.821
55.000	10.000	0.036	0.168	10.882
60.000	9.091	0.033	0.152	12.174
65.000	8.333	0.030	0.135	13.781
70.000	7.692	0.028	0.119	15.833
75.000	7.143	0.026	0.102	18.548
80.000	6.667	0.025	0.086	22.308
85.000	6.250	0.023	0.069	27.857
90.000	5.882	0.022	0.053	36.875
95.000	5.556	0.021	0.036	54.091
100.000	5.263	0.020	0.020	100.002
		Averages:		
52.500	17.739	0.066	0.177	19.115

Column (2) shows that the percentage change is very large when the period is short. The average change falls near the 35-day test, although the middle test is 50 to 55 days, indicating a large imbalance of longer-period tests in which the change is very small. Figure 10-4(a) also shows the large changes in the faster trends, rapidly leveling off to very small changes for most of the remaining tests.

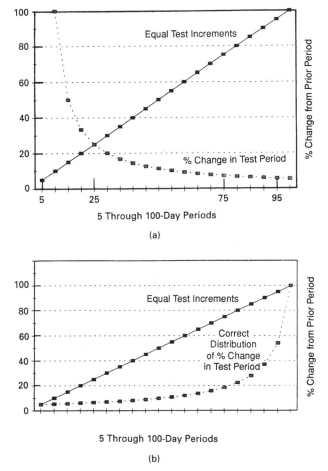

(a)

(b)

Figure 10-4. Trend distribution. (a) *Equal test periods.* Equal test period increments result in very different % changes. (b) *Equal smoothing constants.* Smoothing constants, which can be viewed as a percentage, show how the test periods, in days, are closer together for faster trends.

A series of tests in which the trend speeds change by an equal percentage gives a much better sample of overall performance than equally spaced periods. An exponential moving average is an easier choice
for accomplishing this because an equal spacing of smoothing constants is the same as an equal percentage change. Column (4) has an
equal distribution of smoothing constants, beginning and ending at the
same values as in column (3). Column (5) gives the number of days
approximately equal to the smoothing constants in column (4), converted using

days = (2/smoothing_constant) − 1

Figure 10-4(b) compares the pattern of the test periods in equal days
with the pattern of equal percentages necessary to achieve an even distribution of performance.

- *The number of trades* will show whether there are enough trades to
  have sound results. A rough idea of the accuracy is given by

sample error = 1/@SQRT(number of trades)

- *Maximum drawdown,* on a day-to-day basis measures the peak-to-
  valley decline in equity, and gives the minimum capital needed for
  trading. Although one test may have a smaller equity variation, measured by the standard deviation, the maximum drawdown can
  remain the same because both models were on the same side of a
  severe price shock. The model with the smaller standard deviation
  shows a more acceptable equity variation during normal markets,
  but both require the same investment from peak to valley. It is often
  used for a worst-case scenario. Unfortunately, it is rarely the worst
  case.

- *Risk-adjusted returns* is the most important performance measurement. It compares standardized returns at the same risk level.

- *Percentage of profitable trades* gives an indication of the consistency of
  performance. More frequent profits normally translate into less equity fluctuation. A very low percentage shows dependence on a few
  large price moves. Each type of system, trend-following or countertrend, has a recognizable profile. Trend-following systems should
  have from 35 percent to 45 percent profitable trades, while countertrend programs should exceed more than 60 percent successful
  trades. Variations from these patterns should be examined closely.

- *Time to recovery*, although similar to risk, gives a different interpretation. It measures the time between new equity highs. From a practical view, a larger equity drop but a very fast recovery may be preferable to a smaller decline with a slow recovery.

Step 12. How Will the
Output Be Presented?

If you only saw the most profitable result from a set of 500 historic tests of various parameter combinations, you would have no idea whether the strategy was robust. This chapter tries to stress that the combined performance of a wide range of parameters determines the level of confidence.

Within this total picture, patterns of performance can be used for making the final parameter selection. For example, positions held longer will normally have a higher profit per trade; other tests that limit risk may show a better return/risk ratio.

As the parameters that indicate trading frequency or risk control move from small to large values, performance should change in a continuous pattern. The presentation of test results can make the final parameter selection a much simpler task. Tests are commonly presented line by line, giving the results of the first moving average speed and the incremented stop-loss, similar to the presentation in Table 10-1. By changing the form to a two- or three-dimensional chart, the results become much more useful.

A Two-Dimensional Display.   A bar or line chart is a two-dimensional display. It can show net profits or profits per trade versus trend speed. In Figure 10-5, line a shows that the profits per trade are erratic for a very small stop-loss and trend speeds under 20 days. Results become more consistent above 20 days. The center gray zone holds the best trends. Line b shows the profits per trade from the same trends speeds with a slightly larger stop-loss. Results improve uniformly, but the original pattern remains the same.

The line chart in Figure 10-5 works for this example, but becomes unreadable when many lines are drawn for each stop-loss tested. Instead, a contour map (Figure 10-6(a)) shows the patterns clearly. In Figure 10-6(b), which holds the values plotted in the contour map, the trend speed is the left scale and the stop-loss is along the bottom. The fastest strategy, combining the shortest trend and smallest stop-loss, shows profits per trade of .07 percent in the upper left corner. The slowest strategy and the largest stop-loss give a much larger profit per trade of .22 percent in the lower right corner. Clustered in the center are the peak results.

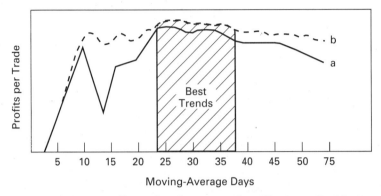

Figure 10-5. A two-dimensional presentation of test results. Moving average results (line *a*) are more erratic using a small stop-loss. A larger stop-loss (line *b*) improves results keeping the same overall pattern.

The white areas in Figure 10-6 have the largest profits per trade, while the black areas have the smallest. It is easy to distinguish that the strategy improves as it moves away from the upper left corner, but falls off near the center right side of the chart. If instead of these clear patterns, there were scattered peaks and valleys, the strategy would be erratic and risky. Other examples of contour maps can be found in the discussion of stops, Chapter 6.

Smoothing the Table and Chart.   In most cases, the contour map seems to be a smooth display of results. However, an isolated peak or valley may make it difficult to choose the best parameters using an automated selection method. The results in Figure 10-6(b) can be smoothed by creating a new table where each entry is the average of the nine boxes for which it is the center. Exceptions can be made for smoothing the entries on the sides using six boxes and the corners with four boxes. Figure 10-7 shows that in this new grid, the shaded box is the average of its surrounding group, including itself. This 2-dimensional smoothing will help parameter selection. For larger tests or more smoothing, blocks of 5 × 5 or 7 × 7 can be used.

PART 3: Evaluating the Results

Using Averages and Maps

The average minus the standard deviation gives the Best Choice Index, which is simply the chance of picking a trading model that will produce an average result. The contour map display can help locate broad areas

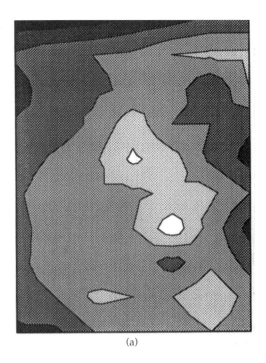

(a)

Fast	0.07	0.07	0.08	0.11	0.13	0.16	0.16
	0.16	0.19	0.20	0.21	0.25	0.26	0.26
	0.12	0.19	0.19	0.21	0.23	0.15	0.25
	0.16	0.17	0.21	0.28	0.20	0.20	0.16
	0.17	0.21	0.24	0.31	0.27	0.19	0.13
	0.19	0.24	0.24	0.24	0.26	0.26	0.20
	0.18	0.23	0.25	0.25	0.33	0.23	0.13
	0.18	0.24	0.21	0.23	0.18	0.24	0.18
	0.17	0.20	0.26	0.25	0.25	0.29	0.23
Slow	0.14	0.14	0.20	0.23	0.22	0.25	0.22

Trend Speed

Small   Stop-Loss   Large

(b)

Figure 10-6. Contour map of test results. (a) This contour map was produced by Mathsoft MATHCAD by importing the spreadsheet shown in chart b. The contour map of test results is similar to a topological map of a mountainous terrain. Areas where profitably jumps from high to low within a few tests resemble jagged, irregular formations. Robust systems and areas of stable performance tend to have larger, more gradual contour changes. (b) This chart shows the profits per trade of a trend system with a percentage stop-loss. The system buys when the trend turns up and sells when the trend turns down. A stop-loss is placed at the time of the original entry point and causes an exit when the trade shows an absolute loss greater than the stop-loss. Once the trade exits, it does not reenter the market until a new trend signal occurs.

Test grid

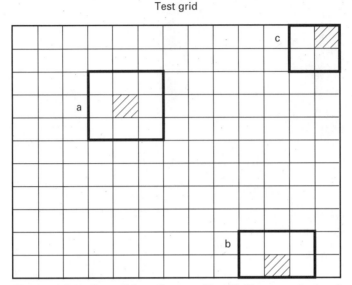

Figure 10-7. Smoothing the results of the raw tests. A smoothed test table and contour map makes parameter selection easier. Each original entry can be replaced by (a) the square of nine boxes, (b) the six boxes along the edge, and (c) the four corner boxes. The shaded box holds the new results.

of success and prevent the selection of a trading model that targets a profit per trade too small for practical use. If the overall picture is good, the strategy is profitable, and results are smooth over most of the map, the chance of choosing a successful model is also good. The following questions will help qualify the results.

Step 13. Are the Calculations Correct?

Before going further, step back and ask yourself whether you have checked all the calculations. Did you manually verify a few lines in the spreadsheet? Did you calculate, in advance, the exact entry and exit prices for a number of trades that used different rules? Do the answers look reasonable? Even the best analyst can make an error typing a formula. Do not waste time running hundreds of tests without verifying the results.

Step 14. Were There Enough Trades to Be "Significant?"

In Step 11, the sample error was given as sample error = 1/@SQRT(number of trades). Therefore, if there are only 16 trades, the error in the performance is ± 25 percent. It requires 400 trades to keep the error to 5 percent, considered the minimum acceptable size, but few systems produce that many trades. The only alternative is to be sure that the underlying premise is sound, and to produce as many sample trades as possible.

Step 15. Does the Trading System Produce Profits for Most Combinations of Parameters?

What are the chances that any selection will be profitable? Are the patterns continuous?

A robust system must be broadly successful. When you look at the test results, you should see mostly profits, and the Best Choice Index must be positive, giving an 84 percent chance of success. Use the average less 2 standard deviations to get the 97.5 percent level, and the average less 3 standard deviations to find the 99.5 percent level. The higher the probability, the more robust. The contour map display should show continuous patterns, as in Figure 10-6(a). Jagged peaks and valleys may be caused by specific rules that work in one test case but not others.

Step 16. Did Logic Changes Improve Overall Test Performance?

When a new rule or calculation is added to the program, the results are robust if they improve the Best Choice Index. This assures that the change in logic was not pointed toward a specific event, but was a general improvement. A higher Best Choice Index occurs when the average of all tests increases while the standard deviation does not increase, or the average remains the same while the standard deviation decreases. A smaller standard deviation indicates improved consistency and makes it easier to select successful parameters. These cases are shown in Figure 10-8.

Step 17. How Did It Perform on Out-of-Sample Data?

At least 10 percent of the test data should have been set aside. Even better, the 10 percent oldest and most recent data should not have been used for testing. Once the trading strategy has been finalized, test that data separately and compare the average of all tests against the average of the final tests of the longer set of historic data. Even in the best of cases, you can expect profits to be lower and risk higher; however, the pattern should be similar to the tested profile.

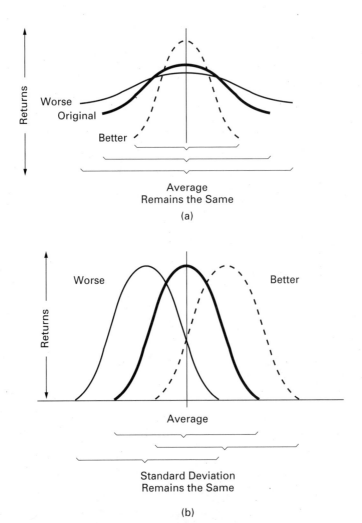

Average
Remains the Same

(a)

Average

Standard Deviation
Remains the Same

(b)

Figure 10-8. Selecting a robust system using the performance curve and Best Choice Index. (a) When the performance curve flattens and widens, the results get worse. The average returns remain the same, but the standard deviation gets larger causing the Best Choice Index to drop. (b) When the average shifts to the right or left, the overall performance gets better or worse, as long as the standard deviation remains the same.

Results of the out-of-sample test that are very different from the other tests must be reviewed carefully. Poor results indicate that the strategy is not working. The use of a chi-square test (see Chapter 11) will show whether this failure is part of the long-term performance profile or indicates that something is wrong. You may have an error in the rules or calculations, but that should have been corrected long before this point. Or, the test period might have been too short, resulting in unstable results.

Feedback Dilemma. Once you have used the out-of-sample data to verify the system, you can no longer use that data again. Inspecting the trades and adding rules may produce a valid improvement, but you have made it work in the "unseen" data; therefore, you have no way to check the results. You might include the new data and omit some other piece; however, the reliability of the results has dropped.

Part 4: Choosing the Specific Parameters to Trade

The final section of a trading model is a combination of profits, risk, and personal preference. A program that holds trades for weeks may produce the highest profits per trade but may not meet the investor's short-term objectives. Even though individuals may choose differently, the most robust systems offer the best platform from which to select. This section asks questions that are important, regardless of your specific goals.

Generally, selecting from models that hold positions longer gives more dependable results. It is also more difficult to assess the expected returns from faster trading models. Figure 10-9 shows the hypothetical results of a trend system, where the fastest trading model is posted at the left. Performance is erratic although a smoothed line can give a better idea of expectations. In actual trading, the 6-day trend may capture the next big profit, while the 4- and 8-day trends post losses.

A comparison of fast and slow strategies shows that:

- Faster trading is more sensitive to current market patterns.

- Faster trading gives up a large percentage of profits and losses to transaction costs.

- Faster trading may have the same large losses due to price shocks, but these losses will be a much larger than typical profits and losses.

Regardless of the trading strategy, taking the long-term view is the more conservative, reliable approach. Although the long-term strategy may have larger absolute losses, it often has a better return/risk ratio than faster programs. This does not mean that you cannot have a system that works well trading fast. The performance must be high when you draw the smooth line through the irregular results. You must also expect real returns to be erratic. Tests plotted in Figure 10-9 show that results can vary significantly from expectations, especially with fast-trading methods. You should expect real returns to vary even more than the tests show.

Step 18. Did the Last Test Include the Most Recent Data?

Having reserved some data for out-of-sample testing (see Step 17), the program should be retested using all data. This is particularly important if the out-of-sample data is the most recent. Once the model is operational, retesting should be performed whenever 5 to 10 percent new data is available, or unique market patterns occur. The model may be adjusted by a small amount, but it will become ever so slightly more robust.

Step 19. Did You Choose from an Area of Broad Success?

Was it the slow selection?
   The contour map shows whether the performance of the strategy has a smooth or irregular pattern with respect to parameter changes. The areas of broad success show stability and are often associated with slower trading models.
   A choice of a faster strategy must be justified by a larger profit per trade and reasonably high reliability to compensate for inherent uncertainty. The worst-performance case in the neighborhood of the selection should still be acceptable. Figure 10-9 shows that erratic results associated with short-term trading should be considered as smoothed when selecting from this region.

Step 20. Are Profits Distributed Evenly over the Tested History?

Study the trades and equity of the final model to see whether profits and losses alternate in a reasonable pattern. A standard deviation of the equity changes, time to recovery, and other statistical measures give the

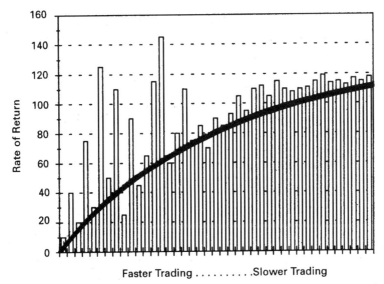

Faster Trading . . . . .Slower Trading

Figure 10-9. The typical results of a trend-following strategy opti-mization. By selecting the peak profits, or return/risk ratio, results often favor isolated returns of short-term trends. The chance of repeating this performance in actual trading is very slim. The smoothed line is the most likely return.

relative merits of one test against another, but only a visual study is good enough before you begin trading. It may be helpful to look at quarterly results to see consistency.

Step 21. Are the Profits per Trade Large Enough to Absorb Errors?

When two tests have similar risks and returns, the best choice is the one with the largest profits per trade. Larger profits absorb unexpected problems (e.g., slippage in a fast market) that result in lost profits when an order cannot be executed. Establish a minimum acceptable profit per trade.

Step 22. Did the Historic Results Show Any Large Losses due to Price Shocks?

Price shocks are unpredictable events. Your program should have an equal number of losses as it has profits due to price shocks, although some may be controlled by a stop-loss. Check the obvious past price shocks against the system trades. If the system profited from all of them, or avoided the losses, the results are overfitted or just lucky. You cannot expect the program to profit from unpredictable events in the future. The danger of trading a system which has not shown losses from price shocks is that the risk is unreasonably small. This leads to greater leverage and large losses.

Step 23. Have You Risk-Adjusted the Returns to Your Acceptable Risk Level?

The return/risk ratio turns absolute performance into relative returns and allows the fair comparison of each model. Traders however must establish their own acceptable risk level. Decide, for example, that you are willing to take a 1 percent chance of losing more than 10 percent during any month. Then the system you trade must show a risk (measured as 1 standard deviation of the monthly equity changes) of less than $3\frac{1}{3}$ percent. Three standard deviations will be 10 percent. Remember that equity changes based on monthly data are already smoothed. You can expect larger mid-month equity fluctuations, sometimes as much as 50 percent greater.

Part 5: Trading and Monitoring Performance

No amount of testing can substitute for trading. As soon as the first position is set, you may realize that the transaction costs used in testing were too low, you cannot execute the full position in the cash market after the New York close, or that a breakout signal produced liquidity gaps. Monitoring the system signals against actual trading provides information that will continue to improve the testing process.

Step 24. Are You Following the Same Rules That Were Tested?

Real trading results often vary from test results because the rules used in testing are not followed. The size of the transaction costs or the liquidity of the market may also prevent you from executing the full position. Most often, it is the execution technique. By waiting until *after* the computer has given a trading signal, the trade price and the theoretical computer signal are far apart. This is solved by anticipating the computer signal. To be a successful system trader, you must execute at the same time the system is executing. Chapter 11 shows how to anticipate a computer signal.

Step 25. Are You Trading the Same Data That Was Tested?

Although it is convenient to test a strategy using a continuation or "perpetual" contract, the results will not be the same when you trade cash or futures contracts. Be sure that you are trading the same market that was tested, and that you tested the same market you are trading.

Step 26. Are You Monitoring the Difference between the System and Actual Entries and Exits?

Understanding how to test a strategy comes from identifying why testing and actual trading results are different. Monitor the theoretical signals, real executions, and the percentage of trades that cannot be executed, then retest the strategy with these improved values. In time, you will be able to show very realistic test results.

Other Important Practical Guidelines

Even the most careful, responsible testing cannot show how the system will perform when it is traded. From the preceding guidelines, experience shows how the following points should be highlighted:

- Slower systems, those using longer periods of evaluation, perform closer to expectations than faster models.
- Avoid systems that do not show downside risk. Absence of risk is an indication of overfitting or a coincidental good fortune that is not likely to be repeated in trading.
- View test results as a smoothed line. In a robust system, expect peak results to be lower, and poor performers better, both moving toward the average when traded.
- Avoid systems with low reliability. They may indicate dependence on a few exceptional trades, rather than steady performance.
- Avoid systems that have only a few trades. They may not yet show an accurate picture of results.

More Data Give
More Predictable Results

It is worth repeating the importance of using more data, rather than less data, for testing. More data contain more price patterns, sustained moves, and price shocks. Many people argue that old data lack relevance—markets have changed. In specific cases, and for some applications, that is true. It is safer to assume that there is more danger than benefit in using small amounts of data.

A system tested over the past 3 years will not see the largest price shocks of the recent 10 years. Yet you must expect that even larger shocks will come. If you capitalize an investment according to recent risk, you will not survive for long. The greatest failure in trading is undercapitalization, and this is the direct result of unrealistic expectations of risk. If recent data are best for maximizing profits, more data are best for risk evaluation.

It is possible to test a strategy twice, once for parameter selection and once for risk. Because tests of more years of data show lower profits and higher risk, they are not viewed as desirable. It is much more pleasing to choose from the high returns and low risk of shorter test intervals. But the reality is that the longer tests are more representative of real trading results. Choosing to ignore these results does not produce greater profits.

Start by Knowing the Answer

The best use of computer testing is to verify a theory. If your idea is good, then testing various time intervals, entry and exit criteria, and risk management parameters should show reasonably consistent returns. It may show that your theory is good for short-term patterns, but not for the longer view; however, it should verify your idea. A concept based on an understanding of the market—whether economic, statistical, or price patterns—is a valid, valuable basis for a system and the best way to begin the development of a trading program. Feeding a test package a multitude of indicators, rules, and prices series, and letting it crunch away until it combines them into a profitable result, has a very low chance of being a successful trading system.

Errors of Omission

"Survivor bias" and the failure to apply a worst-case scenario are two problems classified as *errors of omission*. Omissions constitute an unseen trap for analysts. It is far easier to account for odd patterns and price shocks than to consider situations that do not appear in the data.

Survivor Bias. The selection of certain stocks, funds, and investment managers for testing unconsciously omits the worst cases—those where the company or manager went out of business. A classic case of survivor bias is in the review of investment managers. The one who generates the highest profits may have the highest risk. If you review only those managers currently reporting, you do not find out that all managers with comparably high risk were previously forced out of business by losses. These comparisons result in unrealistically low risk.

Similarly, the selection of specific stock issues means that those firms have not seen the patterns that precede failure. Even the largest firms are no longer as secure as we once thought. Drexel Burnham, E.F. Hutton, Stotler, and the Pennsylvania Railroad (also the Penn-Central, with the most assets of any company in the United States) proved that mismanagement and litigation can ruin even the biggest. IBM, the auto giants, and insurance companies no longer look inviolate. It is difficult to assess risk properly if you only study the winners.

Worst-Case Scenarios. More difficult, yet just as important, is the ability to conceive "worst-case scenarios." What might cause a market to go to new high prices, fall to new lows, or become twice as volatile as the worst period in history? If this happens, what steps do you take to stabilize risk? Or, do you remove those markets from your portfolio? Will the trading strategy perform properly if prices move to levels not seen in historic data? Will previously uncorrelated markets move together?

These scenarios are critical to risk control. Often, there are no immediate answers to these hypothetical cases, but only a general confidence that the current strategy has the flexibility to adapt to market change. That is not always enough. A sharp drop in one market can force a need for capital, causing investors to liquidate unrelated assets to finance the losing ones. This results in a broad reversal in many investment areas.

Data Integrity

The assumption that a historic data series is correct can result in a tremendous loss of time. All data should be scanned for gross errors before being used. Data received electronically or on disk from a reliable vendor may still have problems. Testing and evaluating a system takes time. To find a data error after weeks of work means that all the testing must be done again. A few fast steps can avoid that aggravation and cost.

1. Look at a price chart of all the data to be used. Any serious data problem will be obvious.

2. If you have strategy-testing software, identify opening, high, low, or closing prices that were greater than 3 percent from the previous price. Look at those days one at a time. Many of them will be errors.

3. When the final model has been selected, look at the profits and losses of each trade. Be critical of the largest profits and losses; verify that the entry and exit prices are reasonable.

Patching the Problems

Trading strategies succeed by generalization. Most plans are profitable because they grind out larger profits than losses. The problem with a general or statistical solution is that it is blind to specific cases, but the trader is well aware of the reasons for big price moves.

Each major move and price shock can be explained. By carefully studying the cause and patterns of larger trading losses, indicators and rules can be combined to control the losses, leaving a more profitable performance profile. But the next big move is always different. They can be explained in retrospect, but rarely fit a prescribed pattern. Explaining each loss has intellectual satisfaction but falls short of reducing trading risk. Fixing each case based on its own features is still "overfitting."

Do Not Oversolve the Problem

A young analyst, trying to do his best, produces an answer to four decimal places, when each of the inputs had only two places of accuracy. You cannot create more accuracy than you have. Technical models, based on either price patterns or statistics, do not depend on one price move or a single trade. They succeed over a large number of events. Fine-tuning a moving average can be counterproductive because it moves away from the general solution. A specific trend speed that avoided a large loss has no way of avoiding similar losses in the future. Oversolving or overtesting produces unrealistic expectations of system performance.

Accuracy and Test Time.   For most system tests, there is a direct relationship between accuracy and calculation time. The more time it takes, the better the result. Is it better to test exponential smoothing constants in steps of .1, .01, or .001? There can be 10, 100, or 1000 tests in the range .1 to .9, based on the test increment. But 1000 tests is wasted accuracy, just as testing stop-losses in $5 total investment increments is naive.

Is it important if the one that was not tested showed twice the profit of the two adjacent tests? If you are still trying to find peak profits rather than the best system or contour, then you are wasting your time. Trends are intended to smooth data. Fine-tuning a trend seems inconsistent with the concept of smoothing. If you select a 154-day moving average because a large loss was averted, while a 153-day average was caught, you have a basic misunderstanding about the implied accuracy of a system.

New powerful computers with increased speed have made it painless to run large, meaningless tests. When computers were slower or resources limited, it was necessary to reason out the benefits of each hour spent on the machine. The "broad-brush" approach may still be the most efficient use of time and a way to prevent overfitting.

Summary

The method of finding a trading strategy can increase or decrease your chance for success. Using sound procedures and statistical methods is safe and conservative. This includes long data series that encompass as many unique situations as possible. In addition, global statistics, which average all the tests, are an excellent measure of a robust system and prevent the temptation to seek high-profit simulations. When using averages, it is clear which strategies and new techniques are best.

11

Improving the Performance of Existing Systems

After the completion of tests, measuring and monitoring performance continues the process that results in a successful trading program. A careful comparison of actual results with expectations shows how well the testing was performed. Because there can be a tremendous gap between testing and trading, it should not be surprising that results are different. To be successful, however, they cannot be so divergent that expected profits are turned into real losses. It will be necessary to trade a system to know whether the testing assumptions were realistic. After that, it is necessary to figure out how to improve the program while maintaining its integrity. The following sections discuss some of these improvements.

Measuring and Monitoring Predictability

The most important part of performance monitoring is to discover whether you have correctly measured the risk of loss, and to find out as soon as possible. There are many ways to proceed when there are trading profits, but only one choice when losses are larger than expected. Monitoring actual results gives the only accurate assessment of expectations. Before that, we can only estimate. Burdening tests with slippage and other costs that are too big will make good strategies look bad and increase the time and effort needed to find a good trading method. On the other hand, expecting larger costs is safer than underestimating them.

What Do You Monitor?

We always monitor trading to find the difference between *expected* and *actual* results. Expected performance comes from testing; actual results come from trading. Actual results are not accurate if they reflect the trading of a small position when the intention is to trade a large one.

Deltas. The difference between an expected and an actual value will be called a *delta* (shown as the symbol Δ). There can be execution deltas to compare fill prices, and total performance deltas, as follows:

- Record the difference between the program's estimated trade price and the actual average execution price. Separate the entry and exit values, because there is often more finessing of entries:

  long entry Δ = (system entry − actual entry)

  short entry Δ = (actual entry − system entry)

  long exit Δ = (actual exit − system exit)

  short exit Δ = (system exit − actual exit)

- Record the system profits and losses from those trades not filled at all (unables).
- Calculate the total unit profit and loss for the system and actual trades:

  total unit Δ = (total actual P/L − total system P/L)/number of contracts traded

Although the most important value is the unit difference between the system's expected profit or loss and the actual results, the breakdown of those values provides information to help improve executions. The unit difference should be used to estimate future results, if nothing changes, and to use realistic transaction costs in testing. The other values are all evident. Chapter 2 discussed the impact of *unables* (those orders not filled) on profitability and showed that unables reduce profits but not losses, increasing the diffculty of trading a program successfully.

Liquidity

Execution problems can sometimes be caused by the type of order used to implement the trading system, but they are all related to market liquidity. If your order is too big for the market at the moment it hits, then the execution is bad. It may be necessary to average in over a few hours, or shift the orders closer to the opening or closing of the trading session. *Limit* orders may need to be replaced by *market* orders spaced over a longer period. One thing is certain: If you do not execute each order given by the trading program, you cannot expect to achieve its results.

Feedback

Monitoring performance is the only way to find the real cost of trading. It is valuable information and can be used for testing other systems. Although different types of orders have their own peculiar costs, all of them have some slippage, and all of them have unables. It is most important that we know what they are.

Chi-Square Test

In the spirit of simplicity, it does not require high-powered mathematics to know that your trading is not going as planned. A loss that is larger than any historic one, or a series of losses longer than any before, is sure to get your attention. But not all situations are clear until they become a problem. The *chi-square* test is a simple way to compare historic (expected) and trading (actual) results to find out whether something is wrong.

For example, your new system has had 20 trades and only 4 were profitable, but historic testing showed that 40 percent of the trades should be profitable. What are the chances that something is wrong? Use the chi-square test:

chi-square = @SUM ((actual−expected)^2/expected)

The test is the sum of the percentage difference in the actual versus expected results. When the two numbers are very close, the chi-square value is small. To find out whether a chi-square value is large enough to indicate a problem, Table 11-1 must be used.

If you want to compare the frequency of profits, the expected profit frequency and the expected loss frequency are both used because the chi-square test requires a minimum of two cases:

Table 11-1. Distribution of Chi-Square

Cases	Probability of Occurring by Chance								
Less 1	.70	.50	.30	.20	.10	.05	.02	.01	.001
1	.15	.46	1.07	1.64	2.71	3.84	5.41	6.64	10.83
2	.71	1.39	2.41	3.22	4.61	5.99	7.82	9.21	13.82
3	1.42	2.37	3.67	4.64	6.25	7.82	9.84	11.34	16.27
4	2.20	3.36	4.88	5.99	7.78	9.49	11.67	13.28	18.47
5	3.00	4.35	6.06	7.29	9.24	11.07	13.39	15.09	20.52
6	3.83	5.35	7.23	8.56	10.65	12.59	15.03	16.81	22.46
7	4.67	6.35	8.38	9.80	12.02	14.07	16.62	18.48	24.32
8	5.53	7.34	9.52	11.03	13.36	15.51	18.17	20.09	26.13
9	6.39	8.34	10.66	12.24	14.68	16.92	19.68	21.67	27.88
10	7.27	9.34	11.78	13.44	15.99	18.31	21.16	23.21	29.59

$$\text{chi-square} = \frac{(\text{actual profit freq} - \text{expected profit freq})^2}{\text{expected profit freq}}$$

$$+ \frac{(\text{actual loss freq} - \text{expected loss freq})^2}{\text{expected loss frequency}}$$

where actual is the real trading performance and expected is the tested result. The expected profit frequency and expected loss frequency must total 100 percent:

$$\text{chi-square} = \frac{(20 - 40)^2}{40} + \frac{(80 - 60)^2}{60} = 16.67$$

Referring to Table 11-1, we compare the results of 16.67 with the first line because there are two cases. We see that 16.67 is greater than the value associated with .001 and is considered highly significant. Therefore, there is something wrong with the system if it shows a 20 percent trading reliability. But we have not yet considered the number of trades. Based on 20 trades, the sample error would be 1/@sqrt(20) = .22, or 22 percent. Then the value of 16.67 could fall to 13.00, still above 10.83. Certain levels are considered important for the chi-square test:

chi-square ≥ .001 probability, then it is *highly significant.*

chi-square ≥ .01 probability, then it is *significant.*

chi-square ≥ .05 probability, then it is *probably significant.*

The chi-square test can show whether the actual pattern of price runs (the number of sequences of moves in the same direction) compares

Table 11-2. Chi-Square Evaluation of Price Runs

Length of Run	Expected Results (E)	Actual Results (A)	$\frac{(E - A)^2}{E}$	Chi-Square	Probability
1	1225	1214	.09877	.09877	n/a
2	612	620	.10457	.20334	>.50
3	306	311	.08169	.28503	>.70
4	153	167	1.2810	1.56603	>.50
5	77	67	1.2987	2.86473	>.50
6	38	41	.23684	3.10157	>.50
7	19	16	.47368	3.57524	>.70
8	10	5	1.8947	5.46994	>.70

with a random distribution. Table 11-2 gives the columns of a spreadsheet and the total of the column $(E - A)^2/E$ is the value of chi-square.

For eight cases, Table 11-1 places the chi-square value at a level indicating more than a 50 percent chance of the pattern of runs being random. As more cases are included, the statistic shows that the comparison gets closer.

Anticipation

Theoretical profits can only be realized with anticipation. Chapter 2 tried to point out that screen lag, slippage, and unables could easily change a theoretically sound trading strategy into a losing venture. One solution offered was to target profits per trade that are large enough to absorb the loss. Another way is to anticipate the trading signal. Be prepared to execute an order *at the exact time* the technical system gets its signal, rather than waiting until you get a confirmation. Even better, execute the order *just ahead* of the computer.

To show the importance of anticipating signals, consider a moving average system using the closing prices. The system buys when the trendline turns up, and sells when the trendline turns down. Figure 11-1 and Table 11-3 compare performance of a selection of moving average speeds for entries taken on the *same* day as the moving average calculation with executions on the close of the *next* day. Three very different markets were tested, the Hong Kong Hang Seng Index, the Deutsche mark, and IBM. The trend speeds covered a reasonably broad range of 5 to 75 days.

The results form a clear pattern. Faster trends lose from 50 to 400 percent of their profits when entries are delayed for one day. Slow trends

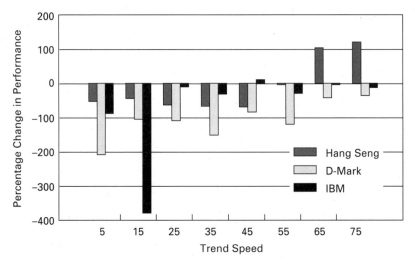

Figure 11-1. Comparison of 1-day lag performance. The three very different markets show similar results from a 1-day entry lag of a trend system. Fast trends have much worse performance while slow trends are not affected.

Table 11-3. Comparison of Same Day and
1-Day Lag Performance

Moving Average Days	Hang Seng			Deutsche Mark			IBM		
	Same Day	Next Day	Percent Change	Same Day	Next Day	Percent Change	Same Day	Next Day	Percent Change
5	106.8	55.2	(48.3)	10.0	(10.7)	(206.8)	38.7	4.9	(87.4)
15	82.7	44.1	(46.6)	23.0	(1.2)	(105.3)	8.7	(25.1)	(387.1)
25	55.9	22.3	(60.0)	35.9	(3.6)	(110.0	9.7	8.6	(11.5)
35	43.4	12.2	(71.8)	21.3	(13.0)	(160.9)	15.0	9.2	(38.6)
45	37.8	7.9	(79.1)	38.3	3.2	(91.8)	18.5	19.9	7.5
55	18.6	18.6	0.2	32.1	(10.3)	(132.2)	24.9	14.5	(42.0)
65	10.2	19.3	90.3	21.6	9.6	(55.7)	24.0	22.8	(5.1)
75	16.3	33.1	102.9	16.3	7.3	(55.0)	38.4	32.7	(14.8)

are not affected. This shows that timing is critical for the 5-day moving average and that the first day holds the largest profits: Hang Seng profits dropped 48 percent, the Deutsche mark fell from a 10 percent profit to a 10 percent loss, and IBM lost 87 percent. Longer trends are not as dependent on a specific entry price, and while the first day may be profitable, it is not a large percentage of the total profit. The profits shown in the 75-day Hang Seng due to the delay should not be expected. It is most likely that it is simply a distortion due to fewer trades.

It seems reasonable that any short-term trading that depends on momentum, or a burst of price movement, to generate a buy or sell signal, will be hurt by a delayed entry. By knowing the price, in advance, at which a trading system will get a new signal, it is possible to eliminate a number of problems. The most important is the ability to execute at the system price, not afterward. Small orders could be placed as stops or resting orders.

The need for better executions with faster trading implies that the bulk of the profits occur early in the trade. This supports the earlier discussion of profit-taking, which argues that holding a trade until the trend reverses causes the return/risk ratio to drop. The amount of profit compared with the risk gets worse as you hold the trade longer.

Windowing Large Orders

Large orders can be executed by creating a *window* around the system calculation time, and entering orders throughout that window. For example, a forex trader has a momentum program based on hourly data. Once the 11:00 calculation has passed, he knows that a new buy signal will occur if prices are above 156.50 at 12:00. Because his experience has shown that an order of 25 million $/sterling should only take 11 minutes to fill at that time of day, he starts buying at 11:55 if the price is safely above 156.50 at that time. If the executions take 10 minutes, the average price should be close to the price at 12:00, when the computer calculates its signal and posts an entry price.

As the hour nears when the system signals are calculated, it usually becomes clear whether or not the order should be placed. Sometimes, prices are right at, or just below the (buy) signal price and you are not certain whether the order should be placed. If you start buying and push prices higher, then you force the system signal yourself. Yet waiting until after 12:00 might mean getting a much worse fill.

The fact that anticipation greatly improves returns tips the balance in favor of executing marginal cases. You begin filling the order slowly, watching for the 12:00 price. If it gives a signal, you finish filling the order; if not, you reverse the position as quickly as possible. Exiting a "false anticipation" is less costly over the long run than waiting until after the signal to begin executing the order.

A false anticipation can occur at any time. Prices can seem safely above a buy signal level, then plummet in the 60 seconds before 12:00, even while you are buying. Once the 12:00 price is fixed, you know whether to continue or reverse the positions that have been set.

Calculating the Anticipated Price

Finding the signal price in advance is straightforward, but it requires some algebra. You write the formula for the moving average, Relative Strength Index (RSI), or other indicators based on the next period price (e.g., tomorrow for daily data), then solve for the next price. For example, a 5-day moving average for today is:

```
@moving_average(price,5)
    = (price + price[1] + price[2] + price[3] + price[4])/5
```

Using the function @sum(price,days), which sums the previous n days of price, we could shorten this to:

```
@moving_average(price,5) = @sum(price,5)/5
```

where price is the last price, price[1] is the prior price, and so forth. Using real numbers, we get:

```
@moving_average(price,5) =
    (154.50 + 153.20 + 153.60 + 152.70 + 152.50)/5
    = 153.30
```

What price is needed for tomorrow's close so that the moving average turns down by .10? The new value of the 5-day moving average @moving_average would need to be equal to 153.20. By moving the calculation forward one day, we can find today's value using simple algebra:

```
@buy_signal = 153.20 = (next_price + @sum(price,4 ))/5
    then next_price = 153.20*5 - @sum(price,4)
```

which solves for next_price by multiplying both sides by 5 and subtracting the sum of the four known values from both sides. The values @sum(price,4) are the most recent four prices. Using the sample prices gives:

```
766.00 = next_price + 154.50 + 153.20 + 153.60 + 152.70

152.00 = next_price
```

Therefore, the moving average turns down by .10 if the price of the sterling closes at 152.00 or lower. Box 11-1 gives a few common formulas and the calculations for anticipating the next price.

Quote Equipment with Programmed Studies

Complicated calculations are not necessary if you use one of the many pieces of quote equipment with preprogrammed studies. *TeleTrac, TradeStation, MarketView, CQG,* and many others already calculate moving averages, stochastics, and other indicators in a way that allows you to change the number of periods in the calculation. The last price is automatically used to find the next value, therefore the machine is constantly telling you whether you *will* get a signal at the next 15-minute, hour, or daily interval. Institutions that plan to customize the process will find the formulas in Box 11-1 to be helpful.

Filtering System Signals

Trading risk increases with high prices and high volatility. Because there are so many unique strategies and time frames, the "high" level associated with risk that is "too high" is likely to be different for each one. One approach to controlling risk is to use a protective stop; however, the market can jump through your risk level at exactly the time you need that safety the most. Financial stops based on personal risk preferences have been discussed as ineffective protection. And, while logical stops (based on significant support and resistance levels, or outside factors such as economic indicators) may reduce day-to-day risk, they cannot protect the loss due to a price shock. Whether you intend to hold a trade for an hour, a day, or a year, a price shock will produce the same loss if you are unlucky enough to be in the wrong position.

Filtering Price Levels

Often, a pattern of trading performance is associated with entering a market at a significantly high or low price. And, while the term "low" is reasonably clear, "high" is not obvious. Physical products can be considered low at levels equal to the lowest prices seen during the past 10 years, or at the cost of production. Controlled markets, such as crude oil, may have a different pattern.

Both low and high price levels vary with inflation and structural change. Again, low prices do not present a difficult problem. If you were trading a long-term moving average for copper, and prices dipped below 50 cents per pound, there would be limited opportunity for profits by going short. Yet a short position at 45 cents would have nearly the

---

Box 11-1. CALCULATIONS FOR
ANTICIPATING SIGNALS

Notation used:

price	"today's" price
price[1]	the previous price
price[n]	the price n-days ago
next_price	"tomorrow's" price, or the next period price
min_move	the minimum rise or fall from the previous indicator value needed to give a signal
uy_signal	the price that would generate a new *buy* signal
sell_signal	the price that would generate a new *sell* signal

Moving Average

@moving_average(price,n) = @sum(price,n)/n

where n is the number of periods.

The next price needed to generate a new buy or sell signal, where the moving average value rises or falls by the min_move:

buy_signal = price[n] + n*min_move

sell_signal = price[n] − n*min_move

Box 11-1. (*Continued*)

For a spreadsheet (in typical row 75), and a 10-day moving average, this becomes

Column A:	Date	
Column B:	Price	
Column C:	@Sum(B75..B66)	Sum of past 10 days
Column D:	+C75/10	10-day moving average
Column E:	@Sum(B75..B67)	Sum of past 9 days (MA less 1)
Column F:	+D75 + 1	Buy signal is minimum upmove for moving average
Column G:	+D75 − 1	Sell signal is minimum downmove for moving average
Column H:	+F75*10 − E75	Lowest price to give a buy signal
Column I:	+F75*10 − G75	Highest price to give a sell signal

Exponential Smoothing

$$@exp\_ma(price, sc) = ema = ema[1] + sc \times (price - ema[1])$$

where sc = the smoothing constant expressed as a percentage

ema = the value of the trendline

The next price needed to generate a new buy or sell signal is:

$$@buy\_signal = ema + min\_move/sc$$

$$@sell\_signal = ema - min\_move/sc$$

Momentum (Price Difference)

$$@momentum(price, n) = price - price[n]$$

The next price needed to generate a new buy or sell signal is:

$$@buy\_signal = price - price[n] + price[n - 1] + min\_ move$$

$$@sell\_signal = price - price[n] + price[n - 1] - min\_move$$

same risk as a short entered at 60 cents. As prices reach absolute lows, the profit potential for short positions decreases faster than the risk.

High prices are different. The tail of the price distribution is very long on the upside, which means that prices can move up to surprisingly high levels. Even adjusted for inflation and other economic factors, it is difficult to tell where a new long position has greater risk than reward. To make it more complex, some programs perform better when prices and volatility are high.

A scatter diagram, as shown in Figure 11-2, can be used to find an entry price for a crude oil trend-following system. It plots the entry price level against the resulting profit/loss. The trades have been separated so that Figure 11-2(a) has only the long positions and (b), only the shorts. Oil is an interesting example because OPEC tried to hold the official selling price at a fixed level, about $20/bbl during this period. Other markets have their own patterns, equally as interesting.

Trend Longs.   Crude oil gives a clear example of the risks associated with entering at a relatively high price. Long positions (see Figure 11-2(a)) generate many small profits and losses, and a few larger profits, below entry levels of $25/bbl. Most losses are clustered together and are less than $4/bbl, while profits net as much as $12/bbl. Frequent small losses and a few large profits comprise a profile typical of a trend-following system. At entry prices above $25/bbl, there are only losses, and those losses have a pattern of getting larger as the entry price increases.

The total picture seems very understandable. There is less opportunity and more volatility when long positions are entered at very high levels. Of course, without a diagram such as this, it would be difficult to know what was "high." Because we know that OPEC targeted an official selling price of about $20/bbl. during this test period, other patterns can be seen. For example, profits dropped as the entry price neared $20. Larger profits were made when oil prices dropped well below the OGSP (Official Government Selling Price). Unfortunately, this analysis benefits from hindsight. If OPEC's target price had dropped to $18/bbl, we could have expected a decline in profits for long positions entered near that level. We could have reasonably expected the same performance pattern, centered around a new level. Had we chosen a longer test period, including oil prices that were stable at $30/bbl, the pattern would not have been nearly as clear because it would have included more than one target area.

Trend Shorts.   We would expect to have more opportunities for profit by setting new short positions at high prices. Figure 11-2(b) shows that one

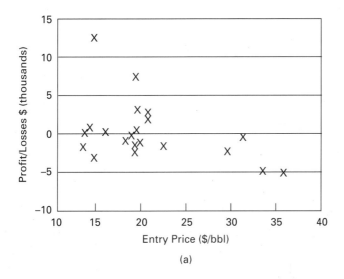

(a)

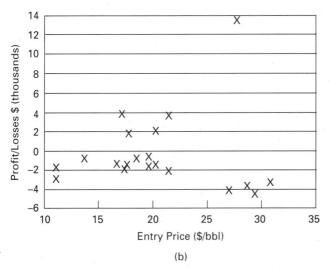

(b)

Figure 11-2. WTI (NYMEX) trend system entry price level versus profit/loss. (a) *Long positions.* (b) *Short positions.* Plotting the entry price against the resulting profits or losses gives you an opportunity to identify, in advance, the trades that should not be taken. For a trend-following system applied to WTI during the period when OPEC's target price was about $20/bbl, we see in (a) that long positions entered above $25/bbl consistently lost. With OPEC's ability to increase supply with relatively short lead time, any immediate imbalance in supply and demand could be corrected quickly. Trend profits had no time to develop. The short positions in (b) showed losses when entered under $15/bbl and higher risk over $25.

trade produced a profit just under $14,000 on a 1,000-bbl contract, and four other short positions, entered above $25, posted larger than average losses. As expected, shorts entered below $15/bbl, a relatively low level, also produced losses. The pattern shows that volatility, for both profits and losses, increases as the price increases.

Price Level, Profits, and Risk.   Unadjusted price levels, plotted against profitability, paint an understandable picture. Neither inflation nor price evolution can alter the fact that entering new shorts at low levels has little opportunity and unattractive risk. Buying at high prices is never as clear, but experience indicates that the risk of a large loss is much greater than the opportunity for any profit. Market factors should prompt periodic reevaluation of those levels, but only a simple analysis is needed to see the obvious benefits.

Filtering Volatility

The volatility at the time of entry is a more dependable indication of expected profits and losses. Even more important, high volatility means high risk. A trade that has a good chance of being a loss, and includes high risk, is an excellent candidate for elimination. Figure 11-3(a) shows plots of the same WTI trades seen in Figure 11-2, this time using entry volatility against profits and losses. Volatility was calculated as the 10-day average of the absolute price changes (in $/bbl).

Filtering Volatile Long Entries.   Figure 11-3(a) shows a similar, but slightly regrouped, pattern as the one in Figure 11-2(a), where entry price was used. A steady pattern of losses appears when long positions are entered during high volatility. The chart shows that these cases of high volatility also occurred at high price levels. Longs set during periods of low volatility were profitable, and some do not correspond to the lowest price levels, which showed some losses.

Filtering Volatile Short Entries.   Short positions are different when plotted against volatility rather than price entry. Many of the trades are pushed to the far left where they are entered at about the same volatility level, and the remaining five trades were set when volatility was from 2.5 to 6 times greater. The trades entered on high volatility were predictably larger losses.

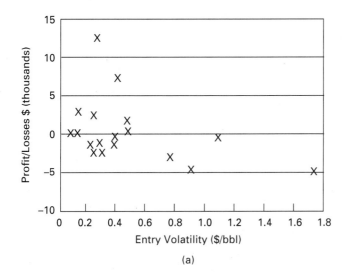

(a)

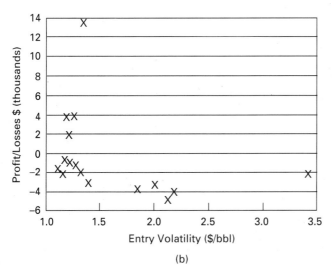

(b)

Figure 11-3. WTI (NYMEX) trend system entry volatility versus profit/loss. (a) *Long positions.* (b) *Short positions.* When entry volatility is plotted against profits and losses, the pattern is clearer. For both longs (a) and shorts (b) losses continue to get bigger, moving down and to the right on the charts as the volatility increases. The large profit from entering a short at $27/bbl in (b) is seen to have occurred during a relatively normal period of volatility. Very low volatility is a reason to filter any trade.

Using Filters

The charts for filtering trend-following trades using entry price and volatility show the simplest choices and the clearest results. Although this example only used crude oil, the same patterns will appear for other commercial and industrial products, where there is a real high and low level. Currencies are different and more complex. There are no absolute levels for exchange rates. The temporary normal levels are set by each country based on their relationship with trade partners. When the currency is at an acceptable level, or equilibrium, volatility is low. When prices move away from equilibrium, by becoming either stronger or weaker, they become more volatile. You might consider a currency price as "high" when it is away from normal, and "low" when it is at the normal level. For currencies, volatility is the only measurement that counts.

Expectations

Filtering trades is a clear way to improve performance, where there are a few concepts are fundamentally sound. Using volatility does not necessarily improve profits, but it should always reduce the risk more than the profits, giving a much better performance profile.

Programming Rules for Filters

This method of filtering was chosen because the volatility calculation can be made at the time of the entry decision. If the volatility is too high (or too low) then the trade is not taken. The following steps are necessary to find the best filters for a trend-following system:

1. Select a trend-following method, such as an exponential moving average.
2. Produce a table of all trades, summarizing the net profit and loss from long and short positions separately.
3. Calculate the volatility at the time of entry. Use the sum of the absolute price changes over, for example, 5 days (as in the crude oil example).
4. Move the position (long or short), entry volatility, and profit/loss to a spreadsheet. Move entry price if you intend to do a price-level analysis.
5. Plot all the long positions on a scatter diagram with volatility versus net profit/loss. Plot the short positions in the same way.

6. Visually identify the levels of highest risk and consistent losses. You may want to eliminate all trades with entry volatility either too high or too low.

7. Add the volatility filter(s) to the trend system by testing volatility at the same time that a trend entry occurs.

Reversing the Optimization Concept

In Chapter 10, broad-based testing (called "optimization") is used to evaluate the merits of a trading strategy, or to see if a change of rules improves overall results. We anticipated large regions of profits, allowing us the latitude of selecting from many parameter combinations, any one of which would trade successfully. Now consider the worst results. It is common to see erratic patterns of profits and losses in the fast trading zone. If these losses are not caused by transaction costs, they indicate a very good place to enter a new trade in the direction *opposite* to the long-term trend position.

For example, a long-term trend produces two trades per year, while a comparable 5-day model generates one new trade each week. Both fast and slow models have a buy signal at the same time. We expect that over the longer interval the trade will be profitable, while the short-term signal has a high likelihood of being a loss. This tells us that, in the short term, prices should be lower than the immediate entry point; otherwise, the short-term trade would tend to be profitable. It is not a good time to enter the long-term trade, nor is the timing of a longer trade particularly important (as seen in the section, "Anticipation," earlier in this chapter).

Trading Rules

Soon after the long- and short-term signals occur, the short term is closed out with a loss. If our timing is right, the faster model now goes short. Because this position is also expected to be bad, we set part of our long position. If the fast system produces a loss, our timing would have been good.

A sensible plan for systematizing entry points that follows from this reasoning is:

1. Select a long-term profitable trading strategy for determining market direction.

2. Select the short-term strategy with low reliability and losses *not* including transaction costs.

3. Enter $\frac{1}{3}$ of the trade when the long-term model gives a (buy) signal.

4. Then enter $\frac{1}{3}$ of the trade when the short-term model closes out a (long) position.

5. Finally enter $\frac{1}{3}$ of the trade when the short-term model enters an opposite (short) position.

The market will give signals when it is volatile, appearing to show immediate profits. Most often, these fast-moving markets have very high slippage, and reverse sharply once the initial momentum lapses. Placing an order for $\frac{1}{3}$ or $\frac{1}{4}$ of the full position gives you an opportunity to decide objectively whether this method improves the performance of the basic approach. The last $\frac{2}{3}$ of the liquidity is set while prices are moving contrary to your objectives; therefore, slippage should be low.

Overnight Risk

Moving through Time Zones

Opening price gaps can cause windfall profits or losses, and increase overall risk. They represent uncontrollable risk. For many financial market and foreign exchange traders who watch the U.S., European, or Far East markets only during their business hours, that risk can be sizable. For the growing number of traders who have facilities to follow a market as it moves through time zones, it is possible to reduce a large part of the risk.

Expanding liquidity in world markets allows nearly continuous, 24-hour trading. Agreements between major exchanges make execution transparent with regard to order placing and margining. You can buy in Chicago during the morning and sell in Singapore 12 hours later by calling the same local trading desk. Or, you can use Globex or any of a number of other electronic exchanges with growing liquidity and great convenience.

To understand the importance of opening gaps, Table 11-4 compares the size of the average opening gap with the daily close-to-close price move for a broad selection of futures markets. Figure 11-4 gives the percentage of the opening gap relative to the net daily move.

Favoring Primary Markets

The results show that primary markets have smaller opening gaps and less risk. U.S. bonds, trading on the Chicago Board of Trade represent the primary market for bonds during its normal business hours.

Table 11-4. Overnight Risk

		Total Points			Pts/	Gap
	Exchange	Open	Close	Days	Day	%
Financials	CBT U.S. Bonds	126.7	515.87	1280	0.10	24.6
	IMM U.S. T-Bills	11.17	20.39	369	0.03	54.8
	LIFFE Euroyen	1.83	8.67	100	0.02	21.1
	LIFFE German Bund	9.91	20.26	142	0.07	48.9
	LIFFE JGB	14.60	22.57	122	0.12	64.7
Currencies	IMM D-Mark (in %)	2.18	3.80	1056	0.21	57.4
	IMM British Pound	0.89	1.07	167	0.01	83.2
Metals	CMX Gold	229	310	242	0.95	73.9
	CMX Silver	2586	4380	1056	2.45	59.0
Other	NYMEX Crude Oil	10.97	20.26	142	0.08	54.1
	CBT Soybeans	1141	2295	597	1.91	49.7
	CME Pork Bellies	416.7	916.8	1056	0.39	45.5

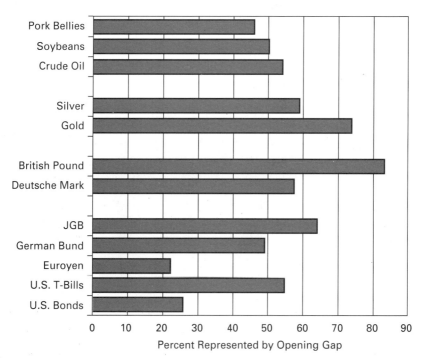

Figure 11-4. Opening gaps as a percentage of the daily move. Markets with active 24-hour trading and those whose primary markets are closed show much larger opening gaps than exchange-traded markets that are open at the same time as their primary cash market. These large opening gaps translate into uncontrollable risk.

Similarly, the Euroyen traded on the London International Financial Futures and Options Exchange (LIFFE) is active during its primary market. These showed the lowest impact of opening gaps, 24.6 and 21.1 percent, respectively.

The worst performer, the British pound trading on the IMM, had 84 percent of its move overnight. We can conclude that during the time between the London opening and the IMM opening about 5 hours later, most of the financial news affecting the sterling was already in the market. Prices had moved to their proper level and the IMM was faced with "catching up." The Japanese Government Bond (JGB) traded in London is similar. Most of the news relevant to the JGB occurs while the LIFFE is closed, therefore 64.7 percent of the daily move is missed due to the opening gap.

The average level of overnight risk might be as high as 50 percent. We can account for the large gaps in gold by recognizing that it is an international store of value; therefore, it is traded around the world. Soybeans and pork bellies are fairly domestic markets, yet show high overnight risk. From this, we should expect that these gaps will add slippage to both entries and exits.

Leverage, Costs, and Trend Speed

Leverage and transaction costs exert an overwhelming influence on a trend system, and they define a basic difference between stock and futures trading. Futures markets require a margin deposit of only 5 percent to trade most markets; it can be much lower for currency spreads and as high as 10 percent for a stock index. Using a slower trend for trading causes positions to be held longer and results in larger equity swings. Faster trends are often used because the risk per trade is reduced although the sequence of profits or losses that form the total equity variation may not change.

The best reason for using a faster trend-following approach is that it offers more distinct opportunities for entering and exiting the market. If you had the choice of two systems, a 25-day moving average and a 50-day moving average, each returning the same profit/risk ratio with transaction costs considered, the faster 25-day program would be the tempting choice. More trades allow the following:

- Profit objectives to be set closer and reached more often
- Smaller individual losses

- The application of trend timing to other objectives, such as hedging
- The variation of position size by trade

In general, more trades mean a better sample, hence a more realistic result. These advantages must be offset against the fact that longer trends are often successful because they parallel government policy and fundamental influences. A 200-day trend in U.S. Treasury bonds might have held a long position for three years, netting exceptionally large profits and offsetting losses in real estate or other weaker parts of a portfolio.

Transaction costs are negligible in the financial and futures markets. A contract with a $100,000 face value can be traded (round-turn) by an active investor for as little as $10, or 1/10,000 of its value, while a 1 percent charge would not be surprising for an individual stock trader. At 1 percent, one stock trade every two weeks takes no less than 26 percent from your trading profits each year. Gross trading profits must exceed 40 percent per year just to be better than a passive stock portfolio.

Because of high commission costs and the slippage associated with frequent trading, many stocks show gross profits (without transaction costs) for tests of fast moving average systems. This profit window exists because small traders cannot benefit from a program where the profit from each trade is less than $\frac{1}{2}$ percent. Institutions cannot trade enough volume, nor would they want to appear that active, in order to take advantage of a small window. Therefore the opportunities remain, waiting for a change in the market or the players.

Figure 11-5 shows how faster trading, which must have smaller profits, is greatly affected by transaction costs, while long-term positions are

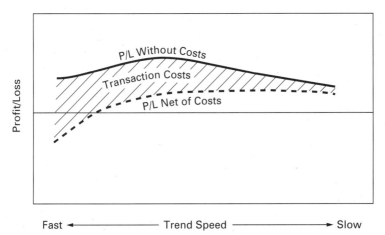

Figure 11-5. Effects of transaction costs on performance. Faster trading must overcome large transaction costs to be profitable.

relatively unaffected. Highly leverage trading, such as futures and forex, exaggerates this pattern further. A cost of .0002 for each entry and exit for the Deutsche mark is only .025 of 1 percent based on full value; however, 5 percent margin makes that .5 ($\frac{1}{2}$ percent), 20 times larger. A small trader can expect to pay more than twice that rate.

It may be difficult to see the advantages of slower trading over faster. The ability to leverage an investment allows smaller profits to be large percentages. Testing without the correct transaction costs, including commission, slippage, and unables, will often make the results appear to favor the faster trends, while the slower ones always hold the advantage. Large profit objectives of 200 basis points will absorb many problems that will hurt fast traders looking for 20 basis points in the Deutsche mark. Results will be more realistic, price shocks will have a smaller effect, and fundamentals will enhance the positions. Being realistic about leverage, profits, costs, and risk translates into staying power and success.

Notation and Terminology

Lotus and *Quattro* spreadsheet notation, Telerate's *TeleTrac,* and Omega's *Easy Language* are used throughout the book. They replace the normal mathematical symbols and should be familiar to most readers. Some of the examples use a general notation, similar to all of them, but not exactly the same. This is shown in the following list. When a specific spreadsheet or computer language is not indicated, the examples use this form.

Mathematical Operators

+	Addition
−	Subtraction
*	Multiplication
/	Division
^	Power

Relational Operators

<	Less than
< =	Less than or equal to
>	Greater than
> =	Greater than or equal to
=	Equal to
<>	Not equal to

Logical Operators (TRUE/FALSE)

NOT	Negates the TRUE or FALSE meaning of the following variable
AND	Both variables must be TRUE
OR	Only one of the variables must be TRUE

Referencing Past Values of Data and Variables

Close or Close[0]	Current value of today's close
Close[1]	Previous value of the close
Close[n]	Value of the close n periods ago

IF Statement

IF condition, then TRUE expression

Example:

IF close > close[1] then BUY at close	If today's close is greater than the previous close, then BUY at the close. (If this statement is not true, go to the next statement)

Functions

Simple trading rules, indicators, mathematical and logical operations are done automatically by most spreadsheets and computer testing programs. Those functions will be shown using an "@" in front of the function name. The ones used most often in this book are:

Mathematical Functions

@abs_val(x)	The absolute (positive) value of x
@power(x,p)	Raises x to the power p
@sqrt(x)	Square root of x

Statistical Functions

@average(list)   Average of list
@count(list)   Number of items in list
@highest(list)   The highest value in list
@lowest(list)   The lowest value in list
@median(list)   The median (middle) value in list
@std_dev(list)   The standard deviation of list
@sum(list)   The sum of values in list

Technical Indicators and Studies

@momentum(series,n)   The n-day difference in the value of series

@average(series,n)   The average of the most recent n-days of series

@exp_ma(series,p)   Exponential smoothing of series by percentage p

@weighted_average(series,n) Preset weighted average of series over n values

@fastK(series,n)   Raw stochastic value of series over n values

@slowK(series,n)   Smoothed raw stochastic (same as %D) of @fastK over n values

@slowD(series,n)   Smoothed @slowK stochastic over n values

@RSI(series,n)   Relative Strength Index of series over n values

Other Terminology

The word "fundamentals" will be used differently when referring to stock market or commodity market situations. Dividends and P/E ratios make up part of equity fundamentals, while supply, demand, and government policy are the fundamentals of forex and commodity markets.

Index

About the Author

Perry Kaufman has more than 20 years of successful trading experience. He is the founder of Kaufman Diamond & Yeong, international consultants to financial institutions. The cofounder of *The Journal of Futures Markets,* he is one of the most highly respected authors of professional trading books today, with six books to his credit.